IN THE SPIRIT OF CRITIQUE

SUNY series in Contemporary Continental Philosophy

Dennis J. Schmidt, editor

IN THE SPIRIT OF CRITIQUE

Thinking Politically in the Dialectical Tradition

ANDREW J. DOUGLAS

STATE UNIVERSITY OF NEW YORK PRESS

Published by
STATE UNIVERSITY OF NEW YORK PRESS, ALBANY

Printed in the United States of America

For information, contact
State University of New York Press, Albany, NY
www.sunypress.edu

Production, Laurie D. Searl
Marketing, Anne M. Valentine

Library of Congress Cataloging-in-Publication Data

Douglas, Andrew J., 1980–
In the spirit of critique : thinking politically in the dialectical tradition / Andrew J. Douglas.
pages cm. — (SUNY series in contemporary continental philosophy)
Includes bibliographical references and index.
ISBN 978-1-4384-4841-1 (alk. paper) 978-1-4384-4840-4 (pbk. alk. paper)
1. Dialectic. 2. Political science—Philosophy. I. Title.
B809.7.D68 2013
142—dc23 2012047513

10 9 8 7 6 5 4 3 2 1

CONTENTS

ACKNOWLEDGMENTS

I have worked on this book off and on for the better part of a decade, and over the years I have managed to incur quite a few debts. I certainly owe special thanks to the friends and colleagues who have read and commented on drafts of various portions of the project, including Paul Apostolidis, Banu Bargu, Michael Bray, Lewis Hinchman, Shannon Mariotti, Dean Mathiowetz, Melvin Rogers, Greta Snyder, and Antonio Vázquez-Arroyo. I likewise owe special thanks to some dear teachers and mentors who have inspired and nurtured my work at my various institutional homes: Marianne Constable, Frederick Dolan, Robyn Marasco, and Nancy Weston at Berkeley; Joshua Dienstag, Allan Megill, Corey Walker, and Denise Walsh at the University of Virginia; Philip Dynia, Luis Miron, and Roger White at Loyola University New Orleans; and Gregory Hall and Preston King at Morehouse College. Justin Rose has been like a brother to me, and certainly this book owes much to his friendship. And I am incredibly fortunate to have come into contact with two outstanding graduate mentors at the University of Virginia; both Lawrie Balfour and Stephen White have nurtured this project from its inception and have exhibited just a remarkable sense of grace and generosity. Of course none of this—the book, the career, the education—could have been possible without the loving support of my father, Edward, for whom I am forever grateful.

Alternative versions of three chapters have appeared elsewhere. An earlier version of chapter 3 was published as "In a Milieu of Scarcity: Sartre and the Limits of Political Imagination," *Contemporary Political Theory* 10, 3 (August 2011), 354–371, an earlier version of chapter 4 was published as "Democratic Darkness and Adorno's Redemptive Criticism," *Philosophy and Social Criticism* 36, 7 (September 2010), 819–836, and an alternative version of chapter 5 was published as "C.L.R. James and the Struggle for Humanism," *Constellations* 20, 1 (March 2013), 85–101. I thank the editors of these journals for their contributions and for allowing me to reprint this material. I also thank Andrew Kenyon, Dennis Schmidt, and the editorial team at State University of New York Press, as well as two anonymous reviewers, both of whom read the manuscript with great care and put forth a range of suggestions that have improved the book tremendously.

Revisions to the original manuscript were rather significant, and in a rather wondrous way, these revisions did not really take off until my daughter was born, or until my time was pressed like never before, indeed until I learned to manage my time, and my work, for the sake of what really matters. For this reason, among many others, I dedicate this book to three women in my life who really matter: my late mother, Kay; my dear wife, Marcie; and my lovely daughter, Juliana.

ONE

INTRODUCTION

Any effort today to revisit the modern dialectical tradition is to set out upon a beleaguered intellectual terrain. To put an ironic twist on the famed words of one of our conversation partners, we might say that the dialectical has become a tradition of dead generations, and one that really only weighs like a nightmare on the brains of the living.[1] Nowadays mention of the dialectical legacy seems only to invoke forlorn specters of closed teleological narratives, presumptuous ontological assumptions, perhaps the delusional hubris of a grand Hegelian style of theorization. We are dealing, it would seem, with a rather forgettable legacy of modernist excess. But of course so much of this is common conjecture, based on a simplistic caricature of an elusive philosophical legacy. And part of the challenge here, a charge that doubles as part of the rationale for this project, is to expose such conjecture for what it is, to tell a broader and richer story about what dialectical thinking entails, in order ultimately to mine a set of intellectual resources that have tended to get buried under the purported dead weight of Hegelian and Marxian modernism.

One objective of this book, then, is to confront a historical problem, to pursue a more generous and nuanced reading of a complex and evolving set of ideas. But ultimately the project is stirred by an increasingly unsettling political problem. Marx's amplification of Hegelian thinking has forever linked the dialectical tradition with revolutionary politics. And this would seem to imply that the tradition sits rather uneasily with the general political ethos of the early twenty-first century. Today we confront a peculiar political moment in which so many seem so fired by discontent and yet so burned by resignation. It is, some have suggested, a kind of postpolitical age, one in which grim prospects for collective action, increasingly fugitive hopes for real structural change, undergird an embrace of the ethical as a preferred site of public engagement. This turn to ethics, to questions of how we might live the established structures rather than contest their hegemony, threatens only to exacerbate a public life increasingly devoid of substance or interest. Certainly the impulse to revisit the legacy of Hegel and Marx, to reconsider a dialectically informed critical theory, is moved by a felt need for some renewed political fervor. But what is referred to here as a *spirit of critique* is intended to address contemporary discourse on its own terms, to address the essentially *ethical* question of *how we engage* the political. The idea, the wager, is that a reconsideration of the dialectical tradition might help to reanimate the critical imagination in our time and to inform a public ethos imbued with a sharper and more politically incisive critical edge.

So the argument put forth in this book is moved by a historical problem and by a political one, and this introductory chapter sets out to elaborate on these twin concerns. Insofar as the overarching concern is to engage with the modern dialectical tradition, it is important to note at the outset that we are dealing with a rich, wide-ranging, and still evolving body of work. Any attempt to fully canvas the tradition today would require a rather Sisyphean sense of determination, and what has worked its way into the pages of this book amounts neither to a general introduction nor to a comprehensive survey.[2] While I engage initially with Hegel and Marx, with the root sources of the tradition, I focus most intently on Jean-Paul Sartre, Theodor W. Adorno, and C. L. R. James, three twentieth-century theorists who have caught my attention in a unique way and who have inspired me to craft a particular story about dialectical thinking and its enduring political import. I will outline the basic contours of this story in a moment. First I will provide some additional context by elaborating further on the two basic concerns that animate the project.

THE DIALECTICAL TRADITION

If already in the foregoing the term *tradition* has appeared too often, there are several reasons for this indulgence. In the first instance, the reference serves a kind of ancillary function, allowing us to manage the delicacy and inherent difficulty of the other terms that are, or could be, for our purposes attached to it. By referring to the *tradition*, we are able initially to simply add the adjective *dialectical* and to avoid immediate connection with what is often referred to more specifically as *the dialectic*. These terminological distinctions are subtle, to be sure. But they are quite significant. As the literary critic Fredric Jameson points out, "the parts of speech offer so many camera angles from which unsuspected functions and implications might be seized and inspected," and "to speak of *the dialectic*, with a definite article or a capital letter," he says, "is to subsume all the varieties of dialectical thinking under a single philosophical system, and probably, in the process, to affirm that this system is the truth, and ultimately the only viable philosophy." In contrast to the noun with the definite article, the adjective *dialectical* can apply more broadly and is often used to describe various modes of apprehension that "rebuke established thought processes" and that challenge "the lazy habits of common sense."[3] There is, of course, far more to it than this. But as regards choice words for an introduction, the adjective provides for our purposes a better initial inroad.

This is not to suggest in some ironic way that *the dialectic*, understood as a grand philosophical system or method, is somehow inessential to the modern dialectical *tradition*.[4] Another reason to emphasize the *tradition* is precisely to indicate that we must wrestle with certain philosophical residues of the nineteenth century, we must trace the established contours, as well as the well-worn conjectures and caricatures, of Hegelian and Marxian modernism, and not merely to cast aside elements of the tradition that may be unfashionable by today's standards, but, more principally, to embed our appreciation for dialectical thinking within an account of its historical emergence. We would do well, as I explain in chapter 2, to focus on Hegel's development of the Kantian "critical" philosophy, for dialectical thinking as we know it emerges in Hegel as part of an attempt to situate the autonomous or self-legislating subject in an experiential and phenomenological milieu, to demonstrate the unfolding process by which human beings wrestle with the given terms of the status quo—the tradition of dead generations, as Marx might put it—in order to resist dogmatic assumptions and blind acquiescence and to work to produce for themselves authoritative reasons for belief and action. Whatever else this complex and evolving dialectical tradition might be said to imply, it must be seen to reflect fundamentally a mode of thinking that is deeply interconnected with the struggle for autonomy, the struggle for individual and collective self-determination.

In terms of our apprehension of the tradition, so much depends on our perception of who is doing this dialectical thinking. The tendency is to focus on the likes of Hegel and Marx, to imagine the dialectician as a high theorist or grand historian set off somehow from the subject matter that she or he seeks to explain. Here the dialectic is perceived as a kind of method, which can, in the hands of the trained observer, reveal a systematic or totalizing process by which these struggles for autonomy pan out. And this perception supports some of the more familiar images associated with the tradition, images of "thesis-antithesis-synthesis," of the "natural laws" made famous by Engels, of the obstetric role of the dialectician in helping to birth historical progress and deliver the inevitable reconciliation of opposing forces, both social and material.[5] This is one perception of the tradition. But the whole thing takes on a slightly different character if we focus more intently on the subject matter, if we locate dialectical thinking at the site of lived experience. Here things become more personal, more intimate and vivid, for we come to see our own lives as situated within a totality of social relations, run up against dissatisfying contradictions of various kinds. Lacking both scholarly distance and historical hindsight, we cannot really bear witness to any grand promise of ultimate reconciliation, nor can we find any real logical pattern implicit to a struggle that presumably we share with those around us. We simply find ourselves mired in the struggle, and dialectical thinking, dialectical critique, emerges as part of a theoretical account, both descriptive and diagnostic, of our human effort to move through the world and to carve out a more self-satisfying and sustainable existence. As we move forward in these pages, we will consider how this site of lived experience is a fundamental, if undervalued, dimension of the tradition going back to Hegel.

Here at the outset it will be helpful to provide a slightly more structured, if still rather terse and provisional, account of what the dialectical tradition means for us, and once again Jameson provides useful reference, in this case a working analytical framework that underscores three characteristic features. First of all, he says, the tradition implies a distinctive orientation toward "reflexivity, or thinking itself." It implies "a recognition of the way in which we are mired in concepts of all kinds and a strategy for lifting ourselves above that situation, not for changing the concepts exactly but for getting a little distance from them."[6] The point here is that we necessarily find ourselves situated in a particular conceptual world—what Hegel refers to as the "understanding" (*Verstand*) or the established contours of "ethical life" (*Sittlichkeit*)—and dialectical thinking, in reflexive fashion and, again, in the service of the struggle for autonomy, refers back to the subject, in order to emphasize the ways in which we may be beholden to a conceptual reality that constrains or limits our prospects for a more substantive enjoyment of our human freedom. Here the philosophical traces of the nineteenth century are on full display, and as we move forward we will have to consider the extent to which dialectical thinking, in its reflexivity, is grounded fundamentally in a set of controversial assumptions about the subject, the presumed self-sovereign subject.

The reflexive character of dialectical thinking reflects a "synchronic" dimension of the tradition, Jameson says, but the tradition also "has to do with telos, narrative, and history: with the story of change, or in other words, with the diachronic, rather than with the structures of consciousness as such."[7] And here we can point to a second feature, which derives from a rather distinctive orientation toward historical narrative and explanation. In a very fundamental sense, to think is to tell a story, and dialectical thinking is said to yield a particular kind of story, a particular kind of narrative, one that unfolds according to the designs of a particular plot structure. Many observers of the tradition, certainly its detractors, focus on the ways in which dialectical thinking engenders, or is perhaps engendered by, a rather determined reconciliatory narrative, one in which, at the end of the day, conflicting elements are resolved and some sort of primordial unity is restored. And certainly this kind of narrative structure is part of the tradition. But, to say it again, we find ourselves obliged to expose certain conjectures, and perhaps dialectical narratives need not be teased along by the promise of ultimate reconciliation, or perhaps this is not the only kind of story brought to life in and through a dialectical mode of apprehension. These questions surrounding "the diachronic" will animate our discussion in chapter 2; for now, I will simply refer again to the context of Hegel's initial turn to dialectical thinking, his effort to situate the autonomous subject within an experiential milieu. If we locate dialectical thinking at the site of lived experience, perhaps its story is less a tale of our self-assured travels on the path toward triumph and accord and more an account of our precarious travails on what Hegel at one point calls "the pathway of despair."[8] After all, if we find ourselves in pursuit of our autonomy, struggling to stake out a self-satisfying and sustainable way of life in the world with others, and if we find ourselves run up at every turn against a conceptual and material reality that complicates and frustrates our best intentions, then it would seem that dialectical thinking is rather poised, in an almost tragic fashion, simply to vivify this complication, this frustration. In any case, we will have to consider, indeed to reconsider, the ways in which dialectical thinking yields a story, an account, of a particular kind.

Finally, as regards a third characteristic feature of the tradition, we need look no further than to the general theme of contradiction. "What defines the dialectic above all," Jameson says, "is the observation—everywhere and always—of contradictions as such. Wherever you find them, you can be said to be thinking dialectically; whenever you fail to see them, you can be sure that you have stopped doing so."[9] To this I would add simply that an emphasis on the *tradition* has the effect of foregrounding a particular set of contradictions, principally that between subject and object, but also, by extension, the contradiction between theory and practice, or form and content. Part of what is distinctive about the legacy of Hegel and Marx is that it encourages us, "everywhere and always," to keep on the lookout for objective conditions, or established terms and features of our given reality, which frustrate or discourage our subjectivity, our humanity. We are encouraged to identify disparities between, on the one hand, our sense of who we are and what we can do, and, on the other, the actual world that we face, our conceptual and material reality. We are encouraged cognitively to "sharpen," as Hegel might say, any perceived disparities into full-fledged contradictions, which, in good dialectical spirit, cannot and should not be sustained. In this way, the dialectical impetus toward seeing, finding, perhaps imagining or creating *contradictions* is, in the tradition going back to Hegel and Marx, an impetus toward critique, toward provocation, indeed toward active political protest.

These three features of the tradition will need to be developed in the ensuing chapters. But perhaps it is apparent already that this rather cursory review, taking its cues from Jameson's analytical framework and adding its own lines of emphasis, is constructed as to highlight the tradition's implicit normative commitments. There is a kind of humanism at work here, which, I wager, may be worthy of reconsideration rather than mere disavowal. Dialectical thinking emerges largely in the service of this humanism, and for our purposes the need to make good on this claim is a driving reason why we refer principally to the *tradition*. With that we can turn now to speak more directly to our political concern, specifically to the need today for a renewed spirit of critique.

A SPIRIT OF CRITIQUE

To be sure, *spirit* is another difficult term, its ambiguity and inherent convolution only confounded by its situation here. So fundamental yet so elusive in Hegel's thinking, so thoroughly disparaged, at least nominally, in Marx's and that of his "materialist" progeny, the term as such does not seem to occupy an especially secure place in the dialectical tradition broadly conceived. Of course I am referring here to a very special sense of the term, the sense of Hegelian *Geist*, which surely is aligned in Hegel's philosophy with the turn to dialectical thinking, insofar as it signals a philosophical perspective that pushes beyond the empirically observable world, beyond the "positive" sciences, a perspective that tries to grasp our human and worldly situation in its totality and in its implicit historical movement toward ultimate reconciliation.[10] This specifically Hegelian concept of spirit will receive some treatment as we move forward, most notably in reference to the reconciliatory plot structure of the dialectical narrative. But generally this concept lies beyond the scope of our concern, not only because adequate treatment would require that we extend the project beyond a manageable size but also, and more significantly, because Hegelian spirit, whether "Absolute" or "objective," has the rather infamous effect of belittling or disavowing the critical capacities of ordinary people.

As I have indicated already, the impulse to strike out on this project derives in part from a concern about a contemporary political situation in which the critical energies of ordinary people have become increasingly belittled and disavowed, a peculiar situation in which many seem at once self-conscious of this impotence, profoundly discontented with it, and yet thoroughly resigned to it. If in our acquiescence we are mere "bearers" or "carriers" (*Träger*) of Hegelian spirit, beholden to what Heinrich Heine once characterized as the "servile" dimension of Hegelian thinking, then it is not clear what we might stand to gain politically from its reconsideration.[11] Part of what is needed today is a spirit or energy that can move citizens to carry themselves through the political world and with an inspired moral sensibility and a corresponding critical edge. It is in this sense that we invoke the term *spirit*, as to signal something like an inspired critical *ethos* that might cash out at the site of lived experience.

But we prefer the term *spirit* over *ethos*, and for a couple of reasons. Thirty years ago, Michel Foucault began to circulate the latter term as part of an attempt to describe a new approach to the practice of critique.[12] He suggested that we might think of critique as a kind of attitude, a tone, a way of thinking and feeling, "a bit, no doubt, like what the Greeks called an ethos."[13] And yet the very idea of a *critical* ethos seems a bit curious, especially in our time. Regarding the term's Greek origins, we can look of course to Aristotle, for whom ethos, like logos and pathos, has to do principally with rhetorical appeal and in particular with the way in which a speaker might cultivate a sense of community with his or her audience, a sense of belonging that encourages the audience to embrace the speaker's character and by extension the speaker's argument.[14] We see here that ethos has to do with community and belonging, with a shared public space, and indeed with a set of public practices that are *characteristic of* established norms, routines, and expectations.[15] This is not to say that a particular ethos, a particular attitude or tone, cannot distress the established contours of its constitutive community and work to transform them in certain regards: the skilled rhetorician does not, after all, merely tell the audience what it wants to hear. But in order to speak of an ethos, one must consider the established community from which that ethos emerges or in which that ethos might realistically take hold. And nowadays, in the throes of neoliberal hegemony, in a world in which the dominant community has become a kind of anti-community of isolated and increasingly self-oriented individuals, one might wonder just how a *critical ethos* could be cultivated or sustained.[16]

Of course public life has never been an expression of a singular or unified community, and if the political ever appears given to consensus, this is likely an effect either of brute physical repression or more subtle and nefarious ideological obfuscation. Our political world is always already torn between winners and losers, always already fractured by competing interests, however complex and obscured these interests may be. And though a particular set of interests may take precedence at a given historical moment, there are always, as Adorno once suggested, certain "gaps" or "waste products" or "blind spots" that elude the jurisdiction of the order of things and that provide some alternative ground, however minimal, for oppositional sentiment.[17] It is from the shaded soil of this alternative ground that something like a critical ethos might take root today, for, as Stephen White has suggested, our "ontological sources," our fundamental commitments about the nature of human being and the world, can be said to "prefigure" our "cognitive perspective, moral bearing, and aesthetic-affective sensibility" and thereby facilitate "an orientation, or disposition, toward everyday life and the ethical and political problems that we encounter there."[18] Part of our objective in mining the dialectical tradition is precisely to unearth a set of basic commitments, what have become by today's standards simply inexpedient "waste products," which might inform an alternative way of engaging the political.

Still, we prefer the term *spirit*, if only because our concern has to do precisely with how we engage *the political*. The question of *how we engage*, plainly the stuff of ethos, is often seen more broadly as the stuff of ethical technique or know-how, and, as such, precisely *not* the stuff of the political. And indeed the language of ethics poses a series of problems that we need to consider.[19] As Raymond Geuss reminds us, "ethics is usually dead politics: the hand of a victor in some past conflict reaching out to try to extend its grip to the present and the future."[20] The concern here, of course, is that by focusing on ethics, by resigning ourselves to the ethical register, we in effect double down on our resignation, for the ethical as such signals little more than a respectful homage at the hand of the political victor. To be sure, this sort of complaint may be a bit overstated. But we should note that a general suspicion of ethics has always been a distinctive quality of the dialectical tradition. As Sartre, one of our featured interlocutors, remarked decades ago, "ethics is a collection of idealistic tricks intended to enable us to live the life imposed on us by the poverty of our resources and the insufficiency of our techniques."[21] If we focus merely on our ethical affairs, if we focus on our daily interactions with those closest to us, we tend, Sartre says, to "*pass over in silence* the injustices of the age, the class struggle, colonialism, Anti-Semitism, etc.," we effectively "*take advantage of the oppression in order to do good*" and any "good that [we] try to do [tends to] be vitiated at the roots . . . turned into radical evil."[22] These general reservations about the ethical provide important context for any consideration of dialectical critique, which, to be sure, is moved by a very different objective. As Max Horkheimer put it in his initial articulation of the program of the early Frankfurt School, the aim of dialectically informed critical theory is not to "eliminate one or other abuse" or to work toward "the better functioning of any element in the structure" but rather to embark on a wholesale appraisal of that structure.[23]

To say it again, ours is a peculiar political moment. The "reign of ethics" today is largely symptomatic of a what is often characterized as a postmodern or neoliberal condition in which political efforts to restore elite class power, efforts to widen inequalities and further erode social capital, are only exacerbated by the presumption, increasingly popular in the wake of Reagan and Thatcher, that, as the old saying goes, "there is no alternative."[24] Nowadays so many are so profoundly frustrated by this state of affairs and yet so resigned to its inertia, and not merely because of the "poverty of our resources and the insufficiency of our techniques," as Sartre would put it, but also because of the sheer magnitude and the bewildering complexities of the problems that we face. These deep challenges to effective democratic renewal are big problems indeed, overwhelming challenges that as such remain inadequately understood, challenges to which the chapters of this slim volume cannot possibly provide a sufficient response. But the story developed here is certainly carved out against this troubled political background, and what I describe as a *spirit of critique* is intended to enrich our sense of *how we engage the political*, our sense of how, in the very act of critique, in the work of thinking itself, we might resist mere resignation to dead politics and instead counsel an energy that can help bring politics as such back to life.

THE STORY

In the chapters to come I look initially to Hegel and Marx and then to Sartre, Adorno, and C. L. R. James in an effort to craft a particular story about dialectical thinking and its enduring political import. The first step in the process entails what I call a "restaging" of the dialectic (chapter 2). If to think is to provide an account of our lives and our world, to gather our sense perceptions and memories and expectations into a coherent narrative of some kind, then we might ask about the *kind of narrative* that our reflections engender or perhaps the kind of narrative that is *engendered by* our mode of reflection. Drawing on literary theory, and specifically on familiar contrasts between different dramatic genres or modes of narrative emplotment, I argue that in the modern tradition going back to Hegel and Marx, dialectical thinking, and indeed the dialectical narrative as such, is shaped by a kind of double plot structure, one that is both *comic*, in its final orientation toward harmonious reconciliation, and *tragic*, in its more proximate attentiveness to the vicissitudes of lived experience. The comic and the tragic are the two platforms—the two dramatic *stages*, as it were—upon which dialectical thinking plays out. And yet popular reception of the dialectical tradition has overwhelmingly privileged the comic stage over the tragic, and in such a way that dialectical thinking has come to be associated almost exclusively with the grand teleological narrative, with the promise of enlightenment and material and intellectual progress, perhaps even, in Hegel's case, with some sort of narrative theodicy in which the fallen qualities of the finite world are always already redeemed by the self-assured prophecy of divine purpose.

This account of dramatic genres is meant simply to facilitate a more generous consideration of how dialectical thinking speaks to political life and to a set of experiences that do not always lend themselves to the lighthearted assurances of comic relief. And here we foreground Hegel's own political commitments, for, as I mentioned already, dialectical thinking emerges in Hegel—and is carried on rather straightforwardly in Marx, despite his avowed hostility toward Hegelian "mysticism"—as part of an attempt both to explain and defend the conditions for the possibility of the autonomous or self-legislating subject. As Robert Pippin has emphasized in a recent work, part of Hegel's great philosophical innovation has to do precisely with the "claim that we require a 'dialectical logic' to do justice to a kind of subjectivity that could be said in some way to be its own normative or self-authorizing 'ground.'"[25] The struggle for individual and collective self-determination, for a more self-satisfying and sustainable freedom, undergirds a distinctive humanist vision, which will demand our attention throughout the book. But at least initially, the shift to the tragic stage helps to reveal this humanism, this struggle for autonomy in the world with others, as an ongoing struggle indeed, one in which we find ourselves implicated, one the success of which is never guaranteed.

"The dialectic," Jameson says, "is not to be understood merely as a success story, nor either as the experience of defeat: it consists in that difficult wisdom in which these two outcomes become one and the same, in which defeat becomes success, and success becomes defeat."[26] The comic and the tragic stages both belong essentially to the dialectical tradition, and as we move into our discussion of the tradition's twentieth-century legatees, we will consider the ways in which these two narrative structures—and the attendant themes of success and defeat, hope and despair—interact with one another in ways that animate and sustain the critical imagination. But the initial challenge—and this is the principal objective of chapter 2, which is the most ambitious essay in the book—will be to recover the tragic as a kind of "blind spot" or "gap" in the conventional reception of the tradition. This initial move yields for our purposes at least three fundamental results. First, it helps us to situate dialectical thinking at the site of lived experience, as opposed to that of high theory or grand history. Second, it allows us to resist the idea that we are dealing only with a logical or formal method, for by embedding our consideration of dialectical thinking within an account of its historical emergence, we expose a mode of reflection imbued with moral substance; we reveal indeed a kind of reflective ethos that draws its sustenance from a series of normative commitments surrounding the struggle for autonomy. And third, this restaging opens a window onto a mode of thinking that is attuned to the uncertain and contentious nature of the political, the nature of a world shot through with power and influence, ever torn between winners and losers, friends and enemies.

The lessons gleaned from this initial visit to the nineteenth century inform our consideration of a series of twentieth-century intellectuals, all of whom indicate various ways in which dialectical thinking can be said to orient, provoke, and sustain the critical imagination. In the case of Sartre (chapter 3), it is a matter of resisting the temptation, especially strong in the age of ethics, to project our thinking beyond the real world of political affairs, to imagine a public life removed or protected somehow from the deep conflicts and sedimented structural constraints that delimit individual and collective freedom. "This world is *difficult*," Sartre admits in his earliest phenomenological work, and the imagination as such affords an "escape from all the constraints of the *world*."[27] And Sartre himself, primarily in his early works, invests quite a bit of confidence in the power of ideas, the power of the imagination, to liberate us, at least existentially, from this otherwise burdensome human condition. But as Sartre becomes more politicized in the postwar period, as he commits himself ever more energetically not only to the class struggle but also to struggles for racial and colonial independence, he comes to embrace the dialectical tradition in a new way. He carves out an account of dialectical thinking that, in "reflexive" fashion, calls the imagination back to the site of thinking itself and indeed to a dialectically stylized figuration of our lived experience, what he refers to as a "milieu of scarcity." Building on the old dialectical adage that we make our history not of our own choosing but under conditions handed down from past generations, Sartre invokes dialectical thinking, at least partly, in an attempt to focus reflective attention on persistent conflicts, on the ways in which our present reality is always already an expression of past conflicts—indeed an expression of "dead politics"—and on the ways in which any critical engagement with this reality demands our own participation in active contestation.[28]

Our treatment of Sartre reveals a mode of thinking oriented almost exclusively toward the tragedies of lived experience. Our turn to Adorno (chapter 4), to a figure likewise known for his somber appraisals of the modern predicament, indicates how dialectical thinking might be teased along, however minimally, by an appeal to the transcendent. The dialectical tradition going back to the nineteenth century very plainly counsels something of a redemptive energy, a pull toward the transcendent that animates and sustains a critical perspective on the present. More fundamental than a set of "theological niceties" that may be tossed out alongside Hegelian "mysticism," this pull toward the transcendent, toward the promise of a radically alternative reality, very clearly moves a dialectical critique intended, as Marx might put it, to change the world. "The dialectic advances by way of extremes," Adorno says.[29] And Adorno reveals how extreme, even exaggerated, figurations of despair and redemption can work together in tension to enliven and sustain critical thinking in dark times. In what Robert Hullot-Kentor has aptly described as an "urgent passage," Adorno says "the only philosophy which can be responsibly practiced in face of despair is the attempt to contemplate all things as they would present themselves from the standpoint of redemption." He says that "perspectives must be fashioned that displace and estrange the world, reveal it to be, with its rifts and crevices, as indigent and distorted as it will one day appear in the messianic light."[30] Ultimately I suggest that the structure of dialectical thinking as such provides a reflective framework for precisely this kind of critically animating interplay. Our dreadful moment is seen to be "indigent and distorted," and thus not good, not true, certainly not worthy of our support or affirmation, and this critical judgment is thrown into the boldest possible relief when fashioned "from the standpoint of redemption," when illuminated by the "messianic light" and thus confronted by the promise of a better world.

The chapters on Sartre and Adorno speak most directly to the structural qualities of dialectical thinking. Of course this is not to suggest that we intend somehow to disavow Sartre or Adorno's substantive moral commitments. Both theorists counsel a vision of human liberation, a vision itself born of the dialectical tradition. Both are affected deeply by a fundamental moral aversion to human pain and suffering. But to flesh out our embrace of the normative commitments at the heart of the dialectical tradition, we turn to C. L. R. James (chapter 5), an inspiring and unduly neglected West Indian writer who offers his own distinctively tragic renewal of the anthropological commitments that undergird dialectical critique.

Born and raised in Trinidad in the early part of the twentieth century, James developed into an original and prolific Marxist theorist and Pan-African intellectual. He is by far the least well known of our featured interlocutors, and we will of course have occasion to speak more fully to his life and background. But our basic objective will be to take cues from James's radically democratic sensibilities and from his rather distinctive postwar reading of Hegel's thinking on human desire and the tragic. As Cornelius Castoriadis once remarked, James "had this wonderful sense of the self-activity of the people, and he was able to translate it in universal terms that were not absolute universals."[31] Influenced certainly by his own colonial background, concerned especially to give voice to the political struggles of Africana peoples throughout the diaspora, James builds upon a deep appreciation for popular political struggle to develop ultimately an account of human agency that is attuned to the ineluctably tragic nature of human action. For James, the struggle for autonomy, the struggle to win for ourselves and for our communities an "actuality" that reflects our desires and talents and energies, is ever run up against challenges, complications, the essential uncertainties of a moving, changing modern world. Indeed our action as such, what makes us who and what we are, is also what exposes our essential vulnerability. For our purposes, these observations—confirmed for James in and through his reading of Hegel, in and through what amounts to a tragic restaging of the dialectical tradition—serve only to temper the humanist imaginary. Dialectical critique is ever teased along by the promise of subjective liberation, the promise of individual and collective autonomy or self-determination, and James for his part will never relinquish this moral vision. And in a way, as I will explain, James conceives of dialectical thinking as a kind of ethos of reflective engagement, a way of "sharpening" our instinctive frustrations into politically incisive contradictions that as such can help move the struggle for autonomy in a practical way. But ultimately what James gives us is a more nuanced conception of human agency, a tempered conception of the self-sovereign subject. Informed by an honest appreciation for the tragic nature of public action, this Jamesian conception can, I argue, provide a more suitable anthropological basis for a renewed spirit of dialectical critique.

Ultimately these chapters tell a sobering and at times rather somber tale. The effort to recover a tragic dimension of the dialectical tradition runs through the project as a guiding thread. And it is important to see that our appeal to the modern dialectical tradition, to a spirit of critique itself born of a bygone historical era, is by no means an expression of what Walter Benjamin once characterized as "left-wing melancholy."[32] While the prospects for revolution or concerted political intervention appear quite grim today, and while we may be inclined to characterize this moment, this age of ethics, in terms of a lamentable loss of the political or the absence of robust democratic publics, the objective throughout this book is not to cling to the revolutionary ideals of a nineteenth- and twentieth-century tradition to the detriment of whatever political action may be available at the start of the twenty-first. What is suggested here as a spirit of critique, grounded in the intellectual resources of the modern dialectical tradition, is meant to inform our engagement with the political, however reduced or fugitive that political has become. In a brief concluding segment (chapter 6), I suggest, in an admittedly speculative fashion, that a shared and distinctive conception of the political, one that is attuned to the fugitive character of meaningful collective experience, may undergird the thinking of Sartre, Adorno, and James, and in a way that speaks rather presciently to our own moment and thus to the timeliness of our efforts throughout these pages.

TWO

RESTAGING THE DIALECTIC

"How do we now stand as regards the Hegelian *dialectic*?" This, Marx said, is "the really *vital* question."[1] For our purposes, we might amend Marx's stylistic emphasis somewhat. Ultimately our purpose in this chapter is to show that "*the* Hegelian dialectic" is not as singular or as monolithic as it is sometimes presumed to be. Taking issue with what has become a rather unduly caricatured reading of the modern dialectical tradition since its inception, we set out to tell a broader and richer story about what Hegelian dialectical thinking entails and ultimately by introducing a literary metaphor, a contrast between the comic and the tragic, as to emphasize two ways in which dialectical narratives have been framed or *staged*. But before we begin, it will be helpful to preface the discussion by commenting briefly on Hegel's inquisitive legatee.

Though Hegel is the evident pioneer, the dialectical tradition as such really takes off with Marx. Clearly the tradition's enduring political import owes an enormous debt to the most impactful of the Young Hegelians, and this is perhaps reason enough to begin with Marx. But ultimately these prefatory comments are called for because one of the obstacles to a fuller appreciation of dialectical thinking derives from Marx's own outspoken assault on Hegelian "mysticism." In these first few pages, before we set out to restage the dialectic and complicate popular reception of the tradition more broadly, I float the idea that Hegel and Marx share an embrace of the basic structure and character of dialectical thinking. This initial observation, which of course will need to be unpacked, will help to preempt any concern that a focused consideration of Hegel, essentially our *modus operandi* in the chapter proper, bespeaks somehow an infelicitous betrayal of Marx or of a mode of critique oriented toward active engagement with the material world.

So how does *Marx* stand as regards the Hegelian dialectic? Early on, in his 1839 "Notebooks on Epicurean Philosophy," Marx speaks sympathetically of "the torrent which smashes." The "dialectic is death," he says, "but at the same time the vehicle of vitality."[2] As a young radical with a famously combative disposition, and ultimately as a mature revolutionary committed to the wholesale transformation of bourgeois society, Marx is ever attracted to the notion of dialectical "negativity," or the driving suspicion of the established contours of extant reality. What Marx refers to as "the moving and generating principle" is said to be the "outstanding thing in Hegel."[3] But Marx is more than just a "negating genius," as his father once described him, and dialectical thinking is for Marx more than just an intellectual sledgehammer.[4] As an alternative to positivism, dialectical thinking cuts against any immediate, unexamined apprehension of the present state of affairs. It sets out to mine beneath the settled terms of the empirically observable world, to get beyond surface appearance (*Erscheinung*) and to a deeper essence (*Wesen*), to the deeper workings of society. It sets out to apprehend the totality of social relations, rather than to consider individual parts in isolation. And for Marx, such an approach lends itself quite naturally to a revolutionary project. That deeper essence, that totality of social relations, does not reveal itself to be a peaceful and harmonious order, at least not immediately, not at the moment. It is rife with contradictions, marred by deep antinomies, indeed burdened by a kind of irrationality that is both unsatisfying and unstable.

"Truly philosophical criticism," Marx says, "not only shows up contradictions as existing, it *explains* them, it comprehends their genesis, their necessity."[5] And dialectical criticism, for Marx truly philosophical criticism, reveals its subject matter as a developmental process, one that follows a "necessary" course. Dialectical thinking turns up contradictions but always under the aegis of an unfolding narrative that has inherent meaning and purpose. These contradictions, in their instability, in their irrationality, are always already prefigured by the prospect of rational reconciliation. This question of what the dialectical narrative can be said to presuppose will be our focus as we turn to Hegel. But for now I want simply to emphasize that Hegel's work gives Marx both a set of intellectual resources with which to condemn what is taken to be the contradictory, even irrational, character of bourgeois society, and a certain confidence that the present conditions cannot endure, that a better and more sustainable future is necessarily on the horizon.

In his initial commentary on Hegel's *Philosophy of Right*, Marx says that in Hegel "lie concealed *all* the elements of criticism, already *prepared* and *elaborated*."[6] For the Marx of 1844, the dialectic emerges as a kind of silver lining to the otherwise dark cloud of Hegelian philosophy. Years later, in his 1873 afterword to the second edition of *Capital*, in what is perhaps his most significant discussion of his own "dialectical method," Marx reiterates this sentiment. He says that "the mystification which the dialectic suffers in

Hegel's hands by no means prevents him from being the first to present its general forms of motion in a comprehensive and conscious manner." The Hegelian dialectic is simply "standing on its head," Marx says, and "it must be inverted, in order to discover the rational kernel within the mystical shell."[7] Part of Marx's project consists in an effort to work through Hegelian mystification and to rescue and mobilize that rational kernel, for dialectic "in its rational form is a scandal and an abomination to the bourgeoisie," Marx says, "and is in its essence critical and revolutionary."[8] And yet part of what suffers from mystification here, indeed part of what is obscured by Marx's own formulation of the problem, is precisely the idea that dialectical thinking can help to shape critical consciousness and thereby help transform the social and political order. Too often Marx's "materialist" critique of Hegel is seen as an attempt to displace a driving emphasis on thinking, on the work of the mind, on the domain of reflective consciousness. Certainly Marx is more focused on material reality and on the labor and lived experiences of flesh and blood individuals. Certainly he worries that Hegel inquires only into the dialectical genesis of ideas, and that ideas are wrongly taken to be constitutive of reality. But Marx's assault on Hegel's idealism has always been somewhat overstated, and it threatens to obscure the extent to which Marx accepts and affirms the basic structure of Hegel's reflective approach.

In one of his earliest references to Hegel, in an 1837 poem, Marx imagines Hegel working against the grain of German Idealism. Assuming the voice of Hegel himself, Marx says that "Kant and Fichte soar to heavens blue / Seeking for some distant land, / I [Hegel] but seek to grasp profound and true / That which—in the street I find."[9] Though Marx later expresses some ambivalence toward his youthful poetry, in many ways this early verse sets the tone for his mature embrace of the Hegelian dialectic. We have here an early indication that, if we can just recognize the genesis of ideas for what it is, if we can just call that "mystification" by its name, we will reveal something of real value in Hegel's work, and that we need not reject Hegel's approach so much as figure out a new way to highlight its real critical import.[10] For Marx, following Feuerbach, our ideas proceed from lived reality, from material experience, ultimately from the relations of production that prevail at any given moment in human history.[11] And to turn the dialectic right side up, to put it on its feet, as Marx's well-known phrase would have it, is simply to emphasize that dialectical conflicts and resolutions are always already prefigured by the given conditions of material reality. In a sense, Marx wants simply to qualify the scope and the philosophical import of the Hegelian dialectic. If "relations of production constitute the economic structure of society, the real foundation, on which arises a legal and political superstructure and to which correspond definite forms of social consciousness," and if "it is not the consciousness of men that determines their existence, but their social existence that determines their consciousness," as Marx says in his famous 1859 preface to *A Contribution to the Critique of Political Economy*, then the dialectic, understood in its demystified and rational form, is but a means to expose and explain the contradictions that plague, not material reality or nature itself, but the "general process of social, political and intellectual life."[12] In other words, we still struggle to generate a self-conscious and sustainable understanding of our proper relationship to reality and to one another, as the Hegelian dialectic would have it, but for Marx these struggles pan out at the level of the superstructure, which is to say that these struggles, these processes that are brought to light through dialectical reflection, are always already *prefigured* by more fundamental material conditions, by the sum total of the relations of production.[13]

To be sure, Marx states explicitly that his "dialectical method is, in its foundations, not only different from the Hegelian, but exactly opposite to it."[14] I would argue that in terms of its relation to reality it may inverted, turned onto a material footing, but in terms of its structure, its form, it is really not all that different.[15] Marx tries to distinguish himself from Hegel by suggesting that, for him, "the ideal is nothing but the material world reflected in the mind of man, and translated into forms of thought," and yet these "forms of thought" are nevertheless said to unfold in a dialectical fashion.[16] These forms of thought are said to be marred by deep contradictions, which, as such, are teased along by the promise of reconciliation.[17] Of course the story is far more complicated than this, and as we turn to Hegel we will consider how, for example, substantive struggles for autonomy and self-determination, struggles against alienation and estrangement, can be said to invite a dialectical mode of analysis. This is true for both Hegel and Marx. But here at the start, I want simply to suggest that Marx's outspoken assault on Hegelian idealism threatens to obscure the extent to which Marx embraces the fundamental structure of dialectical thinking as it surfaces in Hegel. Marx's complaint about Hegelian "mystification" is in some ways simply a rhetorical strategy, a reminder that dialectical conflicts play out at the level of consciousness, at the superstructural level, and that, as Hegel either failed to see or perhaps simply underemphasized, this superstructure, this dialectical unfolding of self-consciousness, is largely conditioned by a deeper material foundation.[18]

As we see in *A Contribution to the Critique of Political Economy*, Marx believes that bourgeois relations of production create the conditions for superstructural contradictions. From a division of labor derive class conflicts, discrepancies between particular and universal interests.[19] And these contradictions express themselves in the superstructural psyche, in legal and political norms and institutions, in philosophy and art, in culture more broadly.

But, Marx says, the relations of production also create the conditions for the resolution of these contradictions.[20] And the task of critical thinking—for Marx, the task of genuinely revolutionary thinking—is to become aware of these contradictions, aware of the irrational afflictions that burden the status quo, indeed aware of the fact, even the essential truth, that these contradictions cannot sustain themselves. When Marx says in his "Theses on Feuerbach" that "the philosophers have only *interpreted* the world" and that "the point is to *change* it," he does not mean to belittle the work of thinking.[21] He does not mean to denigrate the work of the mind and the practical import of critical reflection. The point is that we must think, and we must think *dialectically*, because doing so can help us change the world. A dialectical approach can prompt us to question reality and to mine beneath surface appearances, it can help us expose contradictions embedded in our laws and politics, our culture, our self-understanding, it can help us "explain" these contradictions and "comprehend their genesis, their necessity."

The point here is that in Marx we begin to see how dialectical thinking, born of Hegel's innovations in the early part of the nineteenth century, might contribute to a distinctive spirit of critique. Such a contribution is precisely what this book is concerned to explore. And yet these prefatory comments on Marx also point toward some of the challenges that such a contribution is likely to face. If dialectical thinking sets out to expose contradictions, to what extent are these contradictions really *there* in our intellectual experience? Even if we manage to discover such contradictions, to what extent is our self-consciousness thereby plagued by a kind of *irrationality*? And how can we presume that these contradictions are indeed unsustainable, that by coming to recognize this irrationality we will thereby be moved toward some sort of rational resolution? It would seem that dialectical thinking reveals our lives and our world, or at least our conscious experience of our lives and our world, as part of a distinctive narrative, a process that is said to unfold in a particular kind of way. To invoke a literary metaphor, it is as if a series of tragic conflicts ultimately give way to a rather comic resolution, as if the deep contradictions or antinomies that we experience in the moment, in a particular act, so to speak, are by the end of the drama made into a harmonious reconciliation, resolved into that happy ending that we hoped for or even expected all along.

In this chapter, I pursue this literary metaphor as to flesh out two different ways in which the dialectic has been presented or *staged* in the modern tradition. Taking an important cue from the historian and literary critic Hayden White, I argue that, for both Hegel and Marx, a dialectical approach reveals the human experience as a kind of dramatic performance, one that unfolds both *tragically*, in the dilemmas and conflicts that tear us apart and that bring our lives and our world crashing down upon us, and *comically*, in the broader lessons learned from individual losses and failures, in the ability ultimately to laugh off tragic defeats. Here tragedy and comedy are not so much "opposed ways of looking at reality" but rather "perceptions of situations of conflict from different sides of the action."[22] Taken from the standpoint of the agent, the tragic dimension comes to the fore. When we reflect dialectically upon our own experiences, for example, when we expose dilemmas and conflicts that genuinely tear us to pieces, when we reveal a social reality that smashes our hopes and dreams and foils our best intentions, then ours is a story fit for the tragic stage. But if we take a step back and assume the position of spectators to the drama, if we observe and explain from a distance, as do the dialectical historians and grand theorists, then the emphasis tends to fall on the ultimate point of it all. Dusk sets in and the Owl of Minerva takes flight. The riddle of history is solved. Here the great dialectical resolution is called to center stage and the tragic becomes but a fleeting moment swept up in the rapturous and conciliatory final act, the festive occasion of ultimate triumph.

The basic idea here is that dialectical thinking includes both a tragic and a comic dimension, and these play out together, as a kind of double plot structure. As White puts it, "comedy is the form which reflection takes after it has assimilated the truths of tragedy to itself."[23] And yet throughout the modern dialectical tradition, ever since Hegel and Marx got the whole thing up and running, the comic dimension has tended to overshadow the tragic. Heirs to Hegel and Marx have become largely consumed by the image of the teleological source teasing along the dialectical process, the hidden metaphysical or theological puppeteer tugging at the strings of the grand dialectical narrative. And perhaps this is in the nature of the dialectic as it was originally conceived. Perhaps images of teleological fatefulness are to be expected from a philosopher concerned to expose "the rational and necessary course of the World-Spirit—that Spirit whose nature is always one and the same, but which unfolds this its one nature in the phenomena of the World's existence."[24] But we might caution against perfunctory emphasis on the dialectical resolution. We ought to resist the notion that a dialectical narrative worthy of the name must necessarily jump to its conclusion and privilege the comic stage. This sentiment tends to obscure the tragic subnarratives that are essential to dialectical thinking and that effectively frame dialectical accounts of human conflict, human struggle, human action as such.[25]

The larger book is of course concerned with a spirit of critique. The idea is to expose a distinctive mode of reflective engagement that might vivify and inspire political struggle. And part of what this chapter sets out to suggest is that such a concern is central to the emergence of dialectical thinking, going all the way back to the start of the modern tradition in the nineteenth century. Already we have provided some indication of how and why Marx found himself attracted to the Hegelian dialectic, how and why he turned to a dialectical approach or "method" as part of an effort to explain and confront the conditions of bourgeois modernity. Though we cannot explain the root sources of Marx's radicalism, though we cannot explain his predisposition toward the critique of bourgeois society, we do know that he found in Hegelian thinking certain resources by which to advance that critique. Hegel, for his part, did not exhibit the same predisposition toward radicalism or social critique. He was a philosopher through and through, and ultimately, upon acceptance of Fichte's chair at the University of Berlin, a philosopher laboring in connection with the Prussian state. But there is an important sense in which Hegel and Marx share the same impetus toward dialectical thinking. Marx's critique of bourgeois society was rooted in a commitment to freedom, to autonomy, to a vision of the self-determining human being, and Hegel likewise was driven by a fundamental interest in freedom, albeit for his part a more philosophical desire to explain the nature of the autonomous or self-determining agent. As is well known, Hegel took up and advanced the Kantian project, he set out to provide a richer account of the autonomous subject by underscoring the social and historical dimensions of human experience, and, as Robert Pippin puts it, "he claimed that we require a 'dialectical logic' to do justice to a kind of subjectivity that could be said in some way to be its own normative or self-authorizing 'ground.'"[26] Throughout this chapter, we highlight Hegel's commitment to freedom, his interest in the struggle for autonomy. This will help us see how and why he, like Marx, was drawn to dialectical thinking in the first place. This will help us see how and why dialectical narratives play out on both the tragic and the comic stage. And this will help us see how dialectical thinking can illuminate the complex vicissitudes of lived experience, our ineluctably contentious efforts to secure an adequate and sustainable expression of who we are and what we stand for, as well as the modes of intersubjectivity that might encourage and embrace such efforts.

The chapter is divided into three sections and a brief conclusion. The first section offers an account of the comic structure of dialectical thinking. The idea here is to begin where we should not begin, to get ahead of ourselves by leaping immediately to the reconciliatory moment of the dialectical thought process, as heirs to the dialectical tradition have been wont to do. This will help us see the sense in taking a step back, as we do in the second section, to consider how dialectical narratives also take to the tragic stage. The third section of the chapter puts the dialectical tradition into conversation with Nietzsche, the *other* great nineteenth-century German theorist of the tragic. Regarding his relation to the dialectical tradition, Nietzsche ultimately is a rather ambivalent figure. But certainly in Nietzsche, and in light of his more exclusively tragic perspective, we find important roots of what will become, primarily in the second half of the twentieth century, a kind of late-modern disillusionment with dialectical thinking. In many ways this sense of disillusionment is well founded, based on important concerns about the logic of contradiction and about the status of reason and rationality in dialectical thinking. Any effort to renew a spirit of dialectical critique in our time demands that we take seriously these contentions, and given that this chapter is intended as a kind of prologue to our engagement with a series of twentieth-century intellectuals, a brief engagement with Nietzsche will be helpful

This is an ambitious and challenging chapter. In the course of about twenty pages, it is simply not possible to account for the incredible richness of the foundational figures of the modern dialectical tradition. But the objective here is not to provide a comprehensive survey of dialectical theory in the nineteenth century.[27] The idea, rather, is to expose some of the prejudices that have been heaped upon the dialectical tradition and to show, as Marx might put it, that there may be a worthwhile kernel buried inside that prejudicial shell. My supposition is that if we can manage to restage the dialectic, if we can at least catch a glimpse of that tragic production that necessarily plays out alongside the more familiar comic one, then we will be in a better position to consider a series of more creative twentieth-century theorists in the chapters to come.

DIALECTICAL LIGHTHEARTEDNESS

To say it again, it will be helpful to foreground Hegel's interest in freedom, or, more specifically, his effort to account for the autonomous or self-legislating subject. By itself, dialectical logic can be inordinately dry and abstract, as readers of Hegel know only too well. My sense is that the practical significance of dialectical thinking begins to come alive when we see how, in his development of the Kantian project, in his effort to cash out a theory of freedom as the exercise of practical reason, Hegel is driven to articulate a dialectical logic, a narrative account of the development of the autonomous subject in a broader social and historical milieu. The experience of autonomy emerges in Hegel as a kind of practical ideal, one that is only possible if that dialectical narrative can be said to unfold in a particular kind of way. Ultimately, what I suggest in this section is that any dialectical narrative, and thus any account or explanation that is brought to light in and through a dialectical mode of reflection, can be said to presuppose a specific kind of outcome, ultimately the reconciliation of opposed or contradictory elements. To continue with our literary metaphor, and I will explain as we move along, a dialectical narrative can be said to presuppose a distinctively *comic* plot structure. And due in large part to this implicitly comic dimension, the dialectical tradition has come to be associated with a certain sort of Enlightenment optimism, a sense in which our individual struggles are ultimately swept away by the fateful trajectory of rational progress. By itself, the comic plot structure suggests that dialectical thinking is necessarily bound up with a series of rather untenable teleological assumptions. But this is only part of the story, as will become clear when we turn to consider the tragic dimension later in the chapter.

We begin with a quick detour into Kant's thinking. In recent years, Hegel's relationship to Kant has become a renewed subject of scholarly interest.[28] This relationship of course constitutes a rich and complex chapter in the history of ideas, and a more comprehensive discussion would have to include some consideration of the supporting cast, certainly Fichte and Schelling, perhaps Jacobi and Schiller, among others. For our purposes, it will suffice to focus briefly on the ways in which Hegelian dialectical thinking emerges out of an effort to develop Kant's "critical philosophy," specifically as it pertains to the possibility of the autonomous or self-legislating subject.

It is well known that Kant defines the age of Enlightenment as an "age of criticism, to which everything must submit."[29] He wants to move away from dogmatic presuppositions, to explore the conditions for the possibility of human experience, to allow our knowledge essentially to ground itself in and through rational self-examination. And for Kant, the very activity of critique, the activity of rational self-examination, is said to provide the basis for our liberation, our ability to break free of our "self-incurred immaturity" and to "use [our] own understanding without the guidance of another."[30] Furthermore, for Kant, this kind of self-examination allows us to legislate practical norms that can be considered binding, not just for us, but also for all rationally capacious human beings. "Reason must look upon itself as the author of its own principles independently of alien influences," Kant says.[31] Rather than accept the guidance of some external or contingent influence, in a merely dependent or *heteronomous* fashion, we must give ourselves reasons to think and behave as we do, we must essentially give ourselves the law, as the very language of *autonomy* implies. And insofar as we are able to do this, insofar as we are able to provide authoritative *reasons* to support certain principles and norms, then our principles and norms are quite literally *reasonable*. They make sense to us and to others. They are attractive to us and to others. They motivate us to coordinate our behavior so as to get along peaceably with our fellows. This is all said to follow from the very nature of reason itself, if only we can find the courage, as Kant puts it, to pursue our autonomy, to make independent use of our minds and to give ourselves the law. "The dignity of man," Kant says, "consists precisely in his capacity to make universal law, although only on the condition of being himself also subject to the law he makes."[32]

For Kant, everything turns on our capacity to generate spontaneously certain norms of behavior, to subject our maxims to a test, as he puts it in his famous discussion of the categorical imperative, so as to determine rationally whether we may will our maxims as universal law. This is the practical application of the Kantian critical philosophy, which, as Hegel says, "sets itself the task of investigating just how far the forms of thinking are in general capable of helping us reach the cognition of truth."[33] And again, the idea is that we need not depend upon others, we need not remain slaves to our unruly passions, our sensuous desires, the capricious whims of our contingent interests. This is mere heteronomy. As rationally capacious agents, we can always rely on the formal structure of our cognition to reveal authoritative rules and practices. But herein lies the point at which Hegel sets out to develop, indeed to radicalize, the Kantian project, and by way of a turn to dialectical reason.

Ultimately Hegel is concerned that the Kantian account gets ahead of itself. He is concerned that by focusing on the formal cognitive structure of the individual subject, we threaten "to go into the water before we have learned to swim."[34] After all, in the "age of criticism" we are concerned to eschew unexamined presuppositions, to ward off any immediate embrace of what is merely given to our consciousness in a positivistic fashion. In order genuinely to own up to this critical approach, Hegel says, we must consider how practical reason itself has taken on the particular shape that it has. "If freedom requires a radical self-determination," then we must consider "how a subject *comes* to determine itself as a strictly rational being, as always subjecting its maxims to a test, rendering them universally consistent with the possible actions of other agents."[35] We must pay attention to what Hegel calls "the *activity* of the forms of thinking, and the *critique of them*."[36] We must show how what is reasonable and rational has come to be taken as such, how what exists now as the determinate shape of practical reason, the established character of what Hegel calls "ethical life" (*Sittlichkeit*), has developed as a product of human social and historical activity.[37] For Hegel, it is precisely this "activity of the forms of thinking" that is "taken into particular consideration under the name 'dialectic.'"[38]

This brief detour into Hegel's relationship to Kant is intended simply to provide some context for Hegel's turn to a dialectical mode of inquiry. The key point here is that Hegel is impelled to generate *a particular kind of narrative* in order to explain the conditions for the possibility of the autonomous or self-legislating subject. We require, as Robert Pippin puts it, "a narrative account of why we have come to regard some set of rules or a practice as authoritative," and "our account of our basic sense-making practices is . . . tied to an account of the *aporiai* 'experienced in the life of Spirit,' and so such a justification is everywhere, to use the famous word, 'dialectical,' and not 'logical.'"[39] The concern is to show how we have *come to regard* certain principles or norms as authoritative, as rational and reasonable. And the tendency of course is to look backward, to look into the historical development of ethical life, or into the phenomenological steps of our consciousness, so as to trace the ways in which our "sense-making practices" have become less limited and partial, more self-sufficient and sustainable, less prone to unsatisfying contradictions or *aporiai.* But there is an important sense in which the whole narrative is prefigured, even substantively structured in advance. And this, too, comes into focus when we foreground Hegel's embrace of the Kantian project.

Like Kant, Hegel is concerned to account for the possibility of autonomy, as we have seen. To put it rather bluntly, Hegel wants to show that we can experience an independence that is sustainable in its self-sufficiency. "Freedom is to will something determinate," he says, "yet to be with oneself in this determinacy and to return once more to the universal."[40] In other words, freedom consists in our ability not only to make sense of our own lives, but also to make or allow that sense to resonate with others, in the "universality" that lies beyond our individual "particularity." Freedom consists in our ability to be at home with ourselves and with others, to experience our lives and our community as an expression of our most deeply held principles and norms.[41] As a self-sufficient and sustainable independence, this freedom requires a generally satisfying collective consensus, an achieved condition in which we are able to recognize and honor one another's freedom in a mutually satisfying sort of way. "The freedom of every individual exists only insofar as he is recognized as free by others, and others have in him the consciousness of their own legitimacy," Hegel says. "I am free, insofar as others are free, and I let them count as free just as they let me count as free. . . . This is the realization of self-consciousness as self-consciousness."[42] For our purposes, and without getting into any real detail regarding Hegel's theory of recognition or his broader practical philosophy, we can begin to see that the idea of autonomy, indeed the experience of autonomy, is for Hegel a kind of practical ideal. The same can be said of Marx, for whom bourgeois society is reflective of class interests and thus a merely partial or limited practical rationality, one that necessarily falls short of a sustainable, mutually recognitive collective consensus.[43] The point here is simply that Hegel, like his successor Marx, is committed to a practical ideal, and if this ideal is indeed realizable, then the account of its realization must be shown to unfold in a particular kind of way. By its very nature, the dialectical account is oriented toward a reconciliatory outcome.

So far I have cast this discussion in terms of the experience of freedom, in terms of the conditions that must hold if we are to realize freedom as a practical ideal. To speak more directly in the language of dialectical logic, we might say that the narrative is teased along by the promise of identity. As early as 1801, in his essay on Fichte and Schelling, Hegel says that "the need of philosophy can satisfy itself by simply penetrating to the principle of nullifying all fixed oppositions and connecting the limits to the Absolute. This satisfaction found in the principle of absolute identity is characteristic of philosophy as such."[44] And of course this sentiment is reinforced throughout Hegel's corpus. In the *Phenomenology of Spirit*, for example, he speaks of identity as a kind of goal, one that is not only achieved in the process of its being worked out but that is in fact presupposed by that very process. "Only this self-*restoring* sameness, or this reflection in otherness with itself—not an *original* or *immediate* unity as such—is the True," Hegel says. "It is the process of its own becoming, the circle that presupposes its end as its goal, having its end also as its beginning; and only by being worked out to its end, is it actual."[45] Again, we see that this process of becoming, this narrative account, this *dialectic*, is always already circumscribed by the ideal of autonomy, or by "the need of philosophy" to "satisfy itself."

Keeping with the *Phenomenology of Spirit* for a moment, we might note that, toward the end of the text, in a discussion of precisely this sort of dialectical reconciliation, this restored unity of self and "all that is alien to it," Hegel speaks of how our self-consciousness experiences a sense of "certainty" and a "complete loss of fear." He says that "this self-certainty is a state of spiritual well-being and of repose therein, such as is not to be found anywhere outside of this Comedy."[46] To be sure, Hegel in the *Phenomenology of Spirit* devotes only a few pages to a discussion of comedy as a dramatic genre. The same goes for his treatment of tragedy. But, as we see here, he does characterize the overall dialectical narrative as a kind of comic drama, and this characterization is by no means tendentious. Later on in the 1820s, in his lectures on fine art, Hegel says that "the comical as such implies an infinite lightheartedness and confidence felt by someone raised altogether above his own inner contradiction and not bitter or miserable in it at all: this is the bliss and ease of a man who, being sure of himself, can bear the frustration of his aims and achievements."[47] He says that we should never "come to grief" over any individual character in the comic drama, for "there still remains as a loftier principle the inherently firm personality which is raised in its freedom above the downfall of the whole finite sphere and is happy and assured in itself."[48] We have here a sense of lightheartedness, a certain confidence that, despite any turbulence we may experience along the way, we are always going to land on all four wheels.[49] We have here a sense that any individual sacrifice or failing is simply a kind of farcical misapprehension of the larger storyline.[50] These qualities of the comic drama can be applied rather seamlessly to the overall character of the dialectical narrative.

In his classic account of the historical imagination in nineteenth-century Europe, Hayden White argues that Hegel, like Marx a generation later, tells a certain kind of story. And the meaning of the story can be gleaned, at least partly, from a consideration of the story's plot structure or the way in which its sequence of events is laid out.[51] Certainly Hegel tells a story that moves in a definite direction, a story that is oriented toward the promise of "reconciliations of men with men, of men with their world and their society." He tells a story in which, at the end of the day, "the condition of society is represented as being purer, saner, and healthier," a story in which all the messy and conflicting and opposing elements of our world "are revealed to be, in the long run, harmonizable with one another, unified, at one with themselves and others."[52] We come across a "drama of the unification of man with his own essence, which is to say freedom and reason," a drama "that points to the time in which perfect freedom will be perfect reason and reason freedom, the truth of the whole, which is the Absolute, which is, as Hegel said, nothing but *life* itself in its full comprehension of what it *is*."[53] In terms of its generic form or plot structure, we are spectators to an essentially *comic* drama of dialectical progression. "Hegel's comic conception," White says, "was based ultimately on his belief in the right of life over death; 'life' guaranteed the possibility of an ever more adequate form of social life throughout the historical future."[54] To be sure, and as we will see in the next section, there is also a distinctively *tragic* dimension to the Hegelian dialectical narrative; as White says, for Hegel, as for Marx, "humanity achieves the condition of a comic reconciliation, with itself and with nature, *by means* of tragic conflicts."[55] But the overarching comic trajectory of the dialectical narrative, indeed of any dialectical account, is unmistakable. And this comic staging, as we might put it, has had a rather profound effect on the way in which the dialectical tradition has been received.

These comic qualities give rise to the familiar image of the grand dialectical narrative, the vision of a fateful, teleological progression of Enlightenment rationalism. This is a narrative that is so confident and assured in its direction that its terms are effectively laid out in advance. Ordinary human beings are reduced to predetermined characters playing out predetermined roles, for, as Hegel says, "spirit has actuality, and the individuals are its accidents."[56] Our reflective activity, our "knowing," is reduced, as Hegel remarks at the end of the *Phenomenology of Spirit*, to "this seeming inactivity which merely contemplates how what is differentiated spontaneously moves in its own self and returns to its unity."[57] For our purposes, this comic caricature of what the dialectical tradition is all about is not only burdened by a set of deeply untenable philosophical and historical assumptions, it is, insofar as it backgrounds the critically reflective activities of ordinary individuals, largely out of step with our efforts to articulate a spirit of critique appropriate in the age of ethics. But while this comic staging is a part of what dialectical thinking is all about, *by itself* the comic stage is simply a caricature, indeed an unwarranted exaggeration of a particular dimension of the dialectical tradition. As Gillian Rose reminds us, "Hegelian and Marxist dialectic does not seek to legitimize the phantasy of historical completion with the imprimatur of supra-historical, absolute method." Rather, it "focuses relentlessly on the historical production and reproduction of those illusory contraries which other systems of scientific thought naturalize, absolutize, or deny."[58] In order to create an opening through which we might begin to see potential resources for contemporary thinking, we need to look more carefully at the ways in which the dialectical tradition focuses relentlessly on these illusory contraries.

DIALECTICAL DESPAIR

So far we have considered how dialectical thinking takes to the comic stage. One way to put it would be to say that the progressive trajectory of the dialectical narrative is borne along by a certain insistence on "the right of life over death." As William Desmond points out, "the God of comedy, Comus, was a god of fertility, hence the association of comedy with plenty, with excess, with an agapeic overabundance of being."[59] And as Desmond goes on to say, comic "laughter is quite close to dialectic in that each in its own way tries to say 'It is nothing.' To say 'It is nothing'—and yet to go on, to continue to be, perhaps differently."[60] Indeed, as we have seen, there is a sense in which our confrontations with the unreasonable, with the not yet fully autonomous character of ethical life, amount only to a series of heuristic moments in a broader learning curve. There is a sense in which any "breakdown" we may experience is better understood, indeed properly and dialectically understood, as a kind of "breakthrough." In other words, the transcendental energies of dialectical thinking emerge as the real takeaway. And in Hegel this is simply reinforced, to keep with the context of our literary metaphor, by the fact that the comic is always elevated over the tragic. Throughout Hegel's corpus, the comic is always the later genre, philosophically speaking.[61] That said, there is at least one instance in which Hegel seems to question an elevation of the comic, and this may be suggestive for our purposes.

In his 1803 essay on natural law, specifically in a discussion of the contentious nature of ethical life, Hegel offers a passing remark on both comedy and tragedy. And he expresses some concern that the comic frame may not be able to do justice to the substantive conflicts that so deeply affect our ability to get along in the world. Hegel's concern here is that, in comedy, either "conflicts and the finite are shadows without substance" or else "the Absolute is an illusion." The concern is that comedy "either falls within absolute vitality, and thus presents only shadows of clashes (or mock battles with a fabricated fate and fictitious enemies), or else it falls within non-life and therefore presents only shadows of self-determination and absoluteness."[62] In other words, comedy either lacks conflict or it lacks substance. And in making this claim, it is almost as if Hegel acknowledges the very concern that we have introduced, namely that the comic tends to belittle the lived experiences of ordinary individuals. In a way, Hegel seems to worry that the comic mode, so quick to say "It is nothing" and to laugh it off, is simply too lighthearted to engage honestly with the more serious and somber dimensions of ethical life. In order to account for the substantive conflicts that move our individual and collective consciousness, in order to account for the impassioned disagreements and disappointments that we necessarily endure in our pursuit of autonomy, we must, Hegel says in this early essay, consider that which is "set forth in tragedy."[63]

Certainly conflict is a fundamental element of tragic drama. Tragedy is concerned with serious and determined characters, those who passionately pursue their most deeply held values and principles, but who thereby expose themselves to conditions that they cannot fully control. They confront a world rife with division, a world consumed by clashing values, contrary determinations of what counts as good or just or reasonable. If we bracket for a moment the broader reconciliatory trajectory of dialectical thinking, if we temporarily drop the curtain on the comic stage, we see that tragic motifs afford a rather fitting characterization of the localized movements of dialectical reason, the "negativity" that, as Hegel says, brings us to "complete despair about everything that the understanding holds to be firm."[64] For if we hold fast to a particular belief about justice, or a particular sense of what counts as genuinely reasonable, and if we find that our perspective is at odds with the collective consensus of our broader community, or even with the beliefs of another prominent party or faction, then we find ourselves caught up in the tragic entanglements of ethical life. And by pursuing our beliefs, by defending passionately our deepest and most settled convictions, we implicate ourselves in a rather contentious and conflicted drama, a kind of agonic test that can really tear us to pieces.

My sense is that the tragic dimensions of dialectical thinking are thrown into the boldest possible relief when we focus on individual struggles for autonomy, and once again it will be helpful to foreground Hegel's development of the Kantian critical project. For both Kant and Hegel, as we have seen, autonomy requires a certain strength, a certain courage to think for ourselves. The idea is to question dogmatic assumptions, to challenge authority, to look beyond positivistic surface appearances. In order to do this, we must assume a rather skeptical posture. "*Skepticism*," Hegel says, "is the actual experience of what the freedom of thought is."[65] And for Hegel, this skepticism, this actual experience of freedom, requires an embrace of the rather simple yet existentially disturbing fact that our "understanding" (*Verstand*), to use Hegel's technical language, is constantly challenged by "reason" (*Vernunft*), which "is negative and *dialectical*."[66] To *understand* something is to make it intelligible, to bring it into language, to allow our mind to *stand* still as if *under* the hold of some inertial force. In Hegel's words, "the understanding *determines*, and holds determinations fixed."[67] But if our world is constantly changing, if ethical life is riddled with clashing and contrary determinations, then any genuinely autonomous and sustainably reasonable determination requires our struggle with, and ultimately our synthetic inclusion of, that which lies outside a particular or immediate determination of the understanding. The pursuit of autonomy requires dialectical thinking, which "spoils its own limited satisfaction." Although we may try to hold on to some established determination, eventually our "thought troubles thoughtlessness, and its own unrest disturbs its inertia."[68]

At issue here is not simply an attitude or practice of "doubt," which implies for Hegel a mere "shilly-shallying about this or that presumed truth, followed by a return to that truth again, after the doubt has been appropriately dispelled." Dialectical thinking is more revolutionary than reactionary, and to think dialectically is not to dig in our heels and stubbornly deny difference in the name of tradition. At issue here, for Hegel, is a "thoroughgoing" or "self-completing skepticism [*sich vollbringende Skeptizismus*]," a mode of thinking that puts us, not on the "pathway of doubt [*Zwiefel*]" but on "the way of despair [*Verzweiflung*]."[69] The basic point here is that dialectical thinking, born in Hegel of the post-Kantian pursuit of autonomy, situates our consciousness in a social and historical setting and thus exposes the deeply precarious nature of our beliefs, our values, our sense of who we are and what we stand for. We find ourselves subjected to a world that is complex, rife with multiple and often contradictory determinations of the good, the just, the reasonable. We find ourselves subjected to a world that is always changing. And to pursue our freedom in this world, to pursue our autonomy, our self-determination, to pursue a reasonableness that is self-sufficient and sustainable, is necessarily to expose our thinking to a series of potentially intense confrontations.

Ultimately, and as we would expect, Hegel insists that we will find solace in this "thoroughgoing skepticism." To call this a "way of despair" is perhaps to invoke a bit of a misnomer, or at least to engage in a bit of rhetorical finesse, for our honest embrace of negativity, our embrace of the restless movement of dialectical reason, is said to bring about a "disposition that results in imperturbability and inward repose."[70] Much like the moment of *anagnorisis* in the classical tragic drama, like that moment of enlightenment gleaned through the *sparagmos*, the "tearing to pieces" of the tragic hero, Hegel insists that we arrive at a higher state of consciousness in and through the agony of radical skepticism. "Spirit," Hegel says, "only wins its truth when, in utter dismemberment, it finds itself."[71] This is a sentiment expressed even in the early natural law essay, an essay in which Hegel has not yet committed himself explicitly to the reconciliatory structure of dialectical or speculative logic, an essay in which he seems to want to elevate and privilege the tragic. Even here Hegel says that in suffering and death we rise from the ashes.[72] And certainly tragedy is not *only* about conflict, not *only* about suffering and death. There is a reconciliatory moment, although the tragic reconciliation must be contrasted with comedy, as "the reconciliations that occur at the end of tragedy are much more somber; they are more in the tune of resignations of men to the conditions under which they must labor in the world."[73]

For our purposes, there is an important sense in which the tragic is an apt metaphor only for the moment of dialectical *negation*, and not also for the moment of synthesis, not also for the positive or speculative aspect of dialectical reconciliation. As many commentators have pointed out, there are two ways in which Hegel uses the term *dialectic*. There is a "narrow" sense of the term, which, to borrow Scott Warren's formulation, is restricted to the process of "negation, seen from the perspective of the understanding." And there is a "broader" sense, in which dialectical logic incorporates three aspects: "(1) the abstract, rational form of the understanding; (2) the negative, dialectical form of reason; and (3) the speculative, positive form of reason, or 'concrete comprehension.' "[74] In many ways, tragic motifs seem fit to shed light on dialectical thinking in its "narrow" sense.[75] The language of the tragic seems fit to capture that sense of existential crisis, that feeling of deep despair that we suffer when our life and world is ripped apart, when we find that our most fundamental values and convictions do not jell with mainstream culture, with the "official" laws and customs of our society, or simply with the waves of historical change.

Thus far I have suggested that dialectical thinking takes to both the comic and the tragic stage, although the comic show tends to get all the hype. As Katrin Pahl points out, "most readers prefer a happy ending to the path of despair." But the danger is that "they lose the sense of despair by integrating it quickly into an economy of sacrifice or into the machinery of teleology."[76] It is important to keep in mind, as Hayden White says, that for both Hegel and Marx, "comedy is the form which reflection takes after it has assimilated the truths of tragedy to itself."[77] And it is important to keep in mind that the tragic and the comic do not so much represent two separate moments in the dialectical thought process. Rather, they are like two different ways of making sense of reality, two different perspectives by which we might perceive the action of the drama. Certainly most readers prefer a happy ending, as Pahl says. But so do most actors, so do those involved in the action. The difference is that only the readers, the spectators, are really in a position to belittle or look past tragic suffering, to laugh it off and say, "It is nothing." The actors, those who *live* the tragedy (or the heroes and heroines who die as a result of it), those who *experience* the suffering and take it to heart, they are the ones who have a more difficult time laughing it off. My point here is simply that the tragic dimensions of dialectical thinking come into focus when we consider the lived experiences of the actors, or indeed the experiences of flesh and blood individuals, those struggling to win individual and collective autonomy in a complex and precarious world. One of the fundamental premises of this book is that, in order to draw upon the dialectical tradition to inform our engagement with the political, we must catch sight of the tragic dimensions of the tradition. As I have tried to suggest thus far, this is a fundamental part of the tradition going back to Hegel and Marx, even though it has often been obscured by the comic lightheartedness of the audience, by the grand theorists and historians, those removed from the felt struggles of ordinary women and men and more concerned to synthesize the *longue durée* of rational progress.

NIETZSCHEAN DISILLUSIONMENT

Our discussion thus far has sought to foreground the tragic nature of individual struggles for autonomy. At this point, it will be helpful to welcome another contributor to the discussion, the *other* great theorist of the tragic in nineteenth-century Germany. In many ways, Nietzsche is a more serious student of the tragic, perhaps a more committed student. He takes the lessons of tragic defeat, not as evidence of the sacrificial costs of a broader rational process but as an occasion to question the very idea of rational self-mastery, the very project of rational pursuit. For Nietzsche, this world just is an unruly and uncertain place, better understood as a morally unaccountable game than as an instrument of divine, natural, or human purpose.[78] It is a world marked by multiple and precarious relationships of power and powerlessness, domination and submission. And any attempt to corral these relationships under the aegis of rational coherence, any attempt to impose ultimate form onto the chaos, as Nietzsche might put it, is essentially an effort to control what is uncontrollable. Our attempt at rational determination is not only destined for failure, because the abundance of life always exceeds conceptual determination, such an attempt is also, and perhaps more significantly, a normatively misguided effort, one that has the effect of denying life itself, of thwarting difference and becoming, of foreclosing in advance the possibility of more radically creative energies, passions, and impulses that just might liberate us from the miserable shackles of ascetic discipline or from any other dissatisfying constraint of cultural tradition.

Certainly Nietzsche introduces a range of challenging issues that push far beyond the scope of this project. Our purpose in this section is more focused. The idea is to draw on Nietzsche, or perhaps a Nietzschean sensibility, to address two general concerns regarding the status of reason in early dialectical thinking. The first issue has to do with the logic of contradiction, or what Hegel refers to as the "moving principle" of dialectical reason and what Nietzsche regards as a conceptual straitjacket, the logical domestication of conflict. Nietzsche develops an influential critique here, one that will be significant as we move through subsequent chapters. The second issue has to do with the speculative dimensions of dialectical reason. If dialectical critique is borne along by, on the one hand, an observation that the world as it exists is not fully rational, and, on the other, a sense that the world ought to be rational, a sense that in its *true* character the world *is* rational, then to what extent is dialectical critique simply another moral philosophy, an approach based on a deep metaphysical ideal that cannot really be defended in an age of deep pluralism? My sense is that Nietzsche can help us to articulate this sort of question, although the ultimate objective in the second part of the section will be to defend the speculative dimensions of dialectical thinking against this Nietzschean query.

As we noted at the outset, Nietzsche's relationship to the dialectical tradition is a point of some contention, and before we proceed it will be helpful to say something about where we come down on this issue. Some scholars see Nietzsche as a kind of closet dialectician, one who, despite his explicit condemnation of the Hegelian system, effectively radicalizes dialectical theory. Walter Kaufmann, for example, sees Nietzsche as a "dialectical monist" for whom the will to power, like Hegelian Spirit, is the "single basic force whose very essence it is to manifest itself in diverse ways and to create multiplicity—not *ex nihilo*, but out of itself."[79] On Kaufmann's reading, Nietzsche develops the notion of *Sublimierung* in much the same way that Hegel develops *Aufhebung*. Both terms capture a sense of dialectical "sublimation." In Nietzsche's case, "there is a basic force (the will to power) which is defined in terms of an objective (power) which remains the same throughout all 'metamorphoses.' This essential objective is preserved no less than is the energy, while the immediate objective is canceled; and the lifting up consists in the attainment of greater power."[80] Kaufmann's basic point is that Nietzsche, like Hegel, "expressly denied the peaceful self-identity of the basic cosmic force and considered strife a definitive feature of the 'Absolute.'" For Nietzsche, this basic cosmic force, the will to power, is "always at war with itself," but, and herein lies the key difference between Hegel and Nietzsche, "the battle between reason and impulse is only one of its countless skirmishes."[81] In other words, according to Kaufmann, Nietzsche characterizes the process of worldly becoming as a loosely dialectical process. And Nietzsche's dialectic is thought to be more radical than Hegel's because it goes beyond a mere dialectic of reason.

It is important to keep in mind that Nietzsche's more resolute embrace of the tragic entails a stronger emphasis on artistic or aesthetic expression as the mark of human creative power, and it entails a rather sharp critique of philosophies that focus more exclusively on reasonable or rational self-determination, such as Hegel's or Marx's.[82] What this means for our purposes is that, on the one hand, Nietzsche may well exhibit certain characteristics of dialectical thinking—perhaps in his account of the will to power's *modus operandi*, as Kaufmann suggests, or perhaps in terms of the interconnections between certain oppositions, such as the Dionysian and the Apollonian, or master and slave, or the biological and psychological bases of the will to power. But, on the other hand, Nietzsche is quite plainly a very sharp and determined critic of dialectical *reason*. As Nancy Love points out, "Nietzsche's primary target . . . a target which he refers to as dialectics *per se*—is a dialectics of reason."[83] And given this deep suspicion of reason, and given the centrality of reason to the dialectical tradition that we have been developing, my sense is that we can safely characterize Nietzsche as a critic of the tradition. In this way, there is some real truth to Gilles Deleuze's otherwise provocative contention that "anti-Hegelianism runs throughout Nietzsche's work as its cutting edge."[84] So our purpose here, as I insinuated at the start of the section, is to draw on Nietzsche to address two concerns about dialectical reason. We begin with Nietzsche's critique of the logic of contradiction.

"Generally speaking," Hegel says in *The Encyclopedia Logic*, "it is contradiction that moves the world."[85] This is a bold claim, one that only makes sense in the context of the dialectical tradition. As he puts it in the earlier *Science of Logic*, contradiction is "the root of all movement and vitality," for "it is only insofar as something has a contradiction within it that it moves, has an urge and activity."[86] Keep in mind that for Hegel, dialectical reason is "negative," it is what denies or "negates" any positive determination of the understanding, thereby moving our thinking beyond itself. But for Hegel this negativity only comes alive, our thinking only moves beyond given or established determinations, when it is pushed to the point of contradiction. "Thinking reason," Hegel says, "sharpens the blunt difference of diverse terms, the mere manifoldness of pictorial thinking, into *essential* difference, into *opposition*." And only when these oppositions are sharpened further, "only when the manifold terms have been driven to the point of *contradiction* do they become active and lively towards one another, receiving in contradiction the negativity which is the indwelling pulsation of self-movement and spontaneous activity."[87]

Whenever our consciousness is presented with something new and different—perhaps an ethical claim that does not jell with our established values and convictions, or a maybe a disturbing artwork that upsets our conventional aesthetic sensibilities—then this new and different something becomes significant, it becomes "active and lively" to us, only when it is shown explicitly to contradict our initial position. According to the logic of dialectical reason, our thinking comes alive, our initial doubts graduate to that more radical and thoroughgoing skepticism, only when our mind carries positive identity to its negation. To put it in more formulaic terms, we might say that the meaning of some "X" will come alive only in relation to its other, in relation to what it is not, but because dialectical reason is driven to comprehend this other in terms of pure negation, or pure contradiction, the meaning of "X" will come alive only in relation to *exclusively* "not-X." Or, since we are interested in how the new and different may be said to exceed any established determination, this new something, this difference, can only be thought as the "not-X" of an established "X." In other words, as Deleuze puts it, "difference is already placed on a path or along a thread laid out by identity."[88] Dialectical reason reduces our world to a play of oppositions guided by a rather narrow principle of identity. And the concern here is that the genuinely new and different—any human and worldly possibilities that are neither "X" nor "not-X"—is rendered unthinkable, the excessive remainder to the field of reasonable possibility.

This implicit commitment to a principle of identity is what leads Nietzsche to associate dialectical reason with an "impoverishment of life."[89] For Nietzsche, "there are no opposites, except in the customary exaggeration of metaphysical interpretation."[90] Dialectical reason is simply one more attempt to slow down the tempo of life, to colonize its vitality and render it manageable.[91] In reducing "blunt difference" to contradiction, dialectical reason reduces human and worldly complexity to a manageable coherence.[92] A dialectically reasonable approach may divide the category of the human into an opposition between man and woman, for example, but perhaps such an opposition cannot by itself account for all that is human. Perhaps there are elements to our existence, certain dimensions of our humanity, which push beyond this simple binary division. The broader point here is that dialectical reason, as Nietzsche puts it, is about "fitting new material into old schemes," about "*making* equal what is new."[93] We might say that, for Nietzsche and for his poststructuralist progeny, dialectical reason tries to squeeze reality into Procrustes' bed. And it is not clear, to say the least, that such a reductionist approach is an especially appropriate way to apprehend difference or to orient ourselves toward whatever does not jell with our given sensibilities, whatever does not sit well with the given determinations of the understanding.

This critique of the logic of contradiction is an important and influential one. As Diana Coole says, "it is Nietzsche who sets becoming free from the logical, synthetic march of the dialectic."[94] And in so doing, he helps to usher in a kind of postdialectical school, what has become a rather wide-ranging set of approaches that generally eschew the alleged reductionism of dialectical reason and pursue instead a more radical philosophical orientation toward difference and becoming, a more spirited embrace of ontological excess. But herein lies a concern that we will have occasion to consider in more detail in the next two chapters. This move away from the dialectical tradition emerges from a desire to get beyond the logic of contradiction, beyond the "sterilizing constraints of the dialectic," as Michel Foucault puts it.[95] But I suggest that this move threatens to shift the focus of critique away from the political. And I borrow Coole's helpful formulation here. She notes that, in terms of this Nietzschean critique of dialectical reason, in terms of this suspicion of its reductionist tendencies, "it is no longer the historical fate of a recalcitrant *materiality* that is at stake, with the attendant aim of rendering these ideal terms practically efficacious, but the question of *alterity*: of a radical otherness heterogeneous to reason and thus to the categories of the negative that dialectics employs." And "although this shift is not devoid of political implications, it does generally move the explicit focus of critique from one of changing the real to a question of philosophy's own standing."[96]

We see here that, in an exercise of intellectual housekeeping, the theorist's own mode of reflection is brought under critical suspicion. By itself, this is not a problem, as we ought periodically to take stock of how we think. Such is a fundamental objective of this very book. But in training critical focus on, in this case, a rational thought process that is considered to be too active, too involved, too interventionist, the relationship between theory and practice is called into question in a new way. The idea now is that we need to relax our purposive efforts to change the world, as Marx might put it, and instead work to counsel a more immediate embrace of worldly becoming. We need to take a step back, intellectually speaking, so as to make room for difference. But the problem here is that, in pursuing such an objective, in shifting the focus toward a kind of ontological project, we threaten to let in through the back door a more affirmative political posture, something not unlike what Nietzsche, in his very *least* critical moments, refers to as *amor fati*, a kind of self-satisfactory embrace of the world just as it is.[97] This is a concern that we will take up and develop further in our discussions of Sartre and Adorno in the next two chapters. In the meantime, I want to stay with Nietzsche to address a concern about the speculative dimensions of dialectical reason.

Here we can begin by considering what is perhaps Hegel's most famous claim. "What is rational is actual and what is actual is rational."[98] Put even more simply, "what is, is reason."[99] Of course there is considerable philosophical baggage wrapped up in these seemingly simplistic utterances. But in terms of the dialectical tradition of critical theory, the import of these claims turns on the so-called speculative identification of the rational and the real. "To read a proposition 'speculatively,'" Gillian Rose tells us, "means that the identity which is affirmed between subject and predicate is seen equally to affirm a lack of identity between subject and predicate."[100] The identification of the rational and the real is not the formal identity of an ordinary proposition, but rather a "different kind of identity," one that "must be understood as a result to be achieved."[101] In other words, Hegel wants to capture a sense of the complex interplay between reason, on the one hand, and extant reality, on the other. And insofar as rationality is understood as a reality to be achieved, this speculative projection emerges as an important resource for social criticism.

The idea here is that what is presently real, what we experience as our lived reality, is not *really* real because it is not *rational* or not *yet* rational. Any positive appearance of rationality, what we consider to be reasonable according to dominant terms of established ethical life, is, by the speculative lights of dialectical reason, simply false and illusory.[102] And as such, we cannot rightly *affirm* the conditions of present reality. The status quo must be denied, negated, subject to intense and active critical scrutiny. To put it in the terms that we have been developing, we can say that the limited and partial nature of the understanding must be exposed, brought to consciousness, subject to the negative energy of dialectical reason. Marcuse captures the general point when he says that social critique in the dialectical tradition is "motivated by the conviction that the given facts that appear to common sense as the positive index of truth are in reality the negation of truth, so that truth can only be established by their destruction."[103] And in this way, Marx's dialectical approach is likewise based on a certain speculative identification of the real and the rational. "Marx's dialectical criticism of reality," Marcuse says, is "motivated by the same datum as Hegel's, namely, by the negative character of reality."[104] While for Marx, as we have seen, ideas are not constitutive of reality, and in this sense Marx's materialism is not "speculative" philosophy, surely Marx's dialectical criticism assumes the speculative supposition that our world is not sustainably livable, not true, unless, or until, it is experienced as sustainably rational.

In the dialectical tradition, the rational is not simply an imagined ideal that we drum up out of thin air and impose onto reality, like some arbitrary vision of what ought to be. It is important to keep in mind that for Hegel, as for Marx, and as Simon Jarvis points out, "any attempt radically to separate a purely rational 'ought' from an arational 'is' leaves an 'ought' which is contentless and an 'is' which is unintelligible."[105] But the speculative identification of the real and the rational, this complex interconnection between what is and what ought to be, is meant to capture a desire for transcendence, a sense of the human longing for a better world, that *all too human* longing, as Nietzsche might put it. We engage with this world as it is, for we cannot do otherwise, but, at the same time, we cannot accept this world as absolute. We "penetrate" this reality, as Hegel puts it, "*on the supposition* that at the back of this being there is *something else*, *something other* than being itself, that this background constitutes the truth of being."[106] And in pursuing this something else, in pursing the possibility of worldly transcendence, we "give voice to . . . 'speculation'; to beliefs, surmises, wishes, hopes, imaginings."[107] In this way, Hegel seems to want to tap into a more conventional or ordinary language usage of the term *speculative*. He seems to want to capture a sense of that instinctive desire to look past what is merely present to our senses, that urge to set our sights, our minds, our imaginations, on something more, something better. As Hegel remarks at one point in *The Encyclopedia Logic*, expressing a sentiment that is as timely now as ever, dialectical reason is meant to help the thinker "cultivate one's spirit for higher things and to make efforts on behalf of that. We may hope that in our time a longing for something better has sprung up in the young."[108]

In many ways, we are simply rehashing the theme of comic reconciliation, the idea that dialectical thinking is necessarily teased along by a faith in our ultimate transcendence over the false and illusory here and now. After all, if we are given to our "beliefs, surmises, wishes, hopes, imaginings," it is likely that most of us do look forward to a happy ending. But we can continue to explore the staging of dialectical thinking by subjecting this comic dimension to a distinctively Nietzschean sense of suspicion. Can we really expect human life to play out as if on the comic stage? Can we expect to make the world a rational place? Can we expect to harmonize once and for all the many conflicting and shifting determinations of ethical life, the contrary claims and values that various peoples bring to the table at different times and places? These are big Nietzschean questions, based on the observation that "dialectic and faith in reason still rest on moral prejudices," that by thinking dialectically, by committing ourselves to the strictures of dialectical reason, we take flight from the tragic nature of human life and "are altogether unable to think anything at all just as it *is*."[109]

The concern here is that the dialectical tradition assumes way too much, and despite its advertisements to the contrary, despite its own claims to push the "critical philosophy" to the extreme of presuppositionlessness. The concern is that the tradition assumes the rational nature of the absolute, it passes judgment on the finite as being somehow irrational and therefore untrue, and either it imagines that we are *pulled* toward reconciliation by some sort of divine providence or, in its more critical and proactive iteration, it encourages us to *push* ourselves toward reconciliation in and through our willful struggles to make the world a more rational and mutually recognitive place. The Nietzschean concern, put in its simplest and most basic formulation, is that heirs to the dialectical tradition, like the rabble at the foot of Zarathustra's mountain, simply have not heard the news that God is dead, or, if they have, they don't believe it.[110] The legatees of the tradition implicitly presume, as Hegel for his part says more explicitly, that "God alone is the genuine agreement between Concept and reality; all finite things however, are affected with untruth; they have a concept, but their existence is not adequate to it."[111] And even though dialectical thinking is supposedly attuned to the idea that "God Himself is dead," as Hegel admits in *Faith and Knowledge*, it would seem that a new divine figure, the dialectical subject, is all too eager to stand in as a stunt double, to fill the void, to maintain the world as a unity of opposites and prop up the "ladder to the absolute."[112]

As we move through subsequent chapters, we will try to be mindful of these contentions, these characteristically Nietzschean concerns about strong moral and philosophical foundationalism. Nietzsche reminds us that good theory takes sober stock of the complexities of the human condition and sets out to determine what our political possibilities are and are not. Given the fact of pluralism in the modern world, given widespread disillusionment with grand narratives and the promise of rational progress, it is important that we think seriously about what, really, we can expect of "reason" and of "reasonable" human beings. That said, in terms of the critical import of dialectical thinking, I suggest, now and in the chapters to come, that these concerns about moral or rational foundationalism are overblown or perhaps misguided. And here we can return to Gillian Rose, who argues that "Hegel's thought has no social import if the absolute cannot be thought."[113]

The absolute, Rose says, understood in the speculative sense, "refers to the idea that, as particular individuals, we are not immediately universal, we are not species, not God, not infinite, that we live in societies where our experience as individuals does not correspond to the experience of all, where our empirical consciousness is not pure or universal consciousness, where we are not substantively free."[114] In other words, the speculative interplay between the real and the rational simply encourages our consideration of a human reality that is not absolute. As a resource for critique, this speculative interplay helps to unsettle our commonsensical and unreflective embrace of the status quo, our acceptance of the settled terms of the understanding, our acquiescence to what passes for reason and rationality. This speculative interplay is meant to provoke our critical consciousness, to stimulate political action, and by exposing contradictions that are real, that have a tangible effect on our lives, but that are not absolute. "*Speculative thinking*," Hegel says, "consists solely in the fact that thought holds fast contradiction, and in it, its own self, but does not allow itself to be dominated by it."[115] Such thinking does not signal some moralistic or metaphysical flight from reality or some comic betrayal of the tragic nature of ethical life. Such thinking encourages serious engagement with our lived experiences. And in this way, dialectical thinking, rooted in the speculative dimensions of dialectical reason, keeps the focus of critique trained squarely on the practical affairs of struggling human beings.[116] In this way, dialectical thinking counsels a kind of built-in resistance to that rather uncritical attitude of *amor fati*, that affirmative embrace of a world left to the whims of will to power, an embrace that appears all too resonant with a postpolitical age.

CONCLUSION

We have spoken of comic laughter and tragic defeat, of lighthearted pleasures gleaned from the prospect of a better tomorrow and of sorrows wrought by a more somber assessment of the human situation. These are two dimensions of dialectical thinking, two stages on which dialectical narratives or accounts play out. Yet throughout the modern tradition, going back to Hegel and Marx, the propensity toward reconciliation, toward the ultimate unification of conflicting or contradictory elements, has tended to overshadow the ways in which dialectical thinking attends to the lived experiences of ordinary women and men. If since the nineteenth century the comic has assumed an advantage over the tragic, then there is a sense in which our task, in *restaging* the dialectic, must be to amplify an underrepresented voice. It is not a matter of achieving a new hierarchy of privilege by establishing the superiority of the tragic over the comic. These two dimensions are both essential. In good dialectical fashion, they play off of one another and inform one another in their interaction. Still, in light of challenges posed here in the name of Nietzsche and with an eye toward a spirit of critique that might inform political engagement in our own time, we can explore the possibility of balancing these two dimensions in a particular way.

By itself, the amplification of the tragic stage has a profound effect on our reception of the tradition and thus on our sense of what dialectical thinking is all about. As I mentioned in chapter 1, this initial move yields three significant results. First, it helps to wrestle the tradition away from an exclusive emphasis on high theory or grand history and thus allows us to situate dialectical thinking at the site of lived experience. Second, and by extension, this emphasis on the struggles of flesh and blood individuals, ultimately an emphasis on Hegel's own turn to dialectical thinking as part of a normative defense of struggles for individual and collective autonomy, effectively vivifies the implicit moral substance of the tradition and thus cuts into any simple conjecture that dialectical thinking amounts only to a formal logic or method. And finally, a recovery of the tragic stage helps to restore a dialectical emphasis on conflict, which in turn gives the tradition something of a realist gloss, a more sympathetic disposition toward a political world that is never fully insulated from disagreement or unrest.

Perhaps it will be apparent by now that this amplification of the tragic stage also invites a new relationship with its comic counterpart. The latter, as we have seen, is the site of moral and philosophical presumptuousness. The comic stage puts on full display a self-assured confidence in both the normative commitment to the autonomous subject, what amounts to the humanist moral basis of the tradition, and a philosophical commitment to the narrative unfolding of this humanist vision, the rational working out of conflicting claims to self-legislation, competing reasons for belief and action. In the face of this self-assured confidence, an appreciation of the tragic works to introduce and sustain a sense of doubt or suspicion and in turn encourages a more *rhetorical* embrace of the moral and philosophical commitments that inform a dialectical spirit of critique. To speak of a *rhetorical* embrace here is not to deny the substance of the tradition, which is ever moved by hopes and longings born of a commitment to individual and collective freedom. But this moral and philosophical basis is affirmed in its *plausibility*, as a *working* foundation, and thus is not presumed to be the absolute truth of the human condition or the only viable or authentic account of the human situation at a particular historical moment.[117] This recovery of the tragic stage runs through each of the subsequent chapters, as does an appeal to the rhetorical dimensions of a spirit of dialectical critique.

At this point we might characterize the work undertaken in this ambitious chapter as the work of a necessary and revealing *detour* into the nineteenth century. Our principal focus going forward, indeed the principal focus of the larger book, is to consider a series of twentieth-century theorists and to cull from their works a series of contributions that speak to our own postpolitical moment. While we have identified a tragic dimension implicit to the dialectical tradition going back to Hegel, this dimension, along with a more rhetorical embrace of the moral and philosophical commitments that undergird dialectical critique, find their fullest expression in the twentieth century, in the wake of Nietzsche, and, perhaps most importantly, in response to an evolving, perhaps deteriorating, political landscape. We have spent considerable time with Hegel in order to put ourselves in a better position to appreciate that the more tragic reading of the tradition that we see in the twentieth century can and should be read as a development of, rather than a mere departure from, the works of the nineteenth-century theorists. And so having now taken this detour, having taken stock of "how . . . we now stand as regards the Hegelian *dialectic*," we turn now to counsel—in the works of Sartre, Adorno, and James—a working moral basis and a set of intellectual resources that can be said to orient, provoke, and sustain the critical imagination in trying political times.

THREE

IN A MILIEU OF SCARCITY

In an interview in 1975, when Jean-Paul Sartre was seventy years old and nearly incapacitated by blindness, after he had disavowed Marxism but at a time when he still thought of himself as a kind of dialectician, he was asked to reflect on the notion of scarcity. "I consider that scarcity is the phenomenon in which we live," he replied. "It is impossible to suppress it without changing the conditions of existence, of what is real, of intelligence . . . Even here, among ourselves, there is scarcity in our conversation: scarcity of ideas, scarcity of understanding. I may not understand your questions or may answer them badly—that, too, is scarcity."[1]

Sartre first introduced the language of scarcity in his postwar *Critique of Dialectical Reason*, as part of a broader effort to put existentialism into explicit conversation with Marxist theory. In some sense, the concept helps Sartre jumpstart a certain sort of Marxist historical narrative by calling attention to material conflicts that might be said to motor history along on its path. But the concept of scarcity does not fit easily into Marxist theory, and, as Sartre wrestles with and ultimately moves beyond Marxism, he comes to invoke the language of scarcity as something of an intellectual prod, a way of calling attention not only to debilitating poverty and crippling starvation, but also to a general sense of limitation, imperfection, disappointment, perhaps a more tragic awareness that history does not always follow a given path, that our world does not always conform to our desires or expectations. Sartre's rather distinctive emphasis on scarcity and limitation emerge alongside his evolving embrace of the dialectical tradition, as I explain, and, as I argue, ultimately Sartre's work provides a potentially valuable lesson about the status and role of the imagination in our political thinking.

To think politically is to bring a set of evaluative or normative perspectives to bear on our reality. It is to conjure up, explicitly or implicitly, a set of imaginative projections about what our human situation can and should become.[2] And throughout much of the developed world today, as the maladies of material scarcity get pushed to the margins of public consciousness, unduly relegated to the dustbin of cultural memory, there is a tendency, or at least a temptation, to orient ethical and political reflection away from any driving concern for limitation, whether material or intellectual. Habermasian thinking, for example, tends to privilege notions of mutual understanding and intersubjectivity. Post-Nietzschean thinking, often mobilized in support of a politics of becoming, tends to privilege visions of ontological abundance. Michael Hardt and Antonio Negri, in their recent efforts to imagine the ethical and political possibilities of a shared commons, expressly deride a concern for scarcity as reflective of an "eighteenth-century" sensibility, suggesting that the idea itself "corresponds less and less with our social reality."[3] Whether or not a scarcity of material resources is a genuine, objective fact within any given society today—and these times of recession and economic crisis may signal a real need to rethink the significance of the phenomenon worldwide—we must not allow normative visions of abundance, or imaginative projections of a more peaceful or productive commonality, to background the tragic reality that our world does not always, or even often, conform to our desires or expectations. It is precisely this sort of critical awareness that the Sartrean notion of scarcity, itself brought to light in and through a dialectical mode of reflection, can help to sustain.

My argument in this chapter revolves around two interconnected claims. I have indicated already that Sartre's meditations on scarcity emerge in his 1960 *Critique of Dialectical Reason*, as part of Sartre's postwar turn to Marx and to dialectical thinking. The broader of my two claims has to do simply with the general theme of this book, namely, with what the dialectical tradition might mean in our time. While nowadays theorists tend to reject *the dialectic*, as we have seen, while many have come to express reservation about the reductionism and the determinism of a strong dialectical reason, I argue here that we might remobilize the dialectical tradition by underscoring its rhetorical import and by conceiving of dialectical thinking as a tool with which to orient and sustain a critical engagement with some of the tragic realities of the modern condition. We find at least an indication of this approach in the *Critique*, where Sartre is concerned to vivify the constraining character of our material situation in the world with others. He effectively reveals our modern society as a locus of irreducible conflict—a "milieu of scarcity," as I explain—and dialectical tropes emerge in the text, at least partly, as a set of rhetorical resources, a means of throwing this situation into the boldest possible relief.

My other claim, the more specific one, emerges exclusively from my reading of the *Critique*. I argue that Sartre's particular invocation of the dialectical tradition can be substantively useful in our time insofar as it encourages a sense of reflective limitation. Building upon a political anthropology of the dialectical subject, or the constitutively empty creature struggling to fulfill needs and desires against others trying to do the same, Sartre suggests that we tend to "internalize" conflicts over material resources such that we come to exhibit an almost Hobbesian political sensibility or ethos. Even though we may subscribe to ideals of cooperation and peaceful and productive human interaction, there is a very real sense in which we remain deeply suspicious of one another, often unwilling, perhaps even unable, to make good on our basic ethical and political commitments. By underscoring the psychic significance of our situation in this "milieu of scarcity," Sartre's dialectical lens encourages a sharper attentiveness to some of the material and intellectual constraints that may prevent the ethical and political possibilities that we imagine and defend.

This chapter has five sections and a brief conclusion. In the first section, I establish some distance between a more or less standard Marxist take on the *Critique* and my own effort to read Sartre's dialectical approach as a rhetorical resource with relevance after Marxism. In the second and third sections, I show how Sartre ramps up an engagement with the dialectical tradition in an effort to refine some of his earlier existentialist assumptions and draw reflective attention toward the significance of scarcity and irreducible conflict in complex modern societies. In the fourth section, I provide some further historical periodization of Sartre's turn toward dialectical thinking by showing how this turn maps onto Sartre's evolving postwar engagement with questions of racism and colonial hegemony. Finally, in the fifth section, I put Sartre's reflections on the "milieu of scarcity" into conversation with Hardt and Negri's recent work in an effort to underscore the idea that a reconsideration of Sartre's meditations on scarcity and dialectical reason can help to orient and sustain the critical imagination.

A QUALIFIED READING

The nature and extent of Sartre's intellectual development, specifically the question of whether or not Sartre's thinking reflects any marked turn or break, continues to be a point of scholarly contention. Without delving too deeply into the many chapters of a storied and amazingly prolific career, we might note that our analysis depends on at least a working distinction between, on the one hand, the earlier existentialist works, the contributions of a "writer who resisted, not a resistor who wrote," as Sartre once described his prewar and wartime sensibilities, and, on the other, the works of a more active and engaged postwar political theorist, an intellectual more attuned to the need for collective political struggle, a global figure wrestling with his own involvement in Communist Party politics and battling to work through the theoretical and practical vicissitudes of racial and colonial oppression.[4] While we will at times reference his 1943 *Being and Nothingness* and other works from the earlier existentialist years, the bulk of our analysis turns on a reading of Sartre's 1960 *Critique of Dialectical Reason*. And given that it is not always clear what Sartre is trying to do in the *Critique*, it is important that we qualify our engagement with this difficult and perhaps overly ambitious text.

By the late 1950s, existentialism had become for Sartre an "ideology," an "enclave inside Marxism." As he famously declared in 1957, in an essay on method that would become his prologue to the larger *Critique*, Marxism was to be understood now as "the only philosophy of our time," a philosophy "which we cannot go beyond."[5] Sartre had come to speak of a "fundamental agreement with historical materialism," and in a sense this "agreement," this commitment to historical materialism, constitutes the very essence of his emerging intellectual project. Sartre's objective in the *Critique* is to explain how individual struggles for autonomy, seemingly disparate and unconnected efforts to create and maintain meaningful human lives and communities, might be explained together, in their collective totality, as integral and constitutive components of a singular and universally meaningful human history, a "developmental unity of a single process," as Sartre puts it.[6] "Our historical task, at the heart of this polyvalent world," he says, "is to bring closer the moment when History will have *only one meaning*, when it will tend to be dissolved in the concrete men who will make it common."[7]

Insofar as he is concerned to articulate a singular and universal human history, Sartre turns to the concept of the dialectical "totality" in order to emphasize the significance of the "concrete universal." The idea here is that any universality, any universal history, must necessarily express itself in and through the mediations of concrete particulars, or concrete historical actors, flesh and blood individuals.[8] If a "Truth" of history can exist, Sartre says, "it must be a Truth that has *become*, and it must make itself a *totalization*. It goes without saying that this double requirement defines that movement of being and knowing (or of comprehension) which since Hegel is called 'dialectic.'"[9] In essence, the *Critique of Dialectical Reason* is an attempt to establish an epistemology for historical materialism. It is an attempt to show that dialectical reason can render intelligible a totalizing process by which ordinary human beings collectively fashion and refashion—mostly heteronomously, but at least potentially autonomously—the values and institutional practices that constitute and sustain them.[10]

It is important to see that the *Critique* itself is a struggle, perhaps an impossible challenge, as Sartre himself seems ultimately to admit. Insofar as he moved away from the project in the early 1960s, insofar as he left the *Critique* partly unfinished and largely unrefined, he seems ultimately to have become overwhelmed by the rather Sisyphean nature of the project.[11] As I discuss in further detail later in the chapter, Sartre's disillusionment with the totalizing aspirations of the project coincide with his increasingly active involvement in the Algerian Revolution and indeed with his broader and evolving appreciation for the systemic and increasingly stubborn endurance of racial oppression and a neocolonial world order. While the *Critique* is a reflection of Sartre's sometimes strained efforts to come to terms with Marxism, it is also a testament to the growing pains of a budding decolonial theorist. And in some sense, the deeply tragic character of the colonial and neocolonial situation only contributes to the failures of the Marxist project, for if we embrace honestly the entrenched, institutional complexities of racism and imperial hegemony, we are compelled to qualify our embrace of historical materialism as a rationally comprehensible phenomenon.

Again, we will return to these issues later on in the chapter. For the time being, we might note simply that the *Critique* is motivated by a concern that the human world would fall into a kind of meaninglessness if its history could not be expressed as a unified and totalizing process. And as such, the project is borne along by a vision of ultimate reconciliation, indeed by the residual expectations of what we described in the previous chapter as the comic stage of the modern dialectical tradition.[12] And yet, there is something more to Sartre's contribution, there is indeed another dimension to his turn toward dialectical thinking. Implicitly in the text, Sartre develops something of a dialectical lens that, even when set off from any broader narrative of historical materialism, can help provoke an important and distinctive critical perspective on our human situation.[13]

The very idea that we can provoke a critical perspective, or a certain way of seeing our human situation, has always been an integral part of the modern dialectical tradition. In *The Communist Manifesto*, for example, Marx and Engels envision a sense of reflective clarity, an epistemic condition in which "man is at last compelled to face with sober senses, his real conditions of life, and his relations with his kind."[14] But for Marx and Engels, the assumption is that we can tap into a substantive dialectical reason, unburden ourselves of the afflictions of ideological distortion, and come to see the true economic and social relationships that sustain human living. In our own time, these characteristically nineteenth-century claims and assumptions can be rather hard to swallow. The argument that I develop in what follows depends on a conscious effort to generate some distance between the presumptuous ontological and epistemological assumptions of the modern dialectical tradition, on the one hand, and, on the other, an effort to read dialectical language as a rhetorical resource, a tool with which to provoke and sustain reflective awareness of some of the more unattractive cultural tendencies at work in complex and diverse contemporary societies.

In some sense, this approach folds Sartre's use of dialectical motifs onto his insistence on engaged reflection. The language of "reflection" in Sartre carries a certain ethical significance. It has to do with an honest, even courageous, acceptance of our human situation in the world. But, for Sartre, this is not simply a passive acceptance of things. This is not merely a sidelined "contemplation" of a world that is perceived as more or less inert. Reflection for Sartre implies an active and critical engagement with a situation that is always changing, a situation that is, at least to some extent, always changeable.[15] While Sartre himself tends to speak of "dialectical Reason" or "dialectical rationality" or "dialectical intelligibility," and while the common presumption is that these dialectical references simply map onto a rather strong Marxist narrative, I suggest that dialectical reason provides something of an epistemic supplement to Sartre's insistence on engaged reflection, such that Sartre can be said to inspire a mode of critical reflection attuned to uncertainty, a mode of reflection more appropriate to political thinking after Marxism. To develop this approach, we must first consider how the *Critique of Dialectical Reason* provides a specific frame, a specific dialectical lens, through which we might generate a critical perspective on our social situation in the world.

SARTRE'S DIALECTICAL LENS

Sartre had always underscored the significance of our human "situation." Exhibiting an early attraction to Heidegger's notion of *Geworfenheit*, or "thrownness," Sartre's existentialist writings were concerned to reveal how our situation in the world affects our efforts to generate meaning in our life activities. It will be helpful to provide a few briefs remarks on Sartre's early account of the human situation, because part of Sartre's concern in the *Critique*, part of the reason why he turns to the language and conceptual resources of dialectical thinking, is to address some of the social and political ambiguities implicit in his earlier existentialism.

"Man cannot be distinguished from his situation," Sartre writes in *Anti-Semite and Jew*, "for it forms him and decides his possibilities." But, Sartre continues, "it is he who gives it meaning by making his choices within it and by it."[16] The thought here is that we find ourselves thrown rather fortuitously into a particular historical milieu, shaped by a particular set of social and material circumstances. But in the early work, this thought is often eclipsed by Sartre's more fundamental commitment to the idea of a radical human freedom. In reading the existentialist writings prior to the *Critique*, one gets a sense that we are somehow free to change or transcend our worldly situation simply by refiguring the meaning and significance that we "project" onto it.[17] As creative individuals, full of potential—"I am always beyond what I am," Sartre says in *Being and Nothingness*, "about to come into myself"—we simply confront a mere "resistance of things" or a "coefficient of adversity" offered up by the objective world.[18] This emphasis on a radical human freedom thus risks a certain denigration of *things*, a backgrounding of the very world into which we find ourselves thrown. What takes primacy here is the creative freedom of the transcendental subject, a being able to detach itself from its situation, posit meaning, and project itself forward.

This is perhaps only an unintended ambiguity in the thinking of an existentialist philosopher who is not yet concerned to flesh out the critical or political import of his "phenomenological essay on ontology."[19] But in the postwar period, as Sartre tries to put existentialism into explicit conversation with a more active political agenda, he tempers his earlier thinking on radical human freedom and begins to counsel a more focused and sustained attentiveness to the constraining character of our social and material situation.[20] And he begins to invoke the conceptual resources of dialectical reason to help him do so.

Early on in the *Critique*, Sartre says that "the whole" of dialectical rationality is contained in a single sentence from Marx's *Eighteenth Brumaire*, namely, the well-known statement about how "men make their own history . . . not under circumstances chosen by themselves, but under circumstances directly found, given and transmitted from the past."[21] Sartre wants to bring into focus a "permanent and dialectical unity of freedom and necessity."[22] And if freedom for Sartre is our capacity for self-transcendence, our "going beyond a situation," necessity is our "field of possibilities," which is to be understood now as a "strongly structured region which depends upon all of History and which includes its own contradictions."[23]

"The crucial discovery of dialectical reason," Sartre says, "is that man is 'mediated' by things to the same extent as things are 'mediated' by man."[24] As Mark Poster has pointed out, Sartre wants to navigate a course between two opposing tendencies in twentieth-century Marxist thinking, one that privileges the deterministic character of matter and that threatens to liquidate the role of the human subject, and another that, as exemplified by Lukács in *History and Class Consciousness*, threatens to recoup a kind of Hegelian idealism "in which the object [loses] its power and the dialectic [is] reduced to pure subjectivity."[25] While the Sartre of the *Critique* remains a theorist of radical human freedom, while he continues to underscore our capacities for choice and action and responsibility, his emphasis on a subject-object dialectic brings into focus a constitutive interplay between our human freedom, on the one hand, and historicized, socialized necessity, on the other. Sartre begins now to situate *our* freedom, yours and mine in the here and now, within a field of objectivity, what Sartre calls the "practico-inert," which has been shaped by the freedom of past generations, by the historical choices and actions of the concrete individuals who have come before us.[26] As we noted at the outset, Sartre's ultimate purpose in the *Critique* is to show how these concrete human actions, these expressions of human freedom, can be understood in terms of a singular narrative, a universal or "totalizing" human history. And yet here we can emphasize our qualified reading of the *Critique*. Even if we set aside the larger narrative of a totalizing historical materialism, we see that dialectical reason signals for Sartre something of an interpretive approach, a way of making sense of human being and the world by paying specific attention to the interconnections between subject and object, or between our human activity, on the one hand, and, on the other, the social and material world that we necessarily encounter.

So one way in which Sartre's dialectical lens encourages a critical perspective on our situation is by bringing into focus the constitutive interplays between subject and object. It is important to see that this lens also enriches Sartre's picture of the human subject as such. Again, a brief contrast with the earlier work will be helpful here.

While we do not know for sure whether Sartre attended any of Alexandre Kojève's famous lectures on Hegel in the 1930s, a certain Kojèveian influence is evident in the way that Sartre brings a set of Hegelian motifs to bear on his early account of human subjectivity. We are for Sartre desiring creatures, beings characterized at bottom by a constitutive emptiness, a kind of negativity that provokes our engagement with others and the world. "Human reality," Sartre says in *Being and Nothingness*, "is not something which exists first in order afterwards to lack this or that; it exists first as lack and in immediate, synthetic connection with what it lacks."[27] And for Sartre this lack cannot really be overcome. Striving to fulfill our wants and desires, striving to achieve a negation of the negation, we are simply destined to return again and again to our condition of negativity. We are simply destined to confront again and again further wants, further desires.

In *Being and Nothingness*, this negativity is teased along by desire, which is for Sartre a more or less ontological category. That is to say, this sense of constitutive emptiness is meaningful in Sartre's early work insofar as we desire the security of a stable identity, *for-itself-in-itself*. Rather than merely *become*, we want to *be*. In the *Critique*, Sartre adds a layer of political complexity by emphasizing in addition the category of *need*. "Everything is to be explained through *need* (*le besoin*)," he says now, "need is the first totalizing relation between the material being, man, and the material ensemble of which he is a part."[28]

The language of need does not really change this idea that a constitutive negativity prompts our activity in the world. As a new way of describing the process, this language simply adds a layer of gravity or seriousness to Sartre's account of how we strive to fulfill our emptiness, our lack. And this language works further to vivify our dependence upon others and the material world. The point here is that, insofar as we must address and respond to our basic human needs, we establish a series of connections with others and the world, and our situation becomes meaningful to us in light of these connections. "When [our] project passes through the surrounding world towards it end," Sartre says in the *Critique*, "it unifies the field of instrumentality around itself, so as to make it into a totality which will provide a foundation for the individual objects which must come to its aid in its task."[29] Insofar as our "project" implies the satisfaction of a need for, say, comfortable living arrangements, other human beings and the material world become meaningful to us at least in part because they affect our ability to satisfy this need. As we will see in a moment, Sartre wants to provide a theoretical account of why we tend to reduce others and the world to their instrumental qualities. He wants to account for why we tend to dehumanize one another, why we often come to see others and the world as a potential threat to our own human fulfillment.

To be sure, and to say it again, the Sartre of the *Critique* remains a theorist of radical human freedom. He reinforces the active role of subjective consciousness over and against a material world that is still understood, at least to some extent, as a "coefficient of adversity." But for the earlier Sartre, the material world is *merely* a coefficient of adversity. We see now that the constraining character of this adversity takes on a much stronger significance. By implicating the subject in a social and historical situation, by focusing on our desires and our needs as we experience them against a socially and historically conditioned materiality, Sartre sketches a picture of the modern human condition that is far more challenged and far more challenging, one that reveals a more unsettling experience than that of simple existential anxiety. Dialectical reflection reveals the modern human condition as a "milieu of scarcity," a situation that "first constitutes an initial antagonistic relation between every individual and each and every other," a situation that "produces everyone in a multiplicity as a *mortal danger for the other*."[30] We come to see our situation as one in which "*there is not enough for everybody*."[31] My desires, my needs, make everyone else a threat to my satisfaction, my survival.

This is really the key point of our exposition, this notion of a "milieu of scarcity" that comes into focus in Sartre's postwar work. And the important point for our purposes is that Sartre's dialectical lens reveals our modern human situation as a locus of suspicion, insecurity, and conflict, one that we tend to "internalize" and reflect in our basic political sensibilities. I turn now to flesh this out a bit more.

"IN A MILIEU OF SCARCITY"

Sartre will describe scarcity as a "dialectical fact," a phenomenon that comes into focus through dialectical reflection on our human situation.[32] The language of scarcity provides a way of capturing our social "milieu," a way of describing a "unitary relation of a plurality of individuals" in the modern world.[33] As Fredric Jameson describes it, Sartre's concept of scarcity is "unintelligible in itself, simply a fact to which we cannot assign any metaphysical significance whatsoever," but it "nonetheless is the framework in which we must act, and conditions and alienates our acts and projects in their very conception."[34] Insofar as we project meaning onto the world, insofar as we fashion our life as a project and bring a field of meaning into existence around our project, we do so in a milieu of scarcity, in a situation in which both the world and others, materiality and sociality, become a potential threat to the success of our project, a threat to our fulfillment and to our very being.

"The world exists for anyone," Sartre says, "insofar as the consumption of such and such a product elsewhere, by others, deprives him *here* of the opportunity of getting and consuming something of the same kind." Any given person "can be united with each other indirectly through a series of adhesions, without having the slightest idea of the existence of this or that other person, . . . [but] the other members of the group do exist for him collectively, in that each one of them is a threat to his life."[35] The individual in any given situation "will see everyone *in terms of* the object of consumption or the manufactured product, and, on this basic level, he will recognize them as the mere possibility of the consumption of something he himself needs. In short, he will find each of them to be the material possibility of his being annihilated through the material annihilation of an object of primary necessity."[36]

To be sure, Sartre's language has an almost hyperbolic quality to it. He wants to encourage critical attentiveness to our suspicions, to our insecurities, to the roots of social and political conflict. And his descriptions seem almost exaggerated, intended, perhaps, only to provoke a rather grim perspective on the postwar human condition. I will continue to explore the rhetorical quality of Sartre's language as we move along. But I note here at least one claim that Sartre makes about how our implication in this situation, this milieu of scarcity, comes to affect our basic political sensibilities.

Simply put, we tend to dehumanize one another. While we may subscribe to ideals of democratic equality, while we may underscore notions of a common humanity or an implicit reciprocity at the heart of our interactive or communicative endeavors, Sartre suggests that in a milieu of scarcity such happy ideals amount only to a kind of ideological mystification. "In pure reciprocity," he says, "that which is Other than me *is also the same*." But ours is not an ideal world. We do not experience pure reciprocity. In our situation, "in reciprocity as *modified by scarcity*, the same appears to us as anti-human in so far as *this same man* appears as radically Other—that is to say, as threatening us with death. . . . we understand them as if they belonged to *another species*, our demonic double."[37] While the milieu of scarcity is simply a contingent background condition for Sartre, one to which we cannot ascribe any metaphysical quality, we do find ourselves in this situation, and this situation certainly affects the way that we ascribe meaning to ourselves, others, and the world.

Sartre speaks here of an "internal, dialectical conditioning" or a kind of acculturation that both follows from and serves to reinforce our situation in the milieu of scarcity.[38] As we have seen, we are needy and desiring creatures, we impose our "project" onto the world and allow the meaning of the world to coalesce around our "project," around our given needs and fashioned desires. And this activity does not affect "individuals *subjectively*; on the contrary, it makes everyone *objectively dangerous*." We are "*objectively* constituted as non-human, and this non-humanity is expressed in *praxis* by the perception of evil as the structure of the Other."[39] Sartre seems to suggest here that any attempt to engage honestly with the human situation in our time must include a careful look at "what makes people see each other as the Other and as the principle of Evil."[40] And this attentiveness to need and desire, this figuration of our modern situation as a milieu of scarcity, provides one possible explanation, perhaps one part of a possible explanation, for why we tend to treat one another so miserably, why an entrenched spirit of possessive individualism continues to haunt our political culture.

Whatever else Sartre may be up to in the *Critique*, he certainly offers a remarkable perspective on our human situation, a perspective that is brought to life through a kind of dialectical lens or according to a dialectical structure of intelligibility. By the lights of Sartre's *Critique*, we see that "whatever men and events are, they certainly appear within the compass of *scarcity*; that is, in a society still incapable of emancipating itself from its needs—hence from nature—a society which is thereby defined according to its techniques and tools."[41] Our condition becomes meaningful in a certain kind of way; it becomes ripe for conflict, predisposed, even, to a sense of *irreducible* conflict, given that we pursue our needs and desires against others and against the material world in what we perceive as a milieu of scarcity.

"AN INFERNAL MACHINE"

At this point, it may be helpful to provide some further contextualization of Sartre's postwar perspective. We noted at the outset that this language of scarcity emerges in the late 1950s, initially in *Search for a Method*, which would become Sartre's prologue to the broader *Critique*. And the *Critique*, concerned as it is to articulate an epistemology for historical materialism, is set against the backdrop of Marxist discourse and is often seen as an effort on Sartre's part to stake out his contribution vis-à-vis the "only philosophy of our time." And yet this notion of scarcity, which signals for Sartre a rather tragic embrace of irreducible conflict, does not sit easily with Marxist theory or with the conventional staging of the broader dialectical tradition, both of which are teased along by the promise of abundance, the promise of happy reconciliation.[42] I might suggest that Sartre's rather sobering dialectical lens—which, to invoke yet another of Sartre's many arresting passages, reveals essentially that "all men are slaves insofar as their life unfolds in the practico-inert field and insofar as this field is always conditioned by scarcity"—is affected quite significantly by his evolving thinking about colonialism and the racial dimensions of our historically fashioned proclivity toward conflict and competition.[43]

By the late 1950s, in response specifically to the developing struggle in Algeria, Sartre had begun to reflect more deeply on the constraining character of the colonial situation, what he would describe now as a more complete "system" of exploitation, one that envelops and conscripts both colonized and colonizer, one that must be seen in its systemic character as a kind of "practico-inert hell," an "infernal machine of the practico-inert field."[44] As we have seen already, Sartre's turn toward dialectical reason is part of an attempt to reveal a unity of "freedom and necessity," to show that we freely create history but, as Marx would put it, always under conditions handed down from past generations, always under conditions molded by the praxis of our forebears. In the case of the colonial project, itself born of the milieu of scarcity, Sartre's dialectical lens reveals that past efforts to find cheap labor, which Sartre identifies as the "key condition of the colonial undertaking," have led, over time and through a series of individual acts, to the establishment of socially differentiated groups and indeed to racial differentiation as a most egregious instrument of colonial exploitation.[45] As he puts it in his 1957 preface to Albert Memmi's *The Colonizer and the Colonized*, "Racism is inscribed in the events themselves, in the institutions, in the nature of the exchanges and the production. . . . Racism is *already there*, carried by the *praxis* of colonialism, engendered at every instant by the colonial apparatus."[46]

As the colonial project wears on, Sartre says, race becomes an *Idea-exis*, a still contingent and socially constructed category, but one that is experienced increasingly as an "exigency," an urgent need or demand to reproduce behaviors, habits, routines.[47] And this "exigency" is largely a result of the "serial" nature of the racial collectives constituted and sustained by the colonial system. What is distinctive about the "serial" collective is that its members are held together heteronomously "by the objectified results of the material effects of the actions of others." Members are, as Iris Marion Young puts it, "unified passively by the relations their actions have to material objects and practico-inert histories."[48] In the context of colonialism, we may not consciously will or affirm our racial or colonial identity, but, in our daily pursuits of our individual objectives, our action—our *praxis*, our freedom—is always already manipulated by an objective racial *order*, one that effectively *orders us* anonymously as a particular kind of person, with particular advantages and disadvantages. And insofar as we are conscripted serially into a particular racial category, ordered anonymously by something external to us, we become distanced, not only from members of other races, but, perhaps more significantly, from other members of our own race, and indeed from our own selves, from our own critical capacities. We simply experience ourselves and others as anonymous, interchangeable units in a racial series, and, within a perceived milieu of scarcity, our individual lives become focused almost exclusively on our private concerns, our individual interests. Here Sartre speaks of "impotence as a real bond between members of a series." He says that a "series reveals itself to everyone when they perceive in themselves and Others their common inability to eliminate their material differences."[49]

This conception of race as "seriality," this emphasis on the "exigent" character of racial ordering, especially within the context of the colonial system, is reflective of Sartre's evolving reactions to a changing political world. Throughout the postwar period, as Jonathan Judaken has noted, Sartre finds himself "stumbling toward seeing race not as an idea, but as an ideology, not only as a phenomenon of consciousness, but as a product of behaviors, practices, rituals, folkways, and symbols institutionalized daily." And "by the late 1950s, Sartre conceived of racism not as a mythical blinder that legitimates oppression" but rather as "a central pillar in the structure of exploitation itself."[50] For our purposes, this turn is significant for a couple of reasons.

First of all, the turn itself—this shift from race understood largely as a psychological phenomenon to race understood as an *Idea-exis*, an exigency interwoven into the very fabric of institutional reality—maps directly onto the narrative that we have sought to establish regarding Sartre's intellectual development from the early existentialist writings through the *Critique*. In, for example, *Anti-Semite and Jew*, which was written in 1944, shortly after the publication of *Being and Nothingness*, racism is conceived as an attitude, a reflection of our individual responsibility within a particular situation and not as a reflection of our impotence within the material structures of a broader hegemonic system. It is through a series of enriching experiences during the postwar period—including engagement with Richard Wright and, in a 1945 trip to America, with the institutional character of racial oppression in the Jim Crow South; including evolving engagement with Léopold Sédar Senghor, Aimé Césaire, and the writers of the Negritude movement; including further evolving interactions with Frantz Fanon and Che Guevara and increasingly active support of decolonization struggles throughout the world—that Sartre gradually comes to see that "the essence of racism, in effect, is that it is not a system of thoughts which might be false or pernicious." Racism, for the Sartre of the *Critique*, "*is not a thought at all.*"[51] Whereas in the early 1950s Fanon could say that "Sartre had forgotten that the Negro suffers in his body quite differently from the white man," by the end of the decade Sartre seems to have come to terms with Fanon's testimonial insistence on a more deeply situated, Sartre might say more thoroughly systematized, "fact of blackness."[52] And we might suggest that Sartre's evolving dialectical lens is part of what "makes it clear that *racist ideas*, as structures of the collective opinion of the colonists, are petrified actions," and thus established institutions "manifested as imperatives." In other words, Sartre's dialectical lens helps to reveal that racist practices have become quite literally second nature to us, a fundamental feature of that field of practico-inert "necessity," that imperative delimitation of our human "freedom."

What is especially significant here, for our purposes, is that, by the lights of Sartre's dialectical lens, racism is not something that can be overcome simply by changing our attitude or by thinking differently. Within the colonial system, Sartre says, even the most well-intentioned individuals find themselves "carried along by the colonial apparatus." That is to say, "they *do* each day, *in deed*, what they condemn *in their dreams*, and each of their acts contributes to maintaining oppression."[53] The colonial *system*, in which racism "presents itself as infinite depth," requires something more than individual ethical resistance. It requires a *systematic* response. It requires collective revolutionary action. And yet, insofar as our collective identities are serialized, insofar as we find ourselves isolated, fragmented, "impotent," as Sartre puts it, our "practico-inert hell" is only exacerbated by an incapacity for purposive collective action. As Paige Arthur remarks in her recent study of Sartre on decolonization, in a passage that underscores the multilayered significance of the postwar turn to dialectical thinking, "Sartre's general agreement with Marx concerning a theory of the social reproduction of identities—rather than, as one might have expected from the author of *Being and Nothingness*, more attention being focused on the possibility that individual praxis might disrupt any process of reproduction—is a sure mark of his general pessimism about the human condition in general in 1960, and presumably about the wherewithal of individual[s] . . . to stand up against systems of oppression."[54]

This all sounds rather grim, rather despairing. But such is at least partly the point. As our admittedly very brief detour into Sartre's evolving consideration of race and colonialism indicates, the postwar turn to dialectical thinking elicits, to put it mildly, a rather somber reflective mood. And as I suggest in the remainder of the chapter, such a mood may be more attractive, indeed more productive, than our conventional sensibilities would like to admit.

REFLECTIVE LIMITATION

Thus far we have played up Sartre's emphasis on scarcity and conflict. And we might say that ultimately Sartre counsels a kind of Hobbesian political imaginary.[55] To be sure, such a statement is perhaps a bit misleading, as Sartre plainly denies any "state of nature." Scarcity and conflict are, for him, wholly contingent, socially constructed phenomena.[56] But the comparison with Hobbes is not entirely unfounded either. Throughout the *Critique*, we are told that our political subconscious is more or less haunted by the specter of irreducible conflict, the specter of a war of all against all. And we are given an image of a human situation that is rather nasty and brutish, a life that is, at least potentially, quite short.

More than three decades after his death Sartre remains a familiar name, but he is not today an especially popular figure, nor is he considered to be an especially important political theorist. There are many reasons for this, and certainly one has to do with the loosely Hobbesian tenor of his postwar work.[57] Sartre's more diagnostic orientation seems to have been eclipsed in our time by a kind of prescriptive bias implicit to several prominent strands of contemporary normative theory. The contemporary emphasis on, for example, mutual understanding or commonality or intersubjectivity is reflective of an effort to fashion, or perhaps implicitly to assume, a political imaginary in which ideals of cooperation and peaceful interaction take on a more real and prominent quality. At the outset, I mentioned that one of the more prominent expressions of this trend can be found in the work of Michael Hardt and Antonio Negri, two contemporary theorists who strongly emphasize notions of commonality and human cooperation and who explicitly question the continued relevance of a Hobbesian political imaginary. I will comment briefly on Hardt and Negri's recent work and then suggest that the Sartrean approach might encourage a sense of reflective limitation.

In what could be a line from Sartre's own text, Hardt and Negri indicate that a fundamental part of their objective is to work out a "new theoretical apparatus adequate to our situation."[58] But for Hardt and Negri, this business of scarce resources and this notion of a "war of all against all" hark back to a kind of "eighteenth-century" sensibility, one that "corresponds less and less with our social reality."[59] We might do better, they say, if we simply relax our concerns about scarcity and conflict, not because industrial capitalism has finally delivered its "general plenty" of material abundance, but because "immaterial property" and "immaterial production" have become the more important features of our contemporary economic and political landscape.

"Material property," they say, "such as land or water or a car, cannot be in two places at once: my having and using it negates your having and using it." But "immaterial property, such as an idea or an image or a form of communication, is infinitely reproducible. It can be everywhere at once, and my having it does not hinder yours." Citing Thomas Jefferson, they go on to say that "ideas are enhanced by their communication: when I light my candle from yours they both seem to burn brighter." And while "some resources do remain scarce today, . . . many, in fact, particularly the newest elements of the economy, do not operate on a logic of scarcity." In our own social and political present, "when productive mechanisms rely increasingly on expansive open networks of communication and cooperation, then the notion of a basic conflict with everyone tends to seem increasingly unnatural."[60]

Hardt and Negri ultimately make a kind of Habermasian point, reminding us that "we could not interact and communicate in our daily lives if languages, forms of speech, gestures, methods of conflict resolution, ways of loving, and the vast majority of the practices of living were not common. Social life depends on the common."[61] Incidentally, Habermas himself has criticized Sartre for his blindness toward what is common and mutual and shared in human interaction. "With Sartre, in the last analysis," Habermas says, "all interactions remain something akin to the attempts of world-projecting subjects to objectivate one another, that is, to mutually overpower one another. If one begins with the premises of transcendental philosophy, one cannot comprehend mutual understanding, the commonality of an intersubjectively shared language, tradition, or life-world. . . . Even later, [i.e., in the *Critique*] 'intersubjectivity' remained something, if not entirely foreign, secondary for Sartre."[62]

To be sure, Sartre's notion of the milieu is meant to signify something like an intersubjective commonality, a locus for the generation and resonance of meaning and social objectivity. But Habermas is correct to point out, in effect, that Sartre's texts *privilege* the lived experience of suspicion, insecurity, and conflict over the formal or ideal structures that our human interactions might be said to presuppose. And where this is a problem for Habermas, where this is a distortion of our social reality for Hardt and Negri, I suggest it can be a sign of interpretive strength, a source of reflective sobriety in our time.

Before I elaborate on this claim, I should note that Hardt and Negri do acknowledge that at least ideological conflict has for us both a presence and a future. In some ways, their emphasis on commonality is meant to sharpen ideological opposition by helping to strengthen coalitions among the politically oppressed. An emphasis on what is common, they say, can help to reveal "common methods of combat, common ways of living, and common desires for a better world." Such an emphasis can generate a new kind of "surplus" that "appears monstrous, especially to those in power."[63] But this more or less tactical point does not really affect the broader ways in which a driving emphasis on commonality can be said to orient critical reflection on political life. By emphasizing what is common and mutual and shared, by effectively fashioning the political imagination in terms of surplus, abundance, and peaceful commonality, we risk a subsequent inattentiveness to the darker and less attractive features of our contemporary political landscape.[64]

It may be a characteristic feature of "postindustrial" culture: despite the reality of deep and sustained global recession, our public discourse is saturated with more attractive images of abundance, surplus, the prospect of unfettered growth, even the idea of a coming collective prosperity. Citizens and politicians alike seem to invest a good bit of faith in the idea that we can grow our way out of the maladies of material limitation. There is something of a cultural presumption that we can somehow achieve the sorts of economic, social, and political outcomes that we desire without facing any real challenges to our well-being, our social status, our quality and way of life. But if we come to see our world through Sartre's dialectical lens, if we "situate," as it were, our public culture within the crosshairs of Sartre's dialectical scope, we see that an emphasis on abundance amounts simply to a cultural myth, a "mystifier" that obscures the often very miserable ways in which human beings continue to treat one another.[65] Sartre's thinking encourages our sustained consideration of the unfortunate possibility that while many of us may celebrate the prospect of more abundant futures—perhaps a community committed to principles of equality, mutual understanding, a shared commons, perhaps the prospect of a productively multiracial world—our political sensibilities continue to reflect what Sartre describes as "interiorized, dialectical conditioning," a deep-seated suspicion of one another that lends a sense of disingenuousness to our conscious ethical and political commitments.

To say it again, Sartre's insistence on dialectical reflection reveals our situation in a milieu of scarcity. And to understand our situation as such is to underscore the material dimensions of political life or the lived experience of our social and political interactions. But the real point that I want to make, in this section and in this chapter more broadly, is that Sartre is concerned not only with a material fact of scarcity. He is concerned not only with the fact that, despite the remarkable expansion of productive power in the modern period, we must grapple with limited material resources. He is concerned also with how this material fact plays on our political sensibilities, how it figures into our political subconscious, how it affects the way that we think about one another and treat one another. Sartre's point is that we tend to internalize the struggle over material limitation in such a way that we often do not heed our own ethical and political ideals, our principles, our values. Where Hardt and Negri point out that an idea may not correspond to a logic of scarcity, they are suggesting that ideals of freedom and equality can be shared universally. And in our own time, throughout the liberal, cosmopolitan West, most of us do share, and more or less universally, these principles of freedom and equality. Most of us do subscribe to these ideals, these *universal* ideals. And yet, when push comes to shove politically, these ideals tend to fly out the window. I may champion the principles of freedom and equality, I may defend notions of commonality and mutual cooperation, but not in my backyard, not at a cost to my well-being, my privilege.[66]

Sartre encourages a sense of reflective limitation by reminding us that our political hopes and dreams, our desires and visions for a more humane world, are often already challenged by a material condition and a corresponding ethical and political sensibility that fight against them tooth and nail. In short, at least part of the lesson of Sartre's *Critique of Dialectical Reason*, part of the lesson of his insistence on a dialectical mode of critical reflection, is that our ethical and political interactions are all too often "established and pursued in a climate of fear and mutual mistrust by individuals who are always ready to believe that the Other is an antihuman member of an alien species; in other words, that the Other, whoever he may be, can always be seen by the Others as 'the one who started it.'"[67]

CONCLUSION

Throughout this discussion, Sartre has been cast as a thoroughly critical and eminently diagnostic theorist. His 1960 *Critique of Dialectical Reason* yields, we have suggested, a certain frame of vision, a dialectical lens, which places a rather inordinate emphasis on our human needs and desires, our dependence upon others and the world, and our efforts, indeed our struggles, to satisfy our needs and desires and to master or overcome our dependencies. The perspective that we have sought to elicit, this rather grim depiction of our human situation in a "milieu of scarcity," is not to be understood as an end in itself. This perspective is meant simply to temper the critical imagination, to lend a sense of gravity to any normative projection of what we might wish our political communities to become.

To be sure, Sartre himself does not keep to the diagnostic function of this emphasis on conflict born of human neediness. For Sartre, the very category of need can be understood as the basis of a more prescriptive vision. Need, he says in his 1964 Rome lecture, is "the first rudiment of a dialectical future, the first praxis of the negation of the negation, the first unconditioned end, the first normative structure."[68] And as Robert Stone and Elizabeth Bowman remind us in their important commentary on this as yet unpublished lecture, "need always posits integral or satisfied human life, albeit at some distance from the present."[69] That said, Sartre never really has much to say about how this negation of the negation, this revolutionary praxis born of a milieu of scarcity, might lead to a qualitatively new social reality, other than to suggest that such collective praxis is itself quite unlikely in the modern world and that its "content would be defined in the struggle."[70] Moreover, the normative maxim that "need is its satisfaction's own justification," which Sartre claims to inherit from Marx, would seem only to exacerbate violent conflict in the here and now.[71] For if "the root of morality is *in need*, that is to say in the animality of man," if "it is need which poses man as his own end, and praxis as domination of the universe to be affected through work," then it would seem that Sartre's normative vision never really moves beyond a drive to master or overcome our subjective situation.[72] Nowadays, as I have noted, Sartre's thinking is often thought to be irrevocably dated, perhaps downright passé, and I might wager that this normative orientation toward self-mastery, which William McBride has described as "one of the less attractive or defensible aspects of Sartre's thought from beginning to end, an unfortunate inheritance from the Hegelian [we might say dialectical] tradition," is the primary culprit.[73]

But I might wager also that, for our purposes, we need not get too worked up over these issues, for we might find something of value in a mode of thinking that, by prescriptive normative standards, leads only to a rather displeasing sketch of life in the modern world. The point of our discussion has been to suggest that Sartre's meditations on dialectical reason—which encourage us to see our human interaction "*in its inadequacy, in its imperfections and in its mistakes*"—helps to vivify, in our critical consciousness, a sense of limitation, imperfection, disappointment, perhaps a more tragic awareness that our human world does not always, or even often, conform to our desires or expectations.[74] If normative political thinking by its very nature requires an imaginative projection of what our human situation can and should become, our reading of Sartre's postwar work might help to temper or counterbalance the normative temptation to extend ethical and political thinking beyond the very world in which we find ourselves. This sense of reflective limitation does not quell our hopes and dreams. It simply encourages, to say it again, an inspired and sustained attentiveness to the material and psychic constraints that often delimit the very possibilities we may imagine.

FOUR

BETWEEN DESPAIR AND REDEMPTION

It has become a frequently invoked image, that of Walter Benjamin approaching the Franco-Spanish border in 1940, in the wake of the Hitler-Stalin pact and in possession of his famous "Theses on the Philosophy of History." It is an image of a deeply despondent and ultimately suicidal Benjamin, a man yearning desperately for some sort of salvation, some sort of messianic interruption to what he regarded as the "catastrophe" of human history. And it is an image that helps to explain Benjamin's interest in redemptive criticism, his effort to work theological motifs into a materialist critique of modern society. Confronted by an increasingly barbaric modern world, Benjamin sought to sustain the critical imagination by investing faith in the coming of what he called *Jetztzeiten*, literally "now-times," by which he meant something like the forgotten moments or experiences or semantic potentials that might inspire our reflection, allow us to "blast open the continuum of history" and perhaps rescue the possibility of an alternative future.[1]

Desperate times seem to justify an effort to "enlist the services of theology."[2] But later theorists have struggled to square Benjamin's redemptive and messianic impulses with materialist critical theory.[3] Habermas sums up the general worry when he argues that a "materialist theory of social development cannot be simply fitted into the anarchistic conception of [messianic interruptions] . . . which intermittently come crashing through fate as if from above. An anti-evolutionary conception of history cannot be tacked onto historical materialism as if it were a monk's cowl."[4] And Habermas carries the worry a step further when he says that "a critique which prepares itself for a leap into past *Jetztzeiten* so that it might rescue and redeem semantic potentials has a very mediated relation to political praxis."[5] By departing from a materialist conception of social and economic development, Benjamin's redemptive criticism cannot be understood as "reflection in a formative process," it cannot be understood as a "consciousness-raising" enterprise. Consequently, it remains unclear just how this open-ended redemptive criticism might prefigure a politics or any concerted effort at critical intervention.[6]

Habermas's remarks on the *Aktualität* or contemporary significance of Benjamin's thought were published in 1972, still a period of vibrant critical engagement and democratic activity throughout Europe and the United States. It was also still a time in which it was potentially rhetorically persuasive to go after Benjamin for not being Marxist enough and for not contributing to a critical theory understood as a generally "formative" or "consciousness-raising" enterprise. While our own political moment pales in comparison to what Benjamin must have experienced on his way to Portbou in 1940, some have suggested that we may be gesturing back toward a kind of Benjaminian darkness. Finding ourselves run up against a public sphere marred by a deep sense of democratic demoralization and political apathy, a public sensibility disillusioned with Marxist and other traditional liberation narratives, we seem to have fallen, to borrow a now almost platitudinous phrase, on "dark times" for substantive democracy. Perhaps the present moment signals a need to rethink the political, and indeed democratic, import of a critical sensibility borne along by a certain redemptive vision. Perhaps we might rethink, after Marxism, the possible interconnections between redemption, messianic intervention, these theological motifs, and a materialist critique of our social and political situation.

The possible connections between critique and redemption point toward a deeply elusive dimension of Benjamin's thinking, and these prefatory remarks on Benjamin are meant simply to focus our attention on the question of how we might sustain hope in the face of overwhelming difficulty. Throughout this chapter, we will take cues from Adorno rather than Benjamin, from a figure likewise known for his tussles with melancholy yet more indebted to the dialectical tradition than to any theological one, Judaic or otherwise. Ultimately we are concerned with what Adorno can teach us about dialectical thinking, but we might keep in mind that this "aberrant Marxist, Left Hegelian par excellence, close reader and follower of Nietzsche" nevertheless "insists," as David Kaufmann points out, "on using blatantly religious tropes throughout his career."[7] Take for instance the most frequently cited passage from his wartime *Minima Moralia*—an "urgent" passage, according to Robert Hullot-Kentor, one that we "can hardly help but quote"—which insists precisely on blatantly religious tropes and, in so doing, captures something of that Benjaminian emphasis on the potential redemption of a dark and despairing worldly situation.[8] "The only philosophy which can be responsibly practiced in face of despair," Adorno says, "is the attempt to contemplate all things as they would present themselves from the standpoint of redemption. . . . Perspectives must be fashioned that displace and estrange the world, reveal it to be, with its rifts and crevices, as indigent and distorted as it will one day appear in the messianic light."[9] This is an urgent passage indeed, one that we will use as a guiding thread throughout the chapter. The aim here is not so much to expose or interrogate the theological or religious dimensions of Adorno's work but rather to show how some of Adorno's theological language, certain of his "blatantly religious tropes," can be said to map onto a distinctive style of dialectical thinking, one that might recommend itself to democratic citizens in dark times.

The idea here is that dialectical thinking signals a location at which transcendental claims enter our thinking and that, for Adorno, such thinking provides a locus for a critically animating interplay between opposing or antithetical rhetorical figurations, a simultaneous consideration of despair *and* redemption, darkness *and* lightness, immanent constraint *and* alternative possibility. While readers of Adorno tend to focus on his dealings with the darker side of things—he is often distinguished for his emphasis on suffering and unhappiness, or for his insistence, following Ferdinand Kürnberger, that "life does not live," or for his concern that we have become consumed by a culture of routine and repetition, that our capacities for autonomy and spontaneity have been usurped by the demands of the market and by our internalized drive simply to preserve ourselves amid "the wrong state of things"—we cannot fully appreciate the critical import of Adorno's dialectical approach, or the significance of his insistence on religious tropes, unless we keep sight of the transcendental side of his thinking, what I refer to as the redemptive energy implicit to his dialectical criticism. If for Adorno we find ourselves trapped in a rather dark and despairing moment, it is not as though we have taken up permanent residence in the "Grand Hotel Abyss."[10] Adorno insists on despair, but, more specifically, and like Benjamin, he insists on the "unreality of despair."[11] Our dreadful moment is seen to be "indigent and distorted," and thus not good, not true, certainly not worthy of our support or affirmation, and this perspective, this critical judgment about the nature of our worldly present, is thrown into the boldest possible relief when fashioned "from the standpoint of redemption," when illuminated by the "messianic light" and thus confronted by the promise of an alternative reality.

Simon Jarvis has suggested that we should avoid reading Adorno "too literally," as "many of Adorno's sharpest claims [are] not descriptive attempts to formulate propositions adequate to states-of-affairs, but attempts to provoke readers into just that critical independence of mind."[12] Indeed, these sharp claims are a fundamental component of a dialectical spirit of critique. "Dialectical knowledge [is] taken all too literally by its opponents," Adorno says. "Limitation and reservation are no way to represent the dialectic. Rather, the dialectic advances by way of extremes, driving thoughts with the utmost consequentiality to the point where they turn back on themselves, instead of qualifying them."[13] As I argue later, Adorno's use of theological motifs—his insistence on religious *tropes*, as Kaufmann put it—is only partly intended to be read literally; it is also partly an attempt at rhetorical provocation. In both cases, this vivid and dramatic language helps us see how Adorno's distinctive brand of dialectical thinking can animate and sustain the critical imagination in challenging times. By figuring our thinking *between* the extreme poles of despair and redemption, we maintain hope for alternative possibilities *and* allow that "messianic light" to sharpen and sustain our focus on the psychic and material constraints that may prevent the very possibilities we imagine. It is this double perspective—this simultaneous emphasis on difference and becoming, on the one hand, and psychic and material constraint, on the other—that really comes alive in Adorno's work and that recommends itself as a subtle corrective to contemporary ethical theories focused more exclusively on the embrace of alterity.

Consider for example some of the later work of Jacques Derrida, a figure who suggests himself as a fitting point of comparison here insofar as he is concerned to flesh out a democratic ethical orientation, and he sets out to bring a set of theological motifs to bear on a late-modern reconsideration of Marx.[14] Certainly there is a sense in which Derrida's notion of a "democracy to come," a notion sustained by what he calls a "messianicity," can be said to provide that same sort of critical provocation that we find in Adorno, that sense of an animating redemptive vision or hopefulness in face of any possible political darkness. But Derrida's approach does not always entertain the same attentiveness to material constraint that Adorno's critical provocations do. If Adorno works to vivify an animating dialectical interplay between figurations of despair and redemption, between figurations of material constraint and alternative possibility, Derrida's approach threatens to move beyond dialectical mediation and thus threatens the critical import of this animating interplay. The Derridean approach is much more one-sided, geared toward difference, becoming, natality, often at the expense of any sustained focus on a political and economic situation that may delimit the emergence of alternative possibilities. My point in turning to Derrida in the latter part of the chapter is to underscore what is distinctive about Adorno's approach and also to show how a dialectical mode of thinking might help to sustain a sharper critical edge and thus supplement recent Derridean discourse on radical democracy.

The chapter has four sections. In the first and second, I use the "Finale," the final aphorism from *Minima Moralia*, a passage cited earlier, as a way to anchor a discussion of a dialectical mode of thinking situated between figurations of despair and redemption. I start with Adorno's famous, perhaps infamous, appeals to the dark side, specifically his claim that we find ourselves caught in an arresting "totality" of capitalist exchange relations, dispossessed of any real capacity for autonomous or creative political activity. I then turn to explore how Adorno's appeals to a redemptive energy throw critical light back onto our worldly present and, at the same time, encourage hope and resistance in face of a seemingly impossible political situation. Following a discussion of Derrida, in the third section, I turn finally, in the conclusion, to tease out the practical implications of Adorno's spirit of critique. I suggest that Adorno—a figure whose work is often put at odds with the contemporary ethical turn, a figure not always enlisted in the service of popular political action—may well offer some intellectual resources useful for an account of how we might engage the political today.

"IN FACE OF DESPAIR"

"The only philosophy which can be responsibly practiced in face of despair," to repeat our guiding passage, "is the attempt to contemplate all things as they would present themselves from the standpoint of redemption." While Adorno sometimes seems to give a certain epistemic priority to the experience of despair, or perhaps to a more immediate kind of pain or physical suffering, I suggest that Adorno's figurations of despair and redemption operate in continuous dialectical tension, that we cannot think these figurations apart from one another, and that neither can be said to hold any epistemic or even rhetorical priority over the other.[15] As such, it is almost impossible to unpack the full weight of this passage in any straightforward, linear way. But linear presentation is our medium, and so while the broader picture of Adorno's dialectical style of thinking will eventually come into focus in the next two sections, I begin by engaging the first part of this passage, namely, Adorno's insinuation that we practice philosophy today "in face of despair."

This judgment finds expression in a passage written in America in 1947, in the immediate aftermath of the Second World War. And the context cannot be underestimated. Adorno, like Benjamin and like his Frankfurt School colleagues, was uprooted in a most horrible way in the 1930s, forced into exile at the hands of the Nazi incursions. Adorno fled to England in 1934 and then to America in 1938, where his attitude toward modernity would be further soured by both the news of mounting destruction back home in Europe and by his professional alienation amid a culture and a research community that was becoming increasingly consumed by the "rigors" of empiricism, positivism, and popular opinion. He found himself subject to persistent surveillance and harassment in the United States and was thus given an early indication that authoritarian tendencies were not the exclusive province of overtly fascist regimes but could well flourish under the guise of liberal democracy.[16] It was a desperate time, a painful time, confounded for Adorno by a sense that, at the height of the Enlightenment age of disenchantment, ordinary women and men had become increasingly numb to that pain and to the significance of its desperation.[17] At issue here, for our purposes, is simply the judgment, so central to Adorno's work throughout his life, that critical thinking has become deeply disaffected in the modern age, rendered one-dimensional, to borrow Marcuse's famous phrase. We despair at the sheer hopelessness of critical thinking, to say nothing of the prospects for critically informed political action. It is necessary to say a bit about how and why for Adorno our thinking is rendered one-dimensional, ultimately in order to show how and why the very language of hopelessness, of despair, emerges, rather ironically, as part of an effort to combat an unaffected critical sensibility.

Let us keep in mind that the very word *despair* has a distinctive place within the vocabulary of the modern dialectical tradition. It is perhaps even something of a term of art. As we noted in chapter 2, Hegel in the *Phenomenology of Spirit* suggests that our experience with dialectical reason places our consciousness on a *Weg der Verzweiflung*, a "pathway of despair." According to Hegel's theory, the settled terms of the "understanding" (*Verstand*) are challenged and undermined by the movement of reason (*Vernunft*), which is "negative and dialectical."[18] Insofar as our most intimately held values and beliefs are called into question, challenged by changing historical and social circumstances, our world comes crashing down upon us, we experience a deep sense of uncertainty, something far more existentially troubling than mere skepticism or doubt. But the leitmotif of despair in Adorno is not simply a reflection of intellectual inheritance. And the primary cause of despair is much different in Adorno, very nearly the polar opposite. If Hegel is concerned about the pressures placed upon consciousness by the persistent introduction of difference and becoming against the dead weight of tradition, Adorno is brought to despair by the overwhelming inertia of the established state of affairs, by the suppression of negativity under conditions of capitalist modernity. What might be new or different, what might shock or upset our conventional ways of thinking, is always already discouraged by the logic of an increasingly "total" system of rational domination and capitalist economic exchange. Where Hegel, in characteristically idealist fashion, seems to presume that any spirit of discontent will necessarily fuel active social criticism and fan the flames of negativity and becoming, thereby affecting changes in the "shapes" of social consciousness, Adorno, taking cues from Marx or at least a more materialist reading of Hegel, keeps his sights trained on the material conditions that prevent the efficacy, and before that the very emergence, of critical thinking.

Adorno's materialism, what I describe more specifically as a sustained focus on the material conditions that constrain critical thinking and action, bespeaks a significant departure from traditional Marxist materialism, and it is important that we keep this in mind. Adorno effectively prefaces his *chef d'oeuvre*, his 1966 *Negative Dialectics*, by calling orthodox Marxism into question. "Philosophy," he writes, "which once seemed obsolete, lives on because the moment to realize it was missed. The summary judgment that it had merely interpreted the world, that resignation in the face of reality had crippled it in itself, becomes a defeatism of reason after the attempt to change the world miscarried."[19] Plainly a reference to Marx's "Theses on Feuerbach," Adorno is concerned to reassess the import of philosophy, of interpretation and critical thinking, given that decades of Marxist practice have not exactly emancipated the people or rid the world of human suffering. For Adorno, we still misinterpret this world. We do not yet know what sort of action is called for. We need to reflect a bit more or perhaps a bit differently.[20] While Adorno can be said to exhibit a certain Marxist sense of suspicion, a certain passion for critique, and while he takes up certain Marxist motifs, notably a concern for commodity fetishism and exchange value, Adorno rejects the grand Marxist vision of progressive historical development. And by way of this rejection he makes possible the introduction of a certain mournfulness or melancholy that will shape his approach to dialectical thinking.

At the heart of Adorno's materialism lies the notion of *das Tauschverhältnis*, or the "exchange relationship," that has taken hold of so much of our modern world. Fredric Jameson provides a helpful way of introducing Adorno's concern here. "How is it," Jameson asks, "when the consumption (or 'use') of any specific object is unique, and constitutes a unique and incomparable temporal event in our own lives as well, that we are able to think of such things as 'the same'?" The answer is that we rely on exchange value, "the emergence of some third, abstract term between two incomparable objects."[21] And here Adorno follows a specifically Marxian line, for this is precisely the point of the famous first chapter of *Capital, Volume I*, where Marx argues that the reduction of difference to equivalence is, in effect, a product of the commodity form, a result of the emergence of the exchange relationship in modern society. We may recall here Marx's great arithmetical image—"20 yards of linen = 1 coat or = 10 lb. tea or = 40 lb. coffee or = 1 quarter of corn or = 2 ounces of gold or = ½ ton of iron or = etc."[22] It is only through a process of abstraction, through the establishment of an abstract mediating principle, that we can come to understand any sense of equivalence between these otherwise diverse and differentiated elements.

As this exchange relationship works its way into further corners of our world, we find ourselves reduced ever further to what can be traded or exchanged on the open market. Our sense of self-worth, our sense of who we are as unique and interesting and creative beings, is increasingly reduced to an identity that is effectively constituted by how we fit into this system of economic exchange. "If the standard structure of society is the exchange form," Adorno writes, "its rationality constitutes people: what they are for themselves, what they think they are, is secondary."[23] What really seems to worry Adorno, and I will try to unpack this rather elusive point as we move along, is that the reduction and identification that we experience in our daily lives, by virtue of our participation in this economic exchange relationship, serves as a kind of material model for how we reduce and identify ourselves mentally, in the very act of thinking.

"The 'exchange relationship,'" Jameson notes, "is the *other* great leitmotif that sounds throughout Adorno's work, and it is strictly 'identical' with that more philosophical leitmotif named 'identity.'"[24] As we will see, dialectical thinking for Adorno sets out to unsettle fixed identities and to challenge our impulse or desire to identify by provoking and teasing out what exceeds identification. But it is important to see first that identity, for Adorno, is more than just a philosophical problem. Or rather, identity as a philosophical problem is an expression of identity as a material problem. By placing so much emphasis on exchange value, by placing so much emphasis on the ways in which we are reduced to various sorts of commodities, Adorno seems to suggest that the *material workings* of modern society, the reductionist demands of an exchange economy, have a *constitutive effect* on the way we think, the way we fashion concepts, the way we privilege in our thinking the principle of identity and subordinate what might be different to a kind of sameness.

It is in this sense that Adorno speaks of a "conceptuality which holds sway in reality [*Sache*] itself."[25] Adorno's frequent, almost obsessive allusions to the concept and to conceptuality serve a kind of heuristic purpose; they help to show how the reductionism at work in our ordinary thought process effectively mirrors the reductionism at work in our material experiences, our ordinary economic lives. "The concept," Adorno says, "in itself, previous to any content, hypostasizes its own form against the content."[26] The concept "says what something comes under, what it exemplifies and represents, *but not what it is*."[27] Ordinary conceptual thinking, like the abstract formalism of economic exchange, remains inadequate to the substantial content that it seeks to account for. Rather than grasp particulars as they are, in accordance with their own unique character, conceptual thinking speaks on their behalf and in terms of its pregiven form. And the crucial point here is that conceptual thinking "has its social model in exchange, and it would not be without the latter, through which non-identical particular essences and achievements become commensurable, identical."[28]

While this critique owes much to Marx and to the materialist turn in the dialectical tradition, there is, to say it again, no Marxist theory of historical development. For Adorno, this process of reduction is in no way destined to "burst asunder," as Marx once put it. And it is important that we underscore this "major difference between Marx and Adorno over the universality of the exchange principle," for, as Martin Jay puts it, "whereas the former restricted it solely to capitalism, the latter extended it to a property of the entire Enlightenment, broadly understood," and "the implication of this extension of the exchange principle is, of course, that it would be much harder to abolish."[29] Ultimately Adorno will come to describe our modern condition not as a momentary or passing stage in the larger trajectory of historical development, not as some idiosyncrasy of a particular era or epoch, but rather as a kind of "totality" from which we cannot escape, something akin to "in Hegel's words the all-penetrating ether of society," albeit less ethereal and more of an "*ens realissimum*."[30] As Adorno puts it in a notable and again quite urgent passage from his 1968 address to the German Sociological Association, "the power of that abstraction over humanity," the power of "the exchange relationships, the objective abstractions, which belong to the social life-process," is "far more corporeal than that of any single institution, which silently constitutes itself in advance according to the scheme of things and beats itself into human beings. The powerlessness which the individual experiences in the face of the totality is the most drastic expression of this."[31]

This most drastic expression of powerlessness and totality will bring Adorno in line with Benjamin, or at least with that Benjaminian sense of despair, which we noted at the outset of this chapter. We get a sense that human history, increasingly dominated by the logic of exchange, just is a kind of catastrophic continuum, "wreckage piled upon wreckage." We get a sense that, powerless in face of the totality, only a kind of messianic interruption can now save us. On my reading, what most concerns Adorno, what most worries Adorno here, is that we tend to forget or downplay both the material suffering wrought by the present system of economic exchange and the fact that many of us really do find ourselves caught up in cycles of material constraint, consumed by a routinized existence that prevents us from developing any real critical perspective on the conditions that sustain us. In some ways, Adorno's worry about the *totality* of exchange has to do with a concern for the most vulnerable, for those of us who really are brought to an experience of despair by virtue of an exchange value that is essentially dictated to us as if from above. If my value is what Walmart says it is—maybe, hopefully, $8.50 an hour—then I am in a very real sense powerless in the face of the totality.[32] That said, let us keep in mind that Adorno is not attempting to espouse any kind of economic determinism here. He will grant that this logic of exchange requires our performance and participation. Adorno wants only to emphasize the ways in which the material world of modern bourgeois society, and our deeply fortuitous situation within it, encourage and sometimes require that we continuously conceptualize ourselves and others, as well as the nonhuman world, according to its laws, according to its dominant organizational principles. His remarks about totality, about how the exchange relationship is a material version of Hegel's all-penetrating ether, are at least partly an attempt at rhetorical provocation. These "drastic expressions" have a certain shock value, and this is precisely the point.

Earlier I noted Simon Jarvis's suggestion that we should avoid reading Adorno "too literally." Gillian Rose makes a similar suggestion regarding Adorno's references to powerlessness and totality. She argues that Adorno invokes this language not in order to express some ontological truth but in order to emphasize the material challenges that often stand in the way of our ability to think differently. "If one reads it literally," she says, "it appears to be self-contradictory and self-defeating," for "ideas such as 'the total society,' 'the end of the individual,' and 'complete reification' . . . imply that no critical consciousness is possible." But, Rose continues, critical consciousness is possible, Adorno knows this and wants to underscore this, and in order for us properly to follow Adorno here, "it is necessary to know how to interpret these ideas, in short, to understand the workings of Adorno's dialectic." As Rose points out, "Adorno is dramatizing these ideas, presenting them *as if* they were absolutely and literally true, in order to undermine them more effectively."[33] The key point here is that Adorno often employs figurative language as an integral part of a dialectical mode of thinking, and he does so in order to avoid the literal-mindedness—and thus the positivism, the ideology, the one-dimensional nature—of bourgeois immanence.[34] A certain rhetorical finesse emerges here as a fundamental component of a distinctive approach to critical practice, one that Adorno theorizes and defends throughout his life, from his wartime insistence on the critical import of "exaggeration" and "fantasy" and "provocative formulations" to his later commendation of literature that has the capacity to "shock" our thinking.[35] Furthermore, Adorno's interest in nonliterary art that is said to elicit "shock and trauma"—such as, for example, the "genuinely revolutionary" music of the composer Arthur Schoenberg—is similarly concerned to provoke a certain level of discomfort and to stimulate a critical reappraisal of our culture, our means and relations of production, as well as our modes of apprehension, our listening, our seeing, our feeling.[36] To be sure, Adorno will never commit himself to exaggeration in any irresponsible or unqualified way; on one occasion, during a question-and-answer session following his 1959 lecture on "The Meaning of Working Through the Past," he was careful to "forestall a misunderstanding" on precisely this point. "I would not be able to accept the responsibility for recommending exaggeration in education," he says. Nevertheless, "exaggeration seems to me to be a necessary medium for social-theoretical and philosophical presentation, because the moderate, normal surface existence in general conceals such potentials and because in the face of neutral, average everydayness, to indicate the threat lying below it at first blush always has the character of exaggeration."[37] Implicitly and explicitly in his work, Adorno theorizes this approach to critical practice, he praises its import in the literary and artistic expressions of others, and he practices it himself. And the latter is perhaps nowhere better exemplified than in the reference to "totality," in the insistence that we find ourselves rendered "powerless" by reductive exchange relationships and in the persistent insinuation that such conditions are cause for "despair." These sorts of claims help to provoke our thinking and to interject some intrigue and affect into a critical imagination that has become disenchanted, unaffected, and unmoved.

The general implication here is that Adorno's confidence in the *totality* and thus *necessity* of our utterly despairing modern condition is perhaps only semblance. His dark assessment of modern life is almost always checked by a more subtle ambiguity. If "society's law of motion has for thousands of years been abstracting from its individual subjects, degrading them into mere executors, mere partners in social wealth and social struggle," he notes, "[this] debasement was as real as the fact that on the other hand there would be nothing without individuals and their spontaneities."[38] As he remarks elsewhere, "there would be no exchange without disregarding living human beings."[39] And the implication here is that living human beings are not actually destroyed but merely disregarded, disempowered, drugged into a state of late-modern lethargy. And so "it is only in a *sardonic* sense that the natural growth of exchange society is a law of nature."[40] No matter how deep this process of exchange penetrates into our lives and our world, no matter how "total" its grip becomes, something always escapes it. "As impenetrable as the bane [*Bann*] is, it's only a spell [*Bann*]." And the task of critical theory, which for Adorno means the task of negative dialectical reflection, is "to ensure, be it to ever so modest an extent, that the spell dissolves itself."[41]

I have suggested that Adorno's judgment that we practice philosophy today "in face of despair" derives from his assessment of the material conditions of modern life and specifically from his emphasis on the material constraints that discourage our ability and desire to think differently. And I have indicated that Adorno's despair, heightened by the claim to *totality*, is at least partly understood as a kind of rhetorical strategy or a means of critical provocation. "Everything socially existent today," he says in 1968, "is so thoroughly mediated [by the exchange relationship], that even the moment of mediation is distorted by the totality. . . . There is no standpoint outside of the whole affair which can be referred to, from which the ghost could be called by its name."[42] And yet Adorno calls the spell by its name. He thus seems to follow his own advice, from some thirty years prior, that we must "attempt to contemplate all things as they would present themselves from the standpoint of redemption." I turn now to the latter part of our guiding passage to elaborate on Adorno's remark about the "standpoint of redemption" and his claim that "perspectives must be fashioned that displace and estrange the world, reveal it to be, with its rifts and crevices, as indigent and distorted as it will one day appear on the messianic light."

"FROM THE STANDPOINT OF REDEMPTION"

Adorno calls it an "infinitely ironic description," referring to Benjamin's claim that "theology today, as we know, is wizened and has to keep out of sight."[43] The irony here, of course, is that Benjamin did not exactly hide his theology. There is considerably less irony in Adorno's case, as his theological impulses are mostly kept out of sight, hidden behind or within the apparatus of a dialectical mode of critical reflection. In this section, I highlight two features of Adorno's stubborn and sometimes strained effort to maintain a commitment, however qualified, to the modern dialectical tradition. First, and building on some of what was said in chapter 2, I argue that a certain redemptive energy is implicit to a dialectical mode of thinking, Adorno's included. If we find ourselves run up against the catastrophe that is modern bourgeois immanence, as Adorno certainly suggests that we do, then dialectical thinking signals a location at which transcendental claims enter our thinking. To figure dialectical thinking between despair and redemption, to draw on religious tropes to highlight this, is to train our focus on the complex relationship between immanence and transcendence and on the ways in which these two registers in their interaction can be said to animate and sustain our thinking. The second point I make here is that while dialectical thinking emerges in Adorno as part of a rhetorical strategy, part of an attempt at critical provocation, this turn to dialectics is not simply a rhetorical fabrication. For Adorno, "it is the matter, and not the organizing drive of thought, that brings us to dialectics."[44] That is, the character of modern life, the character of a world inclined materially toward identity and sameness, can be said to encourage our dialectical intervention and its implicit redemptive energies.

Before we proceed, I want to offer a quick point of clarification, as this section may appear to backtrack on some of what was said previously regarding the critical import of Adorno's rhetorical finesse or his use of nonliteral language, exaggeration, hyperbole, and so forth. My intention here is simply to tell the other side of the story. Insofar as we turn now to consider Adorno's insistence on religious tropes, and specifically his appeal to redemption, we begin to see how this language is meant both rhetorically and literally. In a more substantively theological way, Adorno sets out to vivify the distance between the immanent and the transcendent, between the dark times that threaten to consume us and the promise of qualitatively different reality. And again, this is simply the other side of the story; the language of redemption is invoked *both* for its dramatic effect, as we have seen, *and* because its theological context helps us appreciate the ways in which dialectical thinking feeds off of a complex relationship between antithetical registers.

I begin with the idea that a redemptive energy is implicit to the structure of dialectical thinking. I initiated a discussion of this topic in chapter 2 by invoking a passage from Hegel's *Philosophy of Right*. Immediately following the famously ambiguous claim that what is rational is actual and vice versa, Hegel says that "if reflection, feeling, or whatever form subjective consciousness may take, looks upon the present as something vacuous and looks beyond it with the eyes of superior wisdom, it finds itself in a vacuum, and because it is actual only in the present, it is itself mere vacuity."[45] And I noted in chapter 2 that for Hegel, for a thinker still haunted by divine expectation, such vacuity is not exactly a satisfying condition. Presumably we want to do something about our present emptiness, which for Hegel means that we want to pursue the rational and work to make actual what is real and good and true.[46] When I speak of a redemptive energy in the context of dialectical thinking, I mean something like this transcendent expectation, an expectation that prompts both a lament of the present as being somehow negative or untrue (or dark or despairing) as well as a subsequent desire to push forward as to redeem such an unsatisfying vacuity. On a *structural* or *formal* level, this redemptive energy is the driving animus behind a dialectical spirit of critique, Adorno's included.[47]

Certainly Adorno's negative dialectics bespeak a marked departure from Hegel's (and Marx's) substantive philosophy. As Hent de Vries puts it, "Adorno holds *the Hegelian system to be untrue in an emphatic sense, not only in terms of the philosophy of history but also speculatively, as an idea yet to be realized and as an aspiration toward the true, the good, and the beautiful.*"[48] De Vries thus suggests that we cannot rightly describe Adorno as a Hegelian thinker.[49] And these points are well taken. Adorno is not an emphatic rationalist. He is not a system-builder, at least not in an affirmative sense. But there is perhaps a difference between Hegel's dialectic, Hegel's system, Hegel's substantive philosophy, on the one hand, and what will become the more heterogeneous and open-ended, but still quite Hegelian, language and conceptual resources of dialectical criticism, on the other. And by implying that because Adorno rejects the substance of Hegel's dialectic he thereby rejects a broader Hegelian tradition of dialectical criticism, de

Vries threatens to obscure the redemptive energies that animate Adorno's critical approach.

De Vries goes on to say that "the goal of dialectical thinking, if there is one, according to Adorno and in contrast to the tradition, thus becomes qualitatively changed reconciliation, which can no longer be established in an idealistic or materialistically determined yet fundamentally affirmative way. Such reconciliations would respect the singular, the non-identical, the different, the heterogeneous, the individual as the irretrievable and irrevocable other."[50] Again, de Vries's points are well taken, but we must be careful not to background the redemptive motifs that figure, however minimally, in Adorno's thought. Where Horkheimer suggests in 1935 that "the dialectical critique of the world is borne along . . . [by] human impulses which demand something better," Adorno exactly thirty years later will praise his Frankfurt School colleague for having "absorbed the utopian impulse without compromise into the spirit of critique, without affirmative consolation, even without consolation of trust in a future that could not redress past suffering."[51] The point here is that Adorno's dialectical criticism is sustained and provoked by a redemptive (in this particular passage, the word is "utopian") energy. The point here is that if despair is our condition, it is our condition *qua* negativity or untruth, and in the face of such negativity or untruth, we expect "something better." Our critical perspective is maintained by a commitment, however minimal, to that something better.

As we have seen, and to return again to our guiding passage, Adorno insists that we must "contemplate all things as they would present themselves from the standpoint of redemption." He insists that "perspectives must be fashioned that displace and estrange the world, reveal it to be, with its rifts and crevices, as indigent and distorted as it will one day appear in the messianic light." Certainly this language harkens back to a Judaic theological tradition, and these references, these religious tropes, are not invoked only for their shock value, not exclusively in the interest of hyperbole, nor are they merely an occasional response to the unprecedented destruction of the Second World War. My sense is that Adorno intends for this language to be read at least partly in a more literal and substantive way. He wants to underscore a complex relationship between the immanent and the transcendent, something of a separation between two registers that nevertheless remain purposefully related to one another. In an essay on the theological dimensions of Adorno's thinking, David Kaufmann points out that "the separation of the divine from the material is in many ways one of the central tenets—if not *the* central tenet—of normative Judaic thought and organizes the problems that philosophers such as Maimonides and Hermann Cohen confront time and again. . . . They are all born of the same theological impulse: the protection of the transcendent from any incursions by the immanent."[52] And Kaufmann goes on to suggest that, throughout his life, Adorno "shows strongly theological commitments" insofar as he tries "to maintain the dignity of the transcendent while at the same time attempting to make it accessible to experience."[53]

Take for example a reference to the Jewish theological tradition in *Dialectic of Enlightenment*, where Horkheimer and Adorno raise the question of how to name the divine, how to articulate that which bespeaks a genuine transcendence of the given. "In the Jewish religion," they say. "the link between name and essence is still acknowledged in the prohibition on uttering the name of God. The disenchanted world of Judaism propitiates magic by negating it in the idea of God. The Jewish religion brooks no word which might bring solace to despair of all mortality. It places all hope in the prohibition on invoking falsity as God, the finite as the infinite, the lie as truth."[54] In other words, what might be different is precisely that which we cannot articulate or identify in any concrete or determined way. To do so would be to profane the transcendent, to colonize and degrade what necessarily exceeds the bounds of our ordinary sensibilities, indeed the bounds of conceptual thinking, the bounds of material exchange relations. And to imagine alternative possibility in this way, to orient ourselves toward what might be different in a way that is at least reminiscent of a Judaic theological separation between the worldly and the divine, is further to underscore the "despairing" nature of our worldly present. Put more precisely, it is to underscore what Benjamin calls the "unreality of despair." It is to vivify the radically false and unworthy, yet finite and thus not absolutely real or necessary, conditions in which we find ourselves.

This complex relationship between the immanent and transcendent is revisited in a late essay that is worthy of our consideration here, an essay that is concerned more explicitly with the nature of critical thinking as it relates to political practice. I am referring to Adorno's 1969 essay on "Resignation," in which he sets out to defend the import of critical thinking against what he sees as rather blind "actionism" on the part of many young political activists of the late 1960s. Once again, Adorno warns against our quick embrace of the sentiment expressed in Marx's "Theses on Feuerbach." He insists that real resignation lies, not in our philosophical attempt to reinterpret reality, but rather in immediate efforts to change things. "The uncompromisingly critical thinker," he says, one "who neither signs over his consciousness nor lets himself be terrorized into action, is in truth the one who does not give in."[55] The concern here is that, in our effort to achieve tangible results, we tend to accept and reinforce established methods as well as the fetish for what is empirically observable and useful, what can be conceptualized and exchanged. We often set out in pursuit of an established goal, and even if this goal is radical or utopian, once the utopian vision is settled, as a kind of blueprint drawn up and formalized, then, as is the case with conceptual or identity thinking, we foreclose in advance the possibility of, well, possibility. It is worth quoting Adorno at some length here:

> As long as it doesn't break off, thinking has a secure hold on possibility. Its insatiable aspect, its aversion to being quickly and easily satisfied, refuses the foolish wisdom of resignation. The utopian moment in thinking is stronger the less it—this too is a form of relapse—objectifies itself into a utopia and hence sabotages its realization. Open thinking points beyond itself. For its part a comportment, a form of praxis, it is more akin to transformative praxis than a comportment that is compliant for the sake of praxis. Prior to all particular content, thinking is actually the force of resistance, from which it has been alienated only with great effort. . . . Thought is happiness, even where it defines unhappiness: by enunciating it. By this alone happiness reaches into the universal unhappiness. Whoever does not let it atrophy has not resigned.[56]

To be sure, Adorno's ultimate purpose in this essay on resignation is to encourage our consideration of the ways in which immediate political action can sometimes reinforce the very conditions that we seek to change or transcend. His ultimate purpose is to reassess the critical import of reflection, of thinking itself. The key point for our purposes is that, "as long as it doesn't break off, thinking has a secure hold on possibility." There is a certain transcendental energy, indeed a redemptive energy, built into the very structure of thinking, by which of course Adorno means critical thinking, dialectical thinking. The possibility of that which genuinely exceeds the immanent, that which is distinguished and dignified and protected from the incursions of ordinary conceptual thinking and capitalist exchange relationships, is imagined in such a way as to shed critical light back onto the immanent, back onto a conceptual culture and an exchange society that is now seen to be false, and *totally* so, unhappy, and *universally* so, a culture and a society unredeemed but, as such, not yet resigned.

So far in this section I have suggested that Adorno's insistence on religious tropes, especially when read in the context of a Jewish theological tradition, can help us appreciate his sense for how dialectical thinking is animated and sustained by a rather complex relationship between the immanent and the transcendent.[57] And I will continue to explore the nature of this relationship by turning now to the second objective of this section. If a certain transcendental or redemptive energy is implicit to the very structure of dialectical thinking, why does this mode of thinking suggest itself? Why now? Is it simply that dialectical thinking, riding in on the backs of exaggeration and hyperbole, is best suited to shock our thinking, to awaken the critical imagination from a state of late-modern lethargy? Is dialectical thinking simply Adorno's preferred method of critical intellectual intervention? Or is there something more to it?

First of all, the very idea that dialectical thinking amounts to a "method" for Adorno is problematic. "Method in the precise sense," Adorno says, is "an intellectual approach which can be applied everywhere and at any time because it divests itself of any relation to things, i.e., to the object of knowledge."[58] In what is simply a manifestation of ordinary conceptual thinking, formal methodological approaches subsume distinct particulars—unique objects, individual cases—under the aegis of rational domination. As such, formal methods bespeak yet another way in which we equate what might be different and render similar what might be otherwise. Now, this is not to say that Adorno necessarily rejects the idea of a distinctive method or intellectual approach. "Method should be a function of the object, not the inverse," he says. Adorno wants to pursue an alternative "which has been all too simply repressed by the positivistic spirit."[59] As Rolf Tiedemann has suggested, we should avoid trying to recover from Adorno a set of "instructions for thinking." Rather, we should inquire into the "'models of intellectual experience that motivate' Adorno's thinking."[60] We should focus on his "emphatic use of the concept of experience," because "the kind of thinking to which negative dialectics aspires is subject to the primacy of the individual; . . . it consists of the gaze of an individual fixed on individual beings or . . . it at least starts from there."[61] In Adorno's own words, "cognition [when understood in a "dialectical fashion"] always proceeds in principle from below to above and not from the top down; it is concerned with leaving things to themselves and not with a process of deduction."[62] If Adorno recommends a distinctive approach to critical thinking, if dialectical reflection amounts to something like an intellectual method, albeit one that privileges the object over the process of deduction, this is not an approach or method that we introduce from above. We are brought to such an approach by a particular kind of experience. Our individual experiences under conditions of capitalist modernity are said to invite dialectical thinking. "Dialectics is the ontology of the wrong state of things," Adorno says in a particularly memorable passage, and "the right state of things would be free of it: neither a system nor a contradiction."[63] So long as we remain bound up in the wrong state of things, dialectical thinking suggests itself as a critical approach, a kind of nonpositivistic method of intellectual resistance.

What exactly is it about the modern experience that invites dialectical thinking and its implicit redemptive energies? To answer this question we must return, as indicated earlier, to Adorno's seemingly curious infatuation with the concept and conceptuality. We recall Adorno's worry that in *die verwaltete Welt*, "the administered world," in a world dominated by the organizational drive of exchange relations, we are encouraged, forced sometimes, to reduce ourselves, our ideas, our ambitions to that which can be traded and exchanged on the open market. We are compelled to privilege exchange value, which reduces our unique qualities and spontaneous energies to a kind of sameness. What this means for Adorno, as we have seen, is that a certain "conceptuality . . . holds sway in reality [*Sache*] itself." The reductionism at work in our economic lives is a kind of material basis for the reductionism at work in our thinking. It is at this point that dialectical thinking, as opposed to identarian or ordinary conceptual thinking, emerges as a reaction to this experience of conceptuality. Dialectical thinking pushes the reductive tendencies of conceptual thinking to the forefront of the critical imagination and underscores the simple fact that something always escapes its hold. "The name of dialectics," Adorno writes, "says no more than that objects do not go into their concepts without leaving a remainder, that they come to contradict the traditional norm of adequacy."[64] Despite the fact that we find ourselves run up against the totality of capitalist exchange relations, despite the fact that our thinking is compelled toward identity and sameness, our "thinking need not be content with its own legality; without abandoning it, we can think against our thought." And, Adorno adds, "if it were possible to define dialectics, this would be a definition worth suggesting."[65]

Of course Adorno gives us a version of dialectical thinking that is considerably qualified vis-à-vis the tradition. Going back to the nineteenth century, to Hegel and Marx, dialectical thinking is teased along by a positive *telos*, by the promise of reconciliation with what was always meant to be. By contrast, the transcendental animus of Adorno's negative dialectics is better understood as a kind of non- or extra-conceptual redemption. Redemption here is geared not toward reconciliation of the identical but toward a provocation of the nonidentical: "Non-identity is the secret *telos* of identification."[66] Adorno speaks of a "cognitive utopia" that would "use concepts to unseal the non-conceptual within concepts, without making it their equal."[67] And the point, again, is that our concepts can never fully express the particularities that fall under them. Insofar as something exceeds our conceptual mediation, insofar as some substantial value exceeds our conceptual reach, our concepts never fully complete themselves; they are never fully identical with their content and thus always in contradiction with themselves.

For Adorno, this is all part of the experience of modern life, and this is why dialectical thinking recommends itself as an approach to critical intellectual intervention in this particular historical moment. We experience the material and psychic constraints of a society and an intellectual culture that is compelled toward identity and sameness. This is the source of our suffering, our unhappiness, our despair. But we also experience contradiction, we experience, however faintly, the feelings and ideas and creative energies that resist the logic of economic exchange and that exceed the bounds of conceptual reduction. And this experience of contradiction provides, not the basis for any kind of grand Hegelian system, but, as Jay Bernstein puts it, a kind of localized "index" of untruth, an indication that something is wrong here, a sense that "the world is in contradiction with itself, we with ourselves ('The whole is untrue'); it, we, are less or other than we could be."[68] Adorno brings these points together quite nicely in a 1964 conversation with Ernst Bloch on the "contradictions of utopian longing," where he claims that "what people have lost subjectively in regard to consciousness is very simply the capacity to imagine the totality as something that could be completely different. . . . people are sworn to this world as it is and have this blocked consciousness vis-à-vis possibility." And yet, he says, "all human beings *deep down*, whether they admit this or not, *know that it would be possible or it could be different*."[69] In a way that comes to look a good bit like the "instinctive dialectic" of C. L. R. James, which is our focus in the next chapter, Adorno seems to suggest that, by experiencing localized contradictions, we instinctively or intuitively sense the possibility of another reality, of transcendence, indeed of a kind of redemption, and dialectical thinking is a way to raise both the experience of contradiction and the possibility of redemption to the threshold of critical consciousness.

I tie this together by elaborating a bit further on the idea that "dialectics is the ontology of the wrong state of things" and that "the right state of things would be free of it: neither a system nor a contradiction." This passage has a number of implications, all of which shed light on our discussion up to this point. First of all, Adorno's remarks imply that a dialectical approach is not a fixed method to be recommended now as always. It is rather an approach germane to a particular historical moment, an approach that recommends itself in light of the contradictions that we now experience.[70] Before that, these remarks imply that our own particular moment is both systematic and contradictory, and, while these remarks do not refer explicitly to dialectical *thinking*, certainly Adorno's broader implication is that such thinking can help us vivify and resist this "wrong state of things." Negative dialectics is, as Fredric Jameson has noted, a "reintroduction of system or totality . . . as a solution to the closure of identity." It "cannot free us from the latter's illusions and mirages, since no mere thinking can do that, but it suddenly makes these last visible and affords a glimpse of the great magic 'spell' [*der Bann*] in which modern life is seized and immobilized."[71] Adorno's dialectical approach calls our attention to the "totality" of capitalist exchange relations. It vivifies the systematic way in which we reduce our lives and our thinking to a kind of sameness and thus bring the richness of our potential into contradiction with itself. And yet all this is but a "great magic spell," the false despair of the wrong state of things. By figuring the critical imagination between despair and redemption, between the dark times of bourgeois immanence and the open-ended promise of genuinely transcendent possibility, dialectical thinking helps us call the spell by its name. Such a mode of reflection sets out to reawaken the longing for alternative possibility, not by leaping immediately into the new and different, but, somewhat paradoxically, by encouraging our focused and sustained consideration of the cultural and material conditions in which we necessarily think and act, the psychic and material constraints that often prevent the very alternatives we long for.

DEMOCRACY TO COME

Thus far I have suggested that dialectics signals a location at which transcendental claims enter our thinking. For Adorno, dialectical thinking provides a locus for a conscious interplay between figurations of despair and redemption, an interplay that can shape and animate the critical imagination in a particular kind of way. In this section, I begin to explore the political import of this by putting Adorno's approach into conversation with some of Jacques Derrida's recent work. Like Adorno, Derrida is an incredibly rich and complex thinker, one who can inspire our thinking in various ways. I want to put a question to Derrida and to radical democrats inspired by his work. My basic worry is that Derrida's notions of "messianicity" and "democracy to come"—notions that resonate with the kind of redemptive critique that we have been exploring—tend to look past dialectical mediation and the critical interplays mobilized by dialectical reflection. My worry is that what we have unpacked in Adorno, namely, a critically provocative interplay between material constraint and alternative possibility, tends to get backgrounded in Derrida in favor of a rather one-sided attentiveness to possibility and to the political, or perhaps simply ethical, task of trying to anticipate the unanticipatable.[72] If this is a legitimate worry, or perhaps simply a legitimate question for Derrida, we might then welcome Adorno's dialectical spirit of critique, with its more focused and sustained attentiveness to material constraint, as an important and timely critical supplement to recent Derridean discourse on radical democracy.

In *Specters of Marx*, Derrida gives an indication of how we might understand his notion of a "messianicity without messianism." "What remains irreducible to any deconstruction," he says in a now well-known passage, "is, perhaps, a certain experience of the emancipatory promise; it is perhaps even the formality of a structural messianism, a messianism without religion, even a messianic without messianism, an idea of justice—which we distinguish from law or right or even from human rights—and an idea of democracy—which we distinguish from its current concept and from its determined predicates today."[73] This notion of a messianicity—this idea of a weak messianic force without a Messiah, without religion, without *messianism*—is meant to get behind or beyond any substantive doctrine or ideology. It is meant to express what is *undeconstructable*, the "universal structure of experience," by which Derrida means something like the basic condition of temporality.[74]

For Derrida, this appeal to the messianic, to a kind of universal becoming, will ultimately prefigure an ethical-political orientation, a posturing toward a more just, more democratic future. In the same passage I cited from *Specters of Marx*, Derrida refers his reader to an earlier essay, "Force of Law," where he says that "[d]emocracy would be a degeneration of law, of the violence, the authority, and the power of law. There is not yet any democracy worthy of this name. Democracy remains to come: to engender or regenerate."[75] The thought here is that justice and democracy require a sustained openness on our part, a kind of *hospitality* toward future possibilities that are always already moving beyond any effort we might make at institutional codification or closure.

And so we have an appeal to a certain messianic force, an "irreducible emancipatory promise," a kind of promissory vision in the notion of a "democracy to come." Derrida develops all this in the context of a reconsideration of Marx. And there are striking similarities between Derrida here and the young Marx, specifically the early critique of Hegel, where democracy, genuine democracy, takes on a certain promissory character as the "solved riddle of all constitutions," the "true unity of general and particular," something like the communistic utopia, which for Marx, "is not a *state of affairs* to be established . . . [but] the *real* movement which abolishes the present state of things."[76] There is a sense in which democracy emerges in the young Marx as a kind of weak messianic force, something like Derrida's "irreducible emancipatory promise" that is always already moving beyond our political present and its institutional closures.

But Derrida tends to reject or at least background the very mode of critical reflection that Marx, following Hegel, puts into motion and that Adorno takes up and develops for the late twentieth century. In that early commentary on Hegel, Marx goes on to say—and for him this "goes without saying"—that "all forms of state have democracy *for* their truth and that they are therefore untrue insofar as they are not democracy."[77] By invoking a sense of *untruth* and by emphasizing or vivifying the *negativity* of the present, Marx introduces a guiding theme of dialectical criticism. He brings to bear a set of expectations, transcendental or redemptive expectations, that are built into the very structure of dialectical thinking and that motivate the dialectical condemnation of the present. As I suggest throughout this chapter—and to be sure, this is far more evident in Adorno's writings than in Marx's—a dialectical mode of reflection works to *vivify the tensions* between the "present state of things," on the one hand, and alternative futures, on the other, between the psychic and material constraints of our lived reality and the redemptive possibilities that we might imagine. A dialectical mode of reflection introduces transcendental claims so as to bring the baseness—or, as Adorno might put it, the despair—of our lived moment into the boldest possible relief. Such a mode of reflection works to sustain attentiveness to the ways in which this moment may prevent the very possibilities that we desire. And Derrida's project, in trying to communicate the basic condition of temporality, the "universal structure of experience"—and this is very much a continuation of his earlier efforts to articulate *différance*, which "absolutely upsets all dialectics, all theology, all teleology, all ontology"—seems to want to push beyond, or perhaps get behind, the rhetorical and critical work of dialectical reflection.[78]

While Derrida takes inspiration from Marx, while he claims to invoke a certain spirit of Marx, there is a sense in which a more Nietzschean or Heideggerian spirit continues to haunt or perhaps tempt Derrida's thinking. In that earlier work on *différance*, Derrida speaks of an affirmative orientation, specifically of a "sense in which Nietzsche puts affirmation into play, in a certain laughter and a certain step of the dance." And "from the vantage of this laughter and this dance, from the vantage of an *affirmation foreign to all dialectics*," Derrida continues, a kind of "Heideggerian *hope* comes into question."[79] To be sure, in the particular essay in question, Derrida wants to deny any Heideggerian nostalgia for a special word or a language that might grant us some access to the becoming of the world or to the play of *différance*, but he nevertheless seems to counsel a Heideggerian confidence in the becoming of the world, a confidence that certainly resonates with Heidegger's notion of *Gelassenheit*, or that careful and patient "letting be."[80] What is important for our purposes is that this sense of a playful "*affirmation foreign to all dialectics*" implicitly denigrates the very work of conscious, mediated, even rhetorical reflection, and it seems to add an appropriate layer of description to Derrida's notion of a weak messianic force, which requires, as he says, a patient "waiting without horizon of expectation."[81]

I am concerned only with how Derrida's notions of "messianicity" and "democracy to come" can be said to orient, provoke, and sustain the critical imagination in our time. And perhaps I can better articulate my worry by citing an interview from the last year of Derrida's life, in which he describes an "implementation of this messianicity" in the:

> alter-globalisation movements. Movements that are still heterogeneous, still somewhat unformed, full of contradictions, but that gather together the weak of the earth, all those who feel themselves crushed by the economic hegemonies, by the liberal market, by sovereignism, and so on. I believe it is these weak who will prove to be the strongest in the end and who represent the future. Even though I am not a militant involved in these movements, I place my bet on the weak force of those alter-globalisation movements.[82]

To place one's bet on the weak of the earth is to show a sense of solidarity with the fight against human suffering. But it may also be to show a certain confidence in the way that fight is unfolding, a certain confidence in the way frustrations, anxieties, needs, and desires are already being articulated politically. And such a wager may even signal an implicit denigration of the task of sustaining critical attention to the conditions that prevent the articulation of these frustrations, anxieties, needs, and desires. I do not mean to imply that Derridean discourse on radical democracy leads to any sort of political quietism, as an ethics of hospitality certainly requires the cultivation of a sustained openness, even sustained sympathies on our part. And this is no small task. It is an essential task. But in some instances—perhaps in the present American political and economic context, in the face of what has become a rather inert struggle to advance or even defend substantive democracy—we need a bit more attentiveness to the psychic and material constraints that prevent the actualization of the very possibilities we imagine. And it may be that Derrida's effort to look behind or beyond the work of dialectical reflection threatens to imperil the critical and political work of notions such as "messianicity" and "democracy to come." If so, if this is a legitimate worry about the critical and political import of recent Derridean discourse on radical democracy, then we might welcome Adorno's dialectical approach, his spirit of critique, as an important critical supplement. Or more precisely, we might welcome Adorno's mode of critical reflection as a supplementary resource with which to help orient, provoke, and sustain the critical imagination in dark times.

CONCLUSION

In an effort to tie together this discussion, I invoke our guiding passage one last time. "The only philosophy which can be responsibly practiced in face of despair," Adorno says in that final aphorism of *Minima Moralia*, "is the attempt to contemplate all things as they would present themselves from the standpoint of redemption. . . . Perspectives must be fashioned that displace and estrange the world, reveal it to be, with its rifts and crevices, as indigent and distorted as it will one day appear in the messianic light." In a comment on this very passage, the philosopher of religion Jacob Taubes has noted that "you can tell the difference between substantial and as-if, and you can see how the whole messianic thing becomes [for Adorno] a *comme si* affair." On Taubes's reading, Adorno gives us "a wonderful, but finally empty, line."[83] And there is, to be sure, a certain rhetorical quality to this "whole messianic thing" and to the redemptive impulses of Adorno's critical theory. The same can be said of Adorno's figurations of despair and hopelessness, which elicit a certain shock value throughout his writings. But this does not mean that we must denigrate these figurations and deny their substance. The as if, *le comme si*, born of Adorno's insistence that critical insight often must exaggerate its way beyond the comforts of literality, is a fundamental component of dialectical thinking, which, Adorno says, "advances by way of extremes, driving thoughts with the utmost consequentiality to the point where they turn back on themselves, instead of qualifying them."[84] I have suggested that where the exigencies of rhetorical finesse can at least partly explain Adorno's insistence on religious tropes, there is another sense, perhaps what Taubes would regard as a more "substantial" sense, in which theological language is best able to express the nature of the two "extreme" registers, which, in their dialectical interaction, can be said to animate and sustain our thinking.

The tropes of redemption and the messianic allow Adorno to express a distinctive relationship between the immanent and the transcendent, between the ineluctable conditions of our lived experience and the necessary yet undetermined possibility of something beyond. In the first instance the very terrain of the theological—specifically the Judaic separation of the material and the divine as well as the corresponding prohibition on graven images—helps to introduce a tension that is fundamental to the very nature of dialectical reflection. "God, the Absolute, eludes finite beings," Adorno says in a 1963 essay on Schoenberg. "Where they desire to name him, because they must, they betray him. But if they keep silent about him, they acquiesce in their own impotence and sin against the other, no less binding, commandment to name him."[85] Here we have a kind of theological allegory, one that Adorno draws up on a number of occasions and in a number of slightly different ways. In each case he seems to underscore the fact that we can never really think the sorts of transcendent possibilities that our futures may hold, and yet we long for such alternatives because our thinking itself is borne along by their very promise. "If thought is not decapitated," he says elsewhere, "it will flow into transcendence, down to the idea of a world that would not only abolish extant suffering but revoke the suffering that is irrevocably lost."[86] And herein lies the fundamental thesis that I have encouraged us to consider throughout this chapter.

In reading Adorno's work, we see that dialectics signals a location at which transcendental claims enter our thinking. And yet dialectical thinking does not simply cast our imaginations beyond the real situation in which we find ourselves. In the very act of dialectical reflection, according to Adorno's formulation, the transcendent is thrown back onto the immanent in such a way as to vivify the material and psychic constraints that may prevent the possibilities we imagination. We find ourselves caught up in dark times; for Adorno, as we have seen, we are too often overcome by a "totality" of capitalist exchange relations, compelled to reduce our own potential, our creative energies, to what can be conceptualized, and before that what can be valued by and traded on the open market. But our dreadful moment is seen to be "indigent and distorted," and thus not good, not true, certainly not worthy of our support or affirmation, and this perspective, this critical judgment about the nature of our worldly present, is thrown into the boldest possible relief when fashioned "from the standpoint of redemption," when illuminated by the "messianic light" and thus confronted by the promise of an alternative reality. Dialectical thinking, situated between the "extreme" poles of despair and redemption, helps both to vivify the urgency of our despair and orient us toward the possibility of redemption.

In a moment we will turn to C. L. R. James to consider the idea that we counsel a certain "instinct" for dialectical reflection. We will entertain the notion that such an instinct has become repressed in our time and that civic engagement might benefit from a concerted effort to push a certain dialectical sensibility to the forefront of our critical consciousness. I will transition into that discussion first by indicating that Adorno at times seems to gesture in a similar direction and then by teasing out some of the ethical and political, and indeed democratic, implications of his work. Adorno is not particularly known for his contributions to popular politics. He may not immediately come to mind as a figure with whom to sketch in features of a spirit of political engagement. Certainly James, the outspoken radical democrat and lifelong political activist, seems to suggest himself as a more fitting interlocutor on this score. Nevertheless, my sense is that we do a real disservice to Adorno by caricaturing him in the first instance as a depoliticized intellectual, one with little to say to ordinary citizens struggling to make sense of and improve their lives and their communities.

In yet another passage that gets at the driving theme of the present chapter, Adorno says that "[g]rayness could not fill us with despair if our minds did not harbor the concept of different colors, scattered traces of which are not absent from the negative whole."[87] Earlier I called attention to Adorno's insinuation that by experiencing localized contradictions we instinctively or intuitively sense the possibility of another reality. At times Adorno seems to suggest that, by our very nature, we possess a kind of built-in orientation toward the transcendent, something deep down that motivates us to seek out those "different colors" even in the face of overwhelming grayness. It is something of a "speculative element," as Adorno himself describes it, "something quite simple . . . the idea that one should keep on thinking in a motivated way, not blindly, but in a motivated, consistent way, going beyond the point where one's thinking is backed up by facts."[88] For our purposes the latter passage is attractive, not only for what it says, and not only for the ways in which it points toward a set of issues that we will take up in the next chapter, but also because of when and where these remarks were uttered. This is an excerpt from a 1965 lecture course on dialectical thinking. This is Adorno in the classroom in Frankfurt, at work trying to interact with his students, trying to encourage those around him to think about how they think and about the implications of how they think. To read Adorno on dialectics without seeing how such a mode of thinking is informed by and affects our individual experiences, without seeing how such a mode of thinking is meant to inform a public sensibility, is simply to misread Adorno on dialectics. We must keep in mind that, as Adorno remarks to another group of students, "we are not only spectators looking upon this predominance of the institutional and the objective that confronts us." This world that we confront "is after all constituted out of us, this social objectivity is made up of us ourselves," and "in this doubleness, that we are subject and object of this society, surely lies precisely also the possibility of perhaps changing it."[89] A practice of critique, born of dialectical thinking, emerges in Adorno as part of an exemplary democratic response, a spirited response aimed at political contestation.

To be sure, it is at times easier simply to background this dimension of Adorno's work. Images of his run-ins with student activists in the 1960s tend to obscure his embrace of democracy and ethical-political engagement.[90] Certainly he was less than enthusiastic about the prospects of popular politics, less than optimistic about the staying power of democratic institutions. Following his postwar return to Germany, for example, he expressed his concern that "democracy has not become naturalized to the point where people truly experience it as their own and see themselves as subjects of the political process. . . . democracy is not identified with the people themselves as the expression of their political maturity."[91] And if the people lack a collective sense of democratic maturity, if the *demos* is bereft of a democratic *ethos*, then, as noted in chapter 1, the ethical register may not present itself as a well-fueled site at which to set off any sort of democratic brushfire. Furthermore, as we have seen, Adorno is a thinker of "system" and "totality." We find ourselves run up against "the wrong state of things" *en toto*, and "wrong life cannot be lived rightly."[92] To speak of a spirited response here, to speak of an ethos even in the loose sense of a way of living, is to speak of how we might get along with the wrong state of things, perhaps resign ourselves to the status quo, negotiate with untruth rather than negate it. This, anyhow, is the usual reading of the status of both democracy and the ethical in Adorno.

But if Adorno is concerned about a lack of democratic maturity on the part of ordinary citizens, and if this widespread immaturity is something of a cause for despair, such a judgment is, to be sure, and in line with what I have been arguing all along, reflective of a false despair. Adorno routinely encourages us to grow up, and to do so by working to activate the "critical spirit of a democratic society."[93] In a variety of essays and interviews, Adorno underscores the importance of political leadership and educational outreach, "democratic pedagogy" that can inspire, to cite a reference that traces the struggle for autonomy back to Kant, the "courage of each individual to make full use of his reasoning power," his capacities for "critique" and critical intervention.[94] "What we can do," Adorno says, "is give people contents, give them categories, give them forms of consciousness, by means of which they can approach self-reflection."[95] After all, "critique is essential to all democracy," and "democracy is nothing less than defined by critique."[96] If our political interest today entails radical change, deep structural change, this does not mean that we must turn our back on democratic engagement and abandon the essentially ethical question of how ordinary people engage the political. After all, who is responsible for bringing about substantive political change? Any answer that hopes to steer clear of authoritarianism must include ordinary people, ordinary democratic citizens. And the normative implication here is that ordinary citizens must work on a mode of critical reflection that can expose and blast open the continuum of democratic apathy, that sense of democratic demoralization that has far too many caught in its grip. The objective is not simply to counsel *mere* hopefulness. The idea is not simply to wait on the Messiah. "Any attempt simply to wish away [something] in advance of a real change in our experience would amount to a merely hopeful or dishonest declaration that an unfree society is in fact free."[97] Instead, ordinary women and men need to do the heavy lifting, and for Adorno this challenge, this fight, this struggle, begins with the question of how we think, how we bring images and rhetorical provocations to bear on our critical consciousness, how we envision new possibilities and yet vivify at the same time the immanent constraints that may prevent the very transcendence that we seek. It is in this sense that we refer to a spirit of dialectical thinking that is always already part of a spirit of political engagement.

FIVE

THE INSTINCTIVE DIALECTIC

In his early work Marx speaks forthrightly of a "fully developed humanism," which entails, he says, a "reintegration or return of man to himself" and a "complete return of man to himself as a *social* (i.e., human) being."[1] Marx counsels here a certain redemptive or reconciliatory vision, one that emerges in his work alongside growing suspicions of disembodied rationalism and the Cartesian tradition, alongside growing concerns about alienation in the modern labor process, concerns about a liberal ideology that reduces society to "an abstraction vis-à-vis the individual."[2] In many ways, the normative core of Marx's social criticism is borne along by an anthropological vision of a richer, more complete, fully embodied human existence in which "man is affirmed in the objective world not only in the act of thinking, but with *all* his senses."[3] The thought seems to be that as human beings, full of creative potential, we ought to experience our lives, and our social and material world, as a positive expression of our creative talents and energies. If we cannot "reproduce" ourselves "actively, and in a real sense," if we cannot "see" our "own reflection in a world which [we] have created," then, well, we ought to be concerned, we ought to assume a critical posture, for our human situation is not what it ought to be.

Marx's critique of bourgeois society, his "protest" against what has become of the modern way of life, is rooted, Erich Fromm tells us, "in the humanist Western philosophical tradition, which reaches from Spinoza through the French and German enlightenment philosophers of the eighteenth century to Goethe and Hegel, and the very essence of which is concern for man and the realization of his potentialities."[4] On Fromm's take, Marx's philosophy emerges as the "upshot" of this broader humanist tradition, and it does so largely because of its debts to Hegel's dialectical innovations. As Marx himself admits, in a passage that I noted in chapter 2 and that is worthy of slightly fuller consideration here, Hegel's "outstanding" contribution is precisely "the dialectic of negativity as the moving and generating principle." The real contribution, Marx says, has to do with the fact that "Hegel conceives the self-genesis of man as a process, conceives objectification as a loss of the object, as alienation and as transcendence of this alienation; that he thus grasps the essence of *labor* and comprehends objective man—true, because real man—as the outcome of man's *own labor*."[5] As we have seen, both Hegel and Marx turn to dialectical thinking in order to account for self-creative human activity, and not merely in the Kantian, classically liberal sense of the individual pursuit of autonomy but in the broader sense of a species-wide pursuit of collective self-determination.

For both Hegel and Marx, dialectical thinking helps to vivify a process by which we—individuals, communities, the human species as such—come to appreciate and take ownership over our ability consciously to create and recreate our world. In this final substantive chapter, and by way of a return to the framing theme of chapter 2, the theme of "staging," I consider how humanist discourse in the dialectical tradition tends to get swept up in a naïve and perhaps dangerously hopeful reconciliatory narrative. Ultimately, I consider how we might embrace, in our own time, a dialectical way of thinking that appears to be grounded in a set of rather strong assumptions about the nature and trajectory of human "self-activity." I consider how we might embrace a way of thinking that is borne along by a certain promise of, as Marx puts it, "reintegration or return," a promise of atonement, or, as Fromm puts it, "the at-onement of man with himself, with nature, and with his fellow man, based on the fact that man has given birth to himself in the historical process."[6]

By invoking the language of humanism here I mean purposefully to raise a red flag. What we have been referring to as the dialectical tradition represents a significant chapter, perhaps the ultimate chapter, the "upshot," of the broader humanist emphasis on "man" and on the presumed inauguration of a "human" world, an inauguration sold on the promise of liberation and emancipation yet burdened in time by rather pernicious consequences. Throughout the modern period, and perhaps as a constitutive component of Western modernity as such, humanist discourse has been mobilized, often implicitly, as a kind of ideological smokescreen, effectively masking or at least obscuring relationships of power, hierarchies of power. Such discourse, distinctively European in origin and decidedly Eurocentric in character, has often been made to gloss over cultural particularity, to whitewash racial difference, to minimize, indeed to marginalize, the claims of the overpowered. At issue here are potentially violent exclusions that derive from presumptuous claims about what does and does not count as essentially or fully human. Talk of humanism often lapses into talk of universality, and, as Judith Butler reminds us, "universality has been used to extend certain colonialist and racist understandings of civilized 'man,' to exclude certain populations from the domain of the human, and to produce itself as a false and suspect category."[7] Certainly the humanism of the nineteenth-century dialecticians, the humanism of Hegel and Marx, is supposed to be a call to action and a rejection of what Marx might call "fixed, fast-frozen" identities; after all, by the lights of dialectical thinking, man *is* what he *does*. Still, in the face of contemporary suspicions of humanist discourse, it is important that we shore up our understanding of the anthropological assumptions that undergird dialectical thinking. And in what follows, I set out to do so via an engagement with an underappreciated and thus somewhat unlikely figure in C. L. R. James, a West Indian intellectual who brings a rather distinctive perspective to bear on his embrace of Hegel, Marx, and the humanist elements of the dialectical tradition.

C. L. R. James is perhaps best known as the author of *The Black Jacobins*, his 1938 history of Toussaint L'Ouverture and Haitian Revolution.[8] This text, which we will have some occasion to consider later in the chapter, has become a classic statement of anticolonial protest and a foundational contribution to twentieth-century black radical historiography, and yet emphasis on *The Black Jacobins* has tended to overshadow other important elements of James's life and work. Our inquiry will focus primarily on James's writings from the late 1940s and early 1950s, the writings from the tail end of his so-called American sojourn, a fifteen-year period from 1938 to 1953, which many have referred to as James's most original. This is a period in which James established himself as a fairly prominent figure in postwar efforts to interject a younger, more Hegelian Marx into orthodox Marxist political thought. This is a period in which James produced a series of wide-ranging reflections on American popular culture, including commentaries on sports and popular literature, Hollywood films, and comic strips. This is a period in which James described himself as a "profound believer in what is so lightly called by so many democracy."[9] As Cornelius Castoriadis once remarked, albeit without much explanation, James "had this wonderful sense of the self-activity of the people, and he was able to translate it in universal terms that were not absolute universals."[10] As I hope to show, James's radically democratic sensibilities, his emphasis on the spontaneous and often unruly political struggles of ordinary women and men, informs his own independent *restaging* of the dialectical tradition, a restaging that yields something of a renewed humanism, a renewed sense of what it means to be a human being, what it means to take ownership over one's situation, ultimately what it means to critique and take up active protest against, well, dehumanization. The key point, I will argue, is that James manages to *temper* and *enrich* the conventional redemptive or reconciliatory vision of human growth and fulfillment that has beset the modern dialectical tradition, and he does so precisely by moving toward a more *tragic* appreciation for open-ended human activity.

In chapter 2 we sought to transpose onto our analysis the rudiments of an analytical framework established some years ago by the historian Hayden White. White argued that while Hegel and Marx were plainly attentive to the tragic subnarratives of human history, ultimately their visions of historical development assumed a more "comic" emphasis on the fateful reconciliation of opposed or contradictory forces. White went on to suggest that Marx specifically "[carried] this comic conception even further" than Hegel. It "would not be unjust," White said, to play up a more "romantic" dimension to Marx's thinking.[11] I do not wish to scrutinize too much these generic labels; in fact, I want simply to underscore the family resemblances between two kinds of narrative that emphasize ultimate triumph, either through reconciliation or redemption. Whether we invoke the comic or the romantic mode, certainly both genres contrast with tragedy in terms of how they yield an orientation toward the story, toward its meaning, toward its constitutive parts and ultimate outcome. And in the context of a discussion of James, a subtle shift toward the language of romance makes sense, at least initially. As we will see, James comes to the dialectical tradition in the 1930s via a reading of Marx and Lenin and he develops his thinking about socialist humanism by way of an engagement with the *Economic and Philosophical Manuscripts*; only later does he turn to Hegel and to a serious consideration of the tragic. And part of what James seems to develop in and through his initial engagement with Marx is a discernibly romanticized sense of what our human situation ought to look like and thus what ought to be the proper focus of our sustained critical scrutiny.

Throughout his oeuvre, but perhaps most notably in the immediate postwar writings, James articulates a critique of capitalist modernity that bespeaks a marked reaction against an experience of psychic and social fragmentation and division and disintegration. This reaction is animated by a romantic longing for a lost sense of wholeness, what James, following Marx, regards as a more self-satisfactory human condition in which our creative energies are made to function in our daily lives, our daily work, our daily interactions with others. In the first section of the chapter, I sketch in the basic contours of James's romanticized variation on Marxist humanism and I argue that, while these ideas may not be especially original or profound, they do constitute the normative core of James's social criticism. These loosely romantic philosophical commitments undergird a working moral vision against which James can diagnose as deficiencies certain characteristics of a modern, capitalist way of life.

My purpose in this first section is simply to set up a starting position, a kind of raw canvas on which to sketch in some of James's more creative thoughts and considerations. In the remainder of the chapter, the second and third sections, and the conclusion, I show how James provides some additional and more innovative theoretical resources with which contemporary readers can *enrich* and *temper* this romantic humanism. In the mid-1940s, James turns his attention to Hegel, a figure who, somewhat ironically, inspires James to work against the abstractions of grand historical narratives, including, most significantly, the dominant Marxist narrative that had attracted James since his original departure from Trinidad in the early 1930s. James mobilizes elements of Hegelian thinking against any temptation to background the lives, choices, and actions of individual human beings. For our purposes, this rather unique encounter with Hegel *enriches* James's humanism by encouraging a vivification of the psychic and material situation of the concrete individual, and specifically the "instinctive" hopes and frustrations that animate grassroots political activity. Also in the late 1940s, and the early 1950s, James turns his attention to tragic drama. He studies Hegel and Aristotle's thinking on tragedy, as well as tragic motifs in the work of Aeschylus, Shakespeare, Melville, and others. This consideration of tragedy effectively *tempers* James's humanism by encouraging a more nuanced conception of human agency. While James remains firmly committed to the idea of human creative expression as an objective or goal, a source of teleological longing that can help animate and provoke political activity among ordinary women and men, he counterbalances this commitment with a more tragic awareness that we necessarily act in situations that we do not entirely choose, situations that we do not entirely control. James's postwar flirtations with the tragic help to reveal a humanist normative vision that is very much alive, that is exposed to the contingencies of an uncertain world, and that is necessarily open to contestation.

My strategy here is to pick up on a path that James implicitly gestures toward but does not necessarily pursue or even fully recognize. By thinking with and against James, by taking critical inspiration from his life and work and by moving beyond him in certain regards, I hope to create space for a renewed discussion of the humanist commitments that undergird dialectical thinking and criticism, a discussion that shifts focus away from concerns about closed narratives and presumptuous identity claims and toward an emphasis on democratic action. To be sure, James's thinking is enmeshed in a set of philosophical categories that have long plagued humanist discourse. In many ways, James's thinking is an extension of European orthodoxy, of the elevation of the category of class over categories of race and gender, of the conventional comic, or romantic, staging that has come to be associated with the modernist philosophies of Hegel and Marx. In other ways, and here James may be at his best, he places the experiences and the creativity of black women and men at the heart of the humanist imaginary, suggesting that, in the United States as across the history and the geography of the African diaspora, black people have been, and continue to be, uniquely situated to shed critical light on the meaning of oppression, degradation, and inhumanity. At times James seems to suggest that in the struggle against dehumanization, in the struggle for a more fully human experience and a more humane society, black women and men stand at the vanguard, so to speak. I suggest that James's ultimate purpose is to provoke action, to incite democratic protest against a sense of dehumanization, rather than to privilege or exclude any philosophical tradition or specific identity category. By tracing the development of James's thinking about the human, by showing how James's thinking develops in and through an explicit engagement with the vicissitudes of popular political activity, we can put ourselves in a better position to embrace the resources of a dialectical tradition that has long been burdened by strong, often presumptuous, and at times exclusionary anthropological commitments.

CONTOURS OF A ROMANTIC HUMANISM

One interesting way to situate James is to point out the little-known fact that James had access to English translations of at least key pieces of the *Economic and Philosophical Manuscripts* as early as May 1943, some eighteen years before T. B. Bottomore, in 1961, came out with the first widely circulated English-language edition of Marx's most significant "humanist" text.[12] Three sections of the *Manuscripts* were translated in the United States between 1943 and 1947 by Grace Lee (Boggs) and Raya Dunayevskaya and circulated in mimeographed form among James's cadre at the time, the so-called Johnson-Forest Tendency.[13] This is significant, of course, because the rediscovery of Marx's early writings provoked something of an intellectual coup among American and Western European leftists. These writings enabled radical intellectuals to drive a wedge between Marx's philosophy, on the one hand, and Soviet-style communism, on the other. And these writings helped to reveal Marx as a philosopher, as a *humanist* philosopher, and as one indebted in significant ways to the works of Hegel. Finding himself ahead of the curve, so to speak, James began to stake out a humanist Marxism well before postwar socialist humanism really began to take off.[14]

Certainly James's humanism assumes both the spirit and the language of the early Marx. But it is important to keep in mind that James is an eclectic and independent thinker, influenced by European intellectual traditions—but also by the horrors of racism and colonial rule—and by the courageous political struggles of women and men across the history and geography of the African diaspora. The fact that James picks up on some of the more "romantic" dimensions of Marx's early thinking is likely bolstered by the way in which he envisions the trajectory of struggles for black liberation and colonial independence, a vision that, at least in the 1930s and early 1940s, is shaped by the promise of heroic triumph, vindication, redemption. This is an important point, which we will consider in further detail in the third section, as we draw upon some of David Scott's recent work to stake out James's turn from the romantic to the tragic stage. For now, I want simply to show how James develops a rather broad critique of capitalist modernity, a critique that is structured conceptually in terms of a romantic longing for a lost sense of harmony and wholeness, an almost nostalgic longing for some sort of redemption of both a fragmented modern self and a fragmented modern society. My aim in this section is to introduce some of the romantic dimensions of James's postwar humanism and establish something of a starting position, which I'll then *enrich* and *temper* in the latter two-thirds of the chapter.

The romantic dimensions of James's thinking, specifically his emphasis on harmony and wholeness, emerge most notably in his discussions of what he calls the "integrated personality." During the mid-1940s, during the period in which James and his cadre begin to grapple with the writings of the early Marx, James gestures toward a discernibly redemptive normative vision, one that serves to vivify the unsatisfactory, perhaps "unnatural," conditions of fragmentation and division that are said to prevail within both the modern psyche and modern society more broadly. For James, there is something troubling about "the old rationalism with which Descartes ushered in the age of individualism." By placing "body and mind in separate compartments," by placing "the mass of ordinary men on one side and intellect, knowledge, science, method on the other," the dominant strand of modern European thinking effectively "heralded the division of the human personality by the industrial process of capitalism which has now reached the extraordinary stage that it has all over the world."[15]

This concern about fragmentation and division is evident in the way that James tries to vivify the underside of the American dream. In 1949, James began work on his "Notes on American Civilization," what was to be an outsider's assessment of American democracy in the tradition of Alexis de Tocqueville and James Bryce.[16] Throughout the text, which was never published during James's lifetime, James calls attention to the disembodied character of abstract political ideas, describing a "crisis of tens of millions who have only an instinctive conception of life, liberty, and the pursuit of happiness."[17] He calls attention to the social disconnect of American intellectuals and artists, complaining, for example, that Walt Whitman's "rebelliousness was an individualistic gesture and nothing more," that, despite Whitman's otherwise romantic gestures, "he and all who thought as he" were too quick to "leave the workingman and go to follow the Open Road."[18] James calls attention to the monotony and the mindlessness of daily labor, speaking in general of "tremendous antagonisms which are eating away at the core of the personalities of the great masses in the free democratic society of the United States."[19] What is important to see here is that these sorts of concerns are conceptualized theoretically in terms of division and fragmentation. These concerns are constituted and maintained by a philosophically romantic commitment to a sense of psychic and social harmony and wholeness, and perhaps, given the strength of these commitments, a certain *expectation* of harmony and wholeness.

Implicit in James's thinking is a version of what Michael Löwy and Robert Sayre describe as the "two opposite though not contradictory poles" of the romantic critical imaginary. Löwy and Sayre argue that romantic thinking emphasizes, on the one hand, "the subjectivity of the individual, the development and the richness of the human personality, in its full affective depth and complexity, but also in the full freedom of its imaginary." On the other hand, "on the dialectically opposite pole," romanticism underscores "the unity of the self with . . . the human universe, the human collectivity."[20] Throughout James's writings from the 1940s and 1950s, the demand for individuality is inseparable from the demand for community. James's critique of modern life is borne along by the promise of a "movement toward the creation of man as an integral human being, a full and complete individuality with the circumstances and conditions of the fully integrated individuality."[21] While James is never entirely clear as to what he means by "integration," the idea seems to be that, in order to come into our own, in order to work toward our potential and cultivate our personality, we must grow and develop as an integral part of a social whole, for our individuality "can express itself only in common with thousands of others."[22] In other words, our creative energies ought to meet with a sympathetic social circumstance. A self-satisfying human life is one in which we recognize our own creative expression in our daily work, our daily interactions with others, the social whole of which we are an integral part.[23]

This emphasis on human creativity or poiesis points toward another broadly romantic dimension of James's humanism. In their recent survey of various strands of modern humanist thinking, Martin Halliwell and Andy Mousley describe Marx as a "romantic humanist" insofar as he "appeals to a conception of art as a form of human self-magnification." They argue that, for Marx, active poetic expression bespeaks a "heightened sense of the human," which "feeds into Marx's romanticized conception of revolution as the release of hitherto unrealized human powers."[24] James works with a similar, and perhaps even more romanticized, idea of what revolutionary activity might mean. He envisions a kind of natural human longing for poetic expression giving way to expanded poetic possibilities. By striving to become a fully integrated personality in a fully integrated society, by struggling toward a reality in which "the division and antagonisms and madness of an outworn civilization are mercilessly dissected and cast aside," we thus work toward a condition in which "nature, technology, the community of men, science and knowing, literature and ideas are fused into a new humanism, opening a vast expansion of human capacity and human achievement."[25]

As James will admit, this language sounds rather utopian. But this broad, abstract vision is not meant to be any sort of blueprint for a necessarily socialist future. These projections are part of a reaction against what James regards as the generally dissatisfying daily routines to which modern individuals—and for our purposes most notably, the postwar American masses—find themselves subjected. "Somehow," James writes in his commentary on America in the late 1940s, "the creative energies of modern man, the sense of personality of hundreds of millions of modern men, must be made to function in their daily work."[26] And James exhibits here an unmistakable sense of "romantic nostalgia," what Löwy and Sayre describe as a certain longing for "a moment from the actual past in which the harmful characteristics of modernity did not yet exist and in which the human values that have been since stifled by modernity were still operative," a moment that is "transformed into a utopia, shaped as the embodiment of romantic aspirations."[27] Across James's corpus, two such historical moments stand out. One is the democratic "civilization" of classical Athens, which James idealizes as "the most remarkable of all the various civilizations of which we have recorded in history, including our own." Greek democracy, he says somewhat anachronistically, "achieved a balance between the individual and the community that was never achieved before or since."[28] The other prominent instance of nostalgic longing can be found in James's celebration of traditional African societies, or his romanticized account of "the democratic instincts and practices of the African tribes."[29] In some of his later writings on African decolonization, James identifies a certain revolutionary promise in the "purity" of historical traditions that antedate the advent of modernity. Again, James exhibits a romanticized version of, or perhaps a departure from, classical Marxism in that he envisions a new society that, as Robin D. G. Kelley puts it, "need not be built on the logic of modern industrial organization; it can be built on precapitalist traditions of democracy and communal social relations."[30]

This line of thinking may be indicative of a certain tendency among twentieth-century black radical intellectuals. Aimé Césaire, for example, similarly enlists romantic motifs in the service of a renewed humanism. Like James, Césaire focuses on the denial of creative expression under conditions of European imperialism and capitalist modernity, and, like James, he sets out to redeem a truer, purer, what he sometimes refers to as a more "primitive," creative or poetic human capacity.[31] In his 1955 *Discourse on Colonialism*, Césaire encourages a "defense of the non-European civilizations," which he describes as "societies that were not only ante-capitalist, as has always been said, but *anti-capitalist.* They were democratic societies, always. They were cooperative societies, fraternal societies." And for Césaire, these were cooperative societies grounded in lived experience; "they were the fact, they did not pretend to be the idea."[32] We find here not so much a desire for any simple return to premodern social conditions but perhaps a certain use of the romantic motif of nostalgic longing as a means to critique a modern world that has become, when judged against an idealized past, all too inhuman, all too inhumane.[33] At least the structure of Césaire's thinking here seems to resemble that of James, and if a certain set of romantic motifs are an integral part of a tendency within twentieth-century black radical thinking, this is, to be sure, but one dimension of a diverse, multifaceted, and at times internally contentious intellectual milieu. Some, such as Frantz Fanon, will deride any tinge of romanticism or nostalgia in the struggle for a "new humanism."[34] Fanon might describe James's romanticism as but a conservative or reactionary setback to an otherwise radical agenda. In any case, we must keep in mind that James's humanism, which owes much to the early Marx, is nevertheless carved out against an intellectual and experiential milieu that extends beyond the terms of traditional European thinking.[35]

My purpose in this section has been to introduce the context and the basic contours of James's humanism, what amounts, I have suggested, to a kind of romantic variation on the traditional Marxist formulation. This emphasis on harmony and wholeness, this nostalgic longing for some sort of redemption from fragmentation and disintegration, these ideas make up the normative core of James's social criticism. These ideas provide a working moral vision against which James can diagnose as deficiencies certain characteristics of a modern, capitalist way of life. In the remainder of the chapter, I show how James provides some more nuanced and sophisticated theoretical resources with which we can *enrich* and *temper* this humanist vision.

HEGELIAN PASTICHE

Just about all modes of romantic thinking imply at least a suspicion, which I have alluded to already, of a cold, disembodied scientific rationalism. But this is not to say that romanticism necessarily opposes reason. As Halliwell and Mousley point out, romantic thinking simply "sees reason as being incomplete without feeling, for feeling is thought . . . to have more immediate relevance to what being human means."[36] In this section, I turn to explore James's encounter with Hegel, a figure who folds a consideration of feeling and instinct, a consideration of the affective dimensions of human life, into his account of human rationality. But where Hegel is usually thought to denigrate the affective in favor of a rationality that is "essentially human," James, by way of a uniquely eclectic reading, tries to rescue a more "materialist" side of Hegel's thinking, a sharper attentiveness to the "instinctive," an attentiveness that can enrich our picture of James's romantic humanism and help us think further about how dialectical reflection might be put into the service of ethical and political engagement.

I make two claims in this section. One is that James's encounter with Hegel somewhat ironically encourages a vivification of the psychic and material situation of the concrete individual. Hegel inspires James to work against any temptation to allow the abstractions of grand historical narratives to background the lives, the choices, the actions of individual human beings. In this way, Hegel effectively wedges some additional space between James's thinking and the dominant terms of Marxist orthodoxy. The other claim is that the encounter with Hegel, and again somewhat ironically, helps James initiate a turn toward a humanist ethical sensibility by underscoring the need for ordinary individuals to articulate dialectically their own "instinctive" frustrations and desires.

James began to read Hegel in America in the early 1940s, in the midst of his own intellectual uncertainty. Like other independent intellectuals who were drawn to Marxism but who fundamentally rejected Stalinism, James gravitated toward Trotskyism in the 1930s, shortly after he arrived in England from Trinidad. At the request of Trotsky and James P. Cannon, then leader of the fledgling Socialist Workers Party (SWP) in America, James traveled to the United States in 1938 to give a series of lectures on the "Negro question." But after Trotsky's assassination in 1940, James grew increasingly disillusioned with the worn-out terms of the Trotsky-Stalin polemic.[37] "As early as 1941," James recalls, "I began to question the premises of Trotskyism. . . . I was increasingly aware of large areas of human existence that my history and my politics did not seem to cover."[38] James says years later that, during the early 1940s, a new series of questions began to animate his thinking. "What did men live by? What did they want? What did history show that they had wanted? Had they wanted then what they wanted now? The men I had known, what had they wanted? What exactly was art and what exactly culture?"[39]

On the surface, it seems fairly straightforward that James turned to Hegel in much the same way that Lenin did, and for many of the same reasons. In the face of world historical change, caught in the throes of intellectual uncertainty, James sought to get clear on the Hegelian dialectic and to establish a firmer theoretical grasp of the nature of global economic and political development.[40] And certainly in James's most significant text of the period, in his 1948 *Notes on Dialectics: Hegel, Marx, Lenin*, Hegelian philosophy does emerge as a kind of theoretical crutch for a more or less orthodox Marxist historical narrative. But there is something of a minor narrative to *Notes on Dialectics*.[41] As the subtitle to the book indicates, James is concerned with three basic characters in Hegel, Marx, and Lenin, and yet these three characters do not always contribute to the same storyline. James makes a distinction between Hegel, on the one hand, and Marx and Lenin, on the other. The former, he says, is a thinker of the "instinctive dialectic," whereas the latter two are representatives of the "theoretical dialectic."[42] At various points in the text, James makes what he calls "transfers" from the "instinctive" to the "theoretical," presumably as part of a move from the micro to the macro level, as part of an effort to shed light on larger historical processes, most notably the development of the international labor movement.[43] This emphasis on the macro level, the emphasis on Marx and Lenin, has likely caused readers of James to overlook his treatment of Hegel and the subtler, more nuanced, and far more fecund figuration of dialectical reflection that emerges there.[44] James's references to Hegel, specifically his references to dialectical logic, almost always have to do with the mental process by which individual human beings develop a conscious awareness of their own "instinctive" frustrations and desires. Hegel's texts—and in James's *Notes on Dialectics* this amounts to the *Science of Logic*, the first eighty or so sections and additions of the *Encyclopedia Logic*, and at least snippets of the *Phenomenology of Spirit*—help James develop a sense for how ordinary human beings can be said to respond, or perhaps how human beings ought to respond, to the very questions that were now animating James's thinking in general, questions of what ordinary people live by, what they want, and so forth.

The portrait of Hegel that emerges in *Notes on Dialectics* is very much a product of James's own creative exegesis. It is in fact a kind of Hegelian pastiche. James flatly denounces any concern for world-spirit, describing Hegelian *Geist* as "one of the funniest things in philosophy" and saying that "for our purposes it [world-spirit] does not matter a damn. . . . To hell with it!"[45] Ultimately James emphasizes a passage from the *Science of Logic* in which Hegel refers to consciousness as "concrete and engrossed in externality," and though James admits that this is a "curious phrase for the great Idealist," it is here, he says, that "we run up against the dialectic in life."[46] For James, Hegel's repeated gestures toward embodiment and toward a consciousness grounded in the concrete point toward a materialist side of Hegel's thinking.[47] And for James, this materialism issues in a concern for human desire, human need, human feeling, and for the ways in which our thinking is attentive to these. Our thinking, James says, is rooted in "Desire, Will, etc., *human feelings and actions*. We abstract them to think about them. But they come from there. . . . The whole magnificent structure is rooted in the concrete."[48]

I have already alluded to what many would regard as the irony of James's reading. He seems to mobilize Hegel, the great abstract idealist, *against* the very idea of any grand, abstract historical narrative. He seems to use Hegel instead as a kind of lens through which to focus on the intellectual activities of flesh and blood individuals, especially those caught up in a frustrating social circumstance, struggling to articulate politically their own needs, desires, interests, and concerns. I would argue that this is less of an ironic reading of Hegel and more of a reflection of James's independent embrace of what we characterized in chapter 2 as the alternative stage of the modern dialectical tradition. And for our purposes, the contribution worth considering here has to do, not with dialectical logic as such, but with how we might put dialectical thinking into conversation with ordinary experience, how we might use dialectical thinking to give political voice to the instinctive side of our human lives.[49] James is concerned to explore and provoke grassroots political energies by encouraging our consideration of the contradictions between form and content, or between our established concepts, our understanding, the settled terms by which we describe ourselves and our world, on the one hand, and our instinctive frustrations, ultimately our essential negativity, on the other.

I continue to stress this language of *frustration* because this language captures much of what James regards as the characteristic experience of mid-twentieth-century life, and because this language directs our attention to the source of creative energy that James seems to think Hegelian dialectical reflection can help us tap into. We have seen already that James's 1950 study, *American Civilization*, is a story of antagonisms that are "eating away at the core of the personalities" of the American masses. *American Civilization*, written only a year or so after *Notes*, is very much an account of popular frustration, a story of "tens of millions who have only an instinctive conception of life, liberty, and the pursuit of happiness."[50] It is an account of the American proletariat, the industrial workers, but also the homemakers, the students, the artists, and intellectuals who, James says, "are brought up against the contradiction between the theories, principles, ideas, etc. by which they live and the reality which they actually face."[51]

Throughout the text, perhaps in an effort to gesture past dichotomizing debates about class versus race or gender, James speaks in broadly inclusive but imprecise terms.[52] And if we mine beneath the ambivalent language, it seems fairly straightforward that James places the experiences and the creativity of black Americans at the heart of the humanist imaginary. To elaborate on an observation I introduced at the outset, we see here that James's preoccupation with popular frustration is built upon a driving concern for the dehumanization experienced most profoundly by black Americans. Keep in mind that James came to America in 1938, the year in which he published both *The Black Jacobins* and *A History of Pan-African Revolt*, two books that celebrate the autonomous political activities of women and men of African descent.[53] This focus on Africana people, on Africana perspectives, James unquestionably brings with him to the United States. In a way that contrasts rather sharply with the more euphoric tones of mainstream postwar discourse, James seems to focus on the women and men most relegated to the underside of the postwar boom, those most relegated to simply an "instinctive conception" of American democratic principles. James's sobering stories take inspiration from those with the most intimate knowledge of the disjuncture between form and content, those who feel most intensely that sense of frustration between the "theories, principles, ideas," on the one hand, and, on the other, "the reality which they actually face."[54] While James may *explicitly* exhibit some ambivalence regarding his use of specific identity categories, while he may *implicitly* privilege the distinctive perspectives of black Americans, it is important to see that his ultimate purpose, as I noted at the start, is to incite democratic protest against dehumanization rather than to privilege or exclude any philosophical tradition or specific identity category.

It is also important to see that James's emphasis on widespread popular frustration is by no means cause for despair or resignation. He works to interject a series of Hegelian insights into his "wonderful sense of the self-activity of the people," and this experience of frustration provides the fuel for a potentially potent popular response. Part of the task, James seems to suggest, is simply to encourage struggling citizens to begin to conceptualize their lives dialectically, to see their own lives not only in terms of frustrations or fragmentations or disintegrations, but, more pointedly, more "sharply," in terms of *contradictions*, dialectical antinomies that, as such, cannot, or should not, sustain themselves. And here James's Hegelian patchwork becomes a rather delicate balancing act.

On the one hand, James develops his own version of the sort of Nietzschean disillusionment that I spoke of in chapter 2. That is to say, James questions the dialectical tradition's strong ontological commitment to the principle of contradiction. Regarding specifically Hegel's insistence that "contradiction . . . moves the world," regarding Hegel's insistence that "*every* determination, *every* concrete, *every* concept" can necessarily reduce to a play of opposites, James concedes to hyperbole.[55] "Hegel," he says, "as usual you exaggerate."[56] And yet, on the other hand, James seems to pursue Hegel's "broad distinction between the instinctive act and the intelligent and free act," arguing that, if our social and political circumstance induces a sense of instinctive frustration, then we ought to impose the category of contradiction onto our experience, in a perhaps somewhat rhetorical way, as to yield a new kind of intelligence, ultimately as to free ourselves from the shackles of despair.[57] "It is the unbearable nature of contradiction that creates negativity," James says, for "if there is no sharp contradiction, then there is no movement to speak of and there is stagnation, a compromise."[58] In a way, James's notion of the "instinctive dialectic" is meant to put the category of contradiction into conversation with lived experience, specifically with our instinctive dissatisfactions with the settled contours of extant reality, if only because contradiction throws instability into the boldest possible relief. Again, the idea is to incite active protest against an experience of fragmentation, division, and disintegration, and such protestant energy, such critical negativity, comes alive most fully when we see that we cannot and should not sustain disparities between our "theories, principles, ideas," on the one hand, and, on the other, "the reality which [we] actually face."

The broader point here is simply that James invokes Hegel in order to mobilize the idea that individual human beings might cultivate a loosely dialectical, and essentially humanist, response to a dissatisfying social and political situation. Certainly we find here a testament to James's deep-seated commitment to individual self-determination, a testament to the more radically democratic side of his thinking. And we see that James's encounter with Hegel, his initial gestures toward an alternative staging of the tradition, allows him to put romantic humanist commitments into explicit conversation with the political activities of ordinary women and men. This is a move that remains somewhat veiled or at least underdeveloped in James's texts, but it is a move that James gestures toward, and it is one that may be instructive for an effort to reorient and remobilize a humanist discourse in our time. For our purposes, James's encounter with Hegel encourages our consideration of how ordinary citizens engage the political. And it encourages our consideration of how ordinary citizens might engage the political on their own terms by taking up humanist discourse and dialectical reflection as resources, intellectual weapons to be used in grassroots political struggle.

Before we move on, I want to make two quick points of clarification. We have called attention to James's references to the "instincts," specifically his reference to an "instinctive dialectic." We have put these references into conversation with the struggles of the oppressed, specifically the struggles of women and men of African descent. In doing this, we risk giving the impression that James relies on some of the traditionally coded language of European ethnocentrism, that James, much like Hegel, implicitly associates the "instinctive" with a backward primitivism and reserves this category largely for his discussions of non-European, or at least nonwhite, peoples. The worry here is that James assumes a posture not unlike that of Sartre during the late 1940s. In, for example, "Black Orpheus"—a text which, to be sure and as I noted in chapter 3, is reflective of a transitional phase in Sartre's evolving thinking about race and colonialism, a transitional phase in his evolving awareness of his own "situation" as a European intellectual—Sartre, despite his best intentions, effectively relies upon a civilized-primitive dyad and associates blackness with "timeless instincts, a simple manifestation of universal and eternal fecundity."[59] While James has been described disparagingly as a "Black European," while he has been condemned in some circles for his accommodation to European philosophical traditions, it is important to see that his references to the "instinctive" are meant simply to call attention to a deep and fundamental human longing for freedom, for autonomy, for self-determination in the world with others.[60] Certainly James wants to emphasize the ways in which we might work our "instinctive" frustrations into a kind of dialectical picture, "raising," Hegel might say, our immediate impulses to the level of the "intelligent and free act." And certainly James wants to emphasize the insights that African diasporic peoples can provide regarding this instinctive frustration, this fundamentally human discontent with the terms of an inhuman extant reality. But this reference to the instincts, indeed *our* reference to such, is not meant to rehash the coded significance that this language has carried throughout the modern period.

Also, before we move on, I want to be sure to situate James's reading of Hegel vis-à-vis some of the later debates surrounding Hegelian influence on humanist thinking. It should be fairly clear by now that, insofar as James operates within the ambit of the Marxist tradition, insofar as he turns to Hegel in the 1940s to enrich his thinking, insofar as he uses Hegel as a kind of lens to focus on the experiences and the intellectual activities of ordinary individuals, he stands in rather stark opposition to what will become, in the 1960s, the structuralist and poststructuralist suspicions of Hegelian influence. Within the specifically Marxist tradition, this sort of suspicion flows most notably through the work of Louis Althusser. In his grand attack on Hegel and the supposedly "ideological" readings of Marx, Althusser effectively denies or at least downplays the political significance of individual human experience by reducing living human beings to objects, and not subjects, of knowledge. As he suggests famously in *For Marx*, "It is impossible to know anything about men except on the absolute precondition that the philosophical (theoretical) myth of man is reduced to ashes."[61] The idea here is that human beings are better understood as products or artifacts of anonymous social structures, larger historical processes. On my reading, James is simply too much of a radical democrat to pursue this structuralist line of thinking. He is concerned to incite democratic protest against the experience of dehumanization, and, for James, this essentially political project can only be enriched by theoretical inquiry into the nature or the essence of human being. This political project can only be enriched by theoretical reflection about how human beings come to know and interpret their own individual experiences and by reflection about what motivates and inspires human beings to act.[62] I turn now to engage more specifically with James's conception of agency.

THE TRAGEDY OF SELF-ACTIVITY

We must keep in mind that James is a decidedly *modern* thinker, and whether he extracts intellectual resources from Hegel or Marx or Lenin, his thinking is certainly shaped by visions of self-sovereign action, subjective mastery over the objective world, human purpose over chance and contingency. I have already quoted James as saying that "somehow the creative energies of modern man, the sense of personality of hundreds of millions of modern men, must be made to function in their daily work." And this passage is indicative of Marx's more Promethean influence, indicative, perhaps, of a certain commitment to the idea of the authentic self, some sort of true human essence that can and should be expressed more or less authentically, in and through human creativity or production. Certainly these influences loom large in James's thinking, but we have seen that James is very much his own thinker, and, as mere influences among others, these modernist notions and images do not account for all that James has to offer. As I argue in this section, James *tempers* his conception of human agency with a more resolutely tragic awareness of our situation in the world with others.

The key point here is that James's romantic humanism bespeaks a *struggle* for the expression of authentic creativity. Any commitment to authenticity is necessarily contested, caught up in a thicket of existential complexities. While James pursues the notion of human poetic expression as an objective or goal, a source of teleological longing that can help animate and provoke political activity among ordinary women and men, he counterbalances this teleological energy with a more tragic awareness that we necessarily act in situations that we do not entirely choose, situations that we do not entirely control. At the heart of this dynamic is a subtler, more nuanced conception of human agency, one that we can begin to glimpse by turning to James's literary criticism of the late 1940s and early 1950s.

Here it will be helpful to take a cue from some of David Scott's recent work. In *Conscripts of Modernity*, Scott shows that part of James's encounter with Hegel in the late 1940s includes an inquiry into Hegel's thinking on tragedy.[63] And James's interest in tragedy goes well beyond a simple inquiry into just Hegel's thinking. James studies Aristotle and the Greek tragedians—Sophocles, Euripides, and especially Aeschylus. He studies Shakespearean tragedy and tragic motifs in Melville. He lectures on tragedy at Columbia University.[64] Indeed the late 1940s and early 1950s bespeak a kind of tragic turn in James's thinking, a turn that, for Scott's purposes, culminates in a profoundly important set of revisions to the 1963 edition of *The Black Jacobins*.

When James first published his book on the Haitian Revolution, he wanted to inspire his readers to think seriously about colonization and about an enduring imperial presence throughout the modern world. In 1938, he was writing from an anticolonial perspective. By 1963, the year in which James republished *The Black Jacobins*, he was beginning to imagine how his book might speak to a *post*colonial situation. And part of the challenge, as Scott suggests and as James indicates, is that we must rethink the meaning and significance of action and agency. No longer is it simply a matter of fomenting struggles for liberation. No longer is it simply a matter of extending the modernist notion of self-sovereign agency to those who had been deprived of it. Rather, we must imagine a more sustainable conception of human agency, one that continues to draw on the humanist ideal of creative self-activity, but one that is not geared toward overpowering "the other." And so, as Scott points out, James turns to tragedy to help him think through a new conception of agency.

Scott calls attention to a 1953 letter to an unknown critic in which James says, "My ideas of art and society, like my specifically literary criticism, are based upon Aristotle and Hegel."[65] These primary influences help James "put forth a theory of *characters in great fiction*."[66] And "what is most important in this theory," James says, "is the idea that the great tragic writer has to work out an adequate conception of the character in its perfection."[67] It may seem strange that James focuses on *character* in the context of the tragic drama, especially in the context of Aristotle and Hegel's thinking on tragic drama. For both Aristotle and Hegel, tragedy has to do, not with character or *ethos*, but with action, with the Greek notion of *dran*, the very stuff of *dramatic* representation. As Aristotle famously puts it in the *Poetics*, "tragedy is essentially an imitation not of persons but of action and life, of happiness and misery. . . . Character gives us qualities, but it is in our actions—what we do—that we are happy or the reverse. In a play, accordingly, they do not act in order to portray the characters; they include the characters for the sake of action."[68] While James emphasizes the language of "character," he seems to suggest that tragic writers come at character in a certain sort of way. Tragic writers are able to show how character is generally subordinate to action, how character is largely a product of one's activity within a specific social situation. James's theory of characters in great fiction, a theory shaped by a deep appreciation of tragic drama, suggests that *character* is largely an embodiment of the very tensions and frustrations *characteristic of* a given social milieu.

In his discussion of Shakespeare's character Hamlet, for example, James argues that Hamlet's actions are not the product of some settled disposition of character. They are not some flaw or fault or moral idiosyncrasy that can be traced back to an essential or authentic personality. Hamlet is himself a representative of a particular social milieu, what James refers to as the emerging "age of reason." Hamlet is, in other words, an intellectual, an embodiment of isolation and soliloquy. He is a generally impotent figure who has become predisposed to a very specific kind of action, namely the "habit of thought." And on James's reading, this "habit of thought was no flaw in Hamlet's character. It was his character. If it was a flaw, it was a flaw in the whole construction of civilization from the sixteenth century onward." The intellectual, James says, is an "organic part of rationalist society and Hamlet is the organic intellectual."[69]

As Scott has shown, James's theory of character extends beyond his analysis of fiction and into his own biographical sketches of world historical figures. Most significant here is James's account of Toussaint L'Ouverture, a figure who embodies, who is *characteristic of*, the very tensions and frustrations and tragic dilemmas built into the colonial situation.[70] I suggest that this theory of character can help us glimpse certain features of a broader conception of human agency. At least to some extent, James seems to place the doer in the deed. That is to say, a character's intentions are not separable from the action; they come alive in and through the act of expression. And even to entertain the thought that the doer is somehow interconnected with the deed, even to consider an emphasis on action rather than on character or identity, is to challenge the modernist notion of the self-sovereign agent. It is to highlight our essential vulnerability, the tragic fact that the meaning and significance of our actions, and thus our character and identity, depend upon how our action is received by those around us and by the material world itself.[71] To entertain a tragic emphasis on action is to become, as Scott puts it, "acutely sensitive to the vagaries of fortune and the contingencies of circumstance that acting in the world inevitably exposes us to." James's postwar reflections on tragedy help him attend to "the simple but often obscured fact that as human beings we never begin in conditions of our own choosing. And being the mortals that we are, fettered, limited, partial, never fully transparent to ourselves, never fully self-present to our rational consciousness, never fully self-determined in our behaviors, we cannot ever totally overcome these circumstances."[72]

To be sure, these tragic motifs work only to *temper* James's humanist commitments. As we have seen, James is captivated and inspired by a deep appreciation for the autonomous activities of ordinary women and men. He continues to think of popular culture as an expression or "portrayal" of the "moods, desires, aspirations, needs, strengths and weakness" of the people.[73] And throughout James's work, the assumption seems to be that these "moods, desires, aspirations, needs, strengths and weakness" derive more or less organically from the people, or, if we dig deeper, from the authentic expressions of individual human beings. At times, James seems to suggest that all meaningful energy moves outward from the human subject, or the creative fount, the poetic source. On this view, the world and others can very easily be reduced to obstacles, impediments, dead objectivity that we must somehow master or overcome, avoid or deal with in some way. Furthermore, James continues to rely on the labor-centric categories of Marxist thought. Certainly an emphasis on labor and production may discourage James from exploring the ways in which we are often consumers, not only of material goods, but also of "moods, desires, aspirations, needs, strengths and weakness," consumers of our own identity, our "authentic" self.

Still, for our purposes, James at least gestures toward what may be a more fruitful rendition of the humanist imaginary. He provides resources with which to sustain a kind of counterbalance between the longing for creative expression in our daily lives, a longing that may help animate political activity among ordinary women and men, and a more tragic awareness of our situation in the world with others, a more tragic appreciation for uncertainty or worldly contingency. James's flirtations with the tragic help to render dialectical humanism more sustainable as a normative ideal, insofar as we are less concerned to overpower one another and more concerned to acknowledge our vulnerability, our dependence upon the community of which we are an integral part. These flirtations with the tragic add a layer of nuance and philosophical sophistication to a humanist ethical sensibility that might inform and inspire serious consideration of what it means to engage civically, indeed what it means to live our lives as active and engaged citizens.

CONCLUSION

In the preface to his book on Melville, James underscores his concern for "the world the masses of men strive to make sense of." This is a world to be understood, "not as industry, science, politics, economics or psychology, but as a world of human personalities, living as the vast majority of human beings live, not by ideas but by their emotions, seeking to avoid pain and misery and struggling for happiness."[74] This passage captures a good bit of what we have sought to glean from our consideration of James's life and work.

We find in this passage elements of a romantic reaction against a modern, capitalist way of life, a reaction against the frustrations and dissatisfactions that issue from what James regards as a deeply fragmented, profoundly disintegrated society. We see that this reaction is animated, not by ideas, or perhaps not *only* by ideas, but also by emotions, by instincts, by an affective displeasure with the suppression of our creative talents and energies. We find in this passage a suspicion of abstract discourse and an emphasis on ordinary women and men, "human personalities, living as the vast majority of human beings live." And we find here an emphasis on struggle, on contested activity. In his discussion of tragedy Aristotle says that "all human happiness or misery takes the form of action; the end for which we live is a kind of activity, not a quality."[75] What James describes as a struggle for happiness is a testament to a humanist vision that is very much alive, that is exposed to the contingencies of an uncertain world and that, when embraced honestly in its orientation toward action, remains open to, well, re-vision.

In this final substantive installment of the larger discussion, we have traced James's independent restaging of the dialectical tradition in order to show how we might rework the anthropological commitments that undergird dialectical criticism. The tradition that emerges, as Erich Fromm put it, as the "upshot" of the humanist "concern for man and the realization of his potentialities" is, as such, a tradition burdened, or at least threatened, by a kind of built-in orientation toward presumptuous identity claims, an orientation toward allegedly universal but often quite divisive and exclusionary claims about what does and does not count as essentially or fully human. Certainly James takes up the classical nineteenth-century—that is classically Hegelian, classically Marxist—idea that, in order to find satisfaction in our human situation, we must experience our lives and our world as a positive expression of our creative talents and energies, we must, as it were, see ourselves in a world that we have created. Any extant reality that falls short of this "fully developed humanism," as Marx puts it, anything short of this "complete return of man to himself as a *social* (i.e., human) being," is considered to be deficient, irrational, indeed the proper focus of our sustained critical scrutiny. And yet James counsels only a qualified embrace of this more or less romanticized vision of human and worldly redemption, this rather comic expectation of happy reconciliation. As a "profound believer in what is so lightly called by so many democracy," James had, as Castoriadis so aptly put it, a "wonderful sense of the self-activity of the people, and he was able to translate it in universal terms that were not absolute universals." What is remarkable about James, at least when considered in the context of our broader inquiry, is that he both *enriches* and *tempers* the nineteenth-century humanist normative foundation by turning to what I described in chapter 2 as the alternative stage of the dialectical tradition, the site of the lived experiences of ordinary democratic citizens, the site of the uncertain and often tragic struggles that flesh and blood individuals necessarily endure.

Though we have been wrestling primarily with a set of anthropological questions, I must emphasize in closing, and by way of a return to this chapter's namesake, that James's humanism informs a distinctive style of dialectical thinking, what we might call, borrowing James's somewhat underdeveloped phrase, the "instinctive dialectic." The Guyanese writer Wilson Harris once noted that "the genius of art lies, in part, in a 'shock of tone, a shock of beauty, a shock of perception' that helps us to unravel biased habit built into the ways one may have been conditioned to perceive the world" and that "C. L. R. James's preoccupation with such issues makes him a unique Marxist thinker whose dialectic is attuned . . . to necessity for individual originality as much as it is involved in analyses of historical process in the life of the people or the body-politic."[76] Harris is on to something here. James reveals that dialectical thinking can be seen as a kind of *art*, a product of human *artifice*, perhaps a rhetorical fabrication that we, not as grand historians or high theorists, but as ordinary individuals, struggling to realize our originality, impose onto our immediate perceptions, onto the settled terms of the understanding, as to elicit precisely that kind of shock that Harris speaks of. By working our instinctive frustrations into a kind of dialectical picture, by embracing the category of contradiction not as an epistemological or ontological truth but as a rhetorical device, by coming to see, perhaps to imagine, our world in terms of contradictions that cannot and should not sustain themselves, we put ourselves in a better position to "shock" our thinking, to "unravel biased habit," indeed to orient ourselves toward political determination, political action. If today the biased habit has come to reflect a sense of popular political abandon, a sense of resignation, a sense of withdrawal in the face of bewildering and seemingly unalterable social and economic forces, a dialectical style of thinking, a spirit of critique, recommends itself as a potent resource in the struggle for a more human and humane world, the struggle, James might say, for happiness.

SIX

CONCLUSION

"This is a time," Fredric Jameson says, "when people no longer understand what dialectical thinking is or why the dialectic came into being in the first place, when they have abandoned the dialectical for less rewarding Nietzschean positions." There is, he says, "a need today for a revitalized vision of the dialectic," a vision that "would certainly not abandon Marx," but that "would go back to Hegel for an enlargement of the way we have normally understood Marx."[1] These comments were uttered well over a decade ago, but they remain as timely now as ever. And in many ways, the chapters of this book have acknowledged Jameson's concern and sought to heed his call. But the story told here also veers a bit from the path implied by Jameson's comments. In this brief concluding chapter, I initially use these remarks to anchor a recap of the foregoing chapters and to provide some contrast for what may be distinctive about the "revitalized vision" cast in these pages. I also speak, if only speculatively, to an implicit conception of the political that Sartre, Adorno, and James seem to share, a conception that undergirds the felicitousness of the spirit of critique that we have sought to cull from their writings.

At the outset, I identified two basic problems to which this book intends to respond. The first, the *historical* problem, has to do with a prevailing contemporary attitude toward the dialectical tradition. As Jameson says, "people no longer understand what dialectical thinking is or why the dialectic came into being in the first place." And this situation is only reinforced by the common presumption that the legacy of Hegel and Marx, ever given to teleological narratives and the delusional hubris of grand theory, is but an outmoded relic of a bygone philosophical era, an interesting set of ideas perhaps, but worthy nowadays of little more than disinterested historical study. Our efforts to revitalize a sense of what dialectical thinking entails have sought to engage more generously with the tradition's nineteenth-century roots, to reveal anew the rationale behind the tradition's historical emergence. Journeying back through Marx to Hegel, we have sought to amplify an underappreciated dimension of the tradition, a more *tragic* dimension, which helps to situate dialectical thinking at the site of lived experience, to underscore a mode of reflection born of the struggle for autonomy, and to put the tradition generally into more sympathetic conversation with the uncertain and contentious nature of political life. Each of the twentieth-century theorists whom we have considered implicitly counsel something of this tragic dimension, which has allowed us to glean from their works a set of resources that speak more persuasively and propitiously to theorists and citizens in our own time.

This points toward the second problem identified at the start, the *political* problem, which has to do with what a spirit of dialectical critique might mean in a purportedly postpolitical age. And here we begin to wrestle a bit with Jameson's remarks. Presumably the hostility toward "less rewarding Nietzschean positions" derives from a concern about a waning revolutionary spirit, a widespread abandonment in recent decades of an unabashedly systematic critique of global capital, and an increasingly uncontested embrace of the ethical—the individual, the personal—as a preferred site of public engagement.[2] As I noted at the start, any effort to recast dialectical thinking in this moment, in this "age of ethics," is almost certainly an attempt to renew something of the inspired political fervor for which the dialectical tradition, ever affixed to the name of Marx, is so well known. Certainly this is a motivation behind our own efforts. And yet what is referred to here as a *spirit of critique* is meant to speak, as it were, to the spirit of our own moment, this age of ethics. It is meant to address what is, I believe, an ethical issue, namely *how we engage* with public life. The story developed in these pages is less hostile to the sorts of moral and philosophical concerns raised in the name of Nietzsche, less hostile to the site of the ethical as a location at which ordinary women and men—as individuals, moved by what is most intimate and personal—choose publically to think and act. The idea here, the wager, as I mentioned in the introduction, is that a spirit of dialectical critique, a spirit informed by a set of intellectual resources drawn from a fresh look at the modern dialectical tradition, might contribute to a public *ethos* imbued with a sharper, more politically incisive critical edge.

Once again, the amplification of the tragic dimension is the crucial device that opens a window onto these resources and thus onto a renewed tradition that presents itself more compellingly to readers disillusioned by self-assured philosophical narratives, readers more fully attuned to pluralism and complexity in late-modern societies. As C. L. R. James's work indicates, an appreciation of the uncertain and contentious nature of human action, an appreciation itself reinforced by James's unique reading of Hegel, facilitates an embrace of a more normatively defensible moral foundation for dialectical critique. The implicit humanism at the heart of the tradition—the moral vision that grounds the struggle for individual and collective autonomy, the vision that grounds the dialectical condemnation of an as yet irrational and untrue world—is affirmed as a *working* moral foundation, something akin to what Stephen White has described as a "weak ontological source," a foundational commitment that is taken to be both "fundamental *and* contestable."[3] In this way, a dialectical spirit of critique invites a cautious application of the politically invigorating notion that we *ought* to experience our lives and our world as a positive expression of our creative talents and energies, that we *ought* actively to contest a world still marred by pervasive unfreedom.

If James's work provides for our purposes a fresh take on dialectical humanism and the moral basis of dialectical critique, Sartre and Adorno speak more directly to a reconsideration of the structural qualities of dialectical thinking. And as regards our engagement with Sartre and Adorno, the irony of the appeal to the tragic dimension is that, far from signaling a spirit of resignation born of absolute defeat and despair, far from counseling our flight from the political, this appeal, as a constitutive component of dialectical critique, helps to orient, provoke, and sustain active political engagement.

In the case of Sartre, dialectical thinking holds open a reflective window onto the ever contentious nature of the political world, a world that theorists and citizens alike too often prefer only to forget, disavow, or imagine away, and often at their own peril. As Raymond Geuss has suggested recently, "to think politically is to think about agency, power, and interests, and the relations among these." It is to ask, "Who does what to whom for whose benefit?"[4] For Sartre, this is effectively the *modus operandi* of dialectical thinking, which calls attention to the thinker's own situation in a social and historical milieu. And in our own time this is a "milieu of scarcity," a world always already given to competition and struggles for comparative advantage. I reemphasize here in the conclusion that such thinking can be understood as a reflective component of an ethics or ethos of public engagement. If, as Geuss says elsewhere, "ethics is usually dead politics: the hand of a victor in some past conflict reaching out to try to extend its grip to the present and the future," then perhaps Sartre indicates how dialectical thinking can help cut into ethics as usual and, ultimately, awaken dead politics.[5] Perhaps dialectical thinking, as an approach to political life, can help to vivify the role that conflict has played in shaping the reality that we now experience, ultimately in order to emphasize the role that our own active contestation must play going forward.

In the case of Adorno, an appreciation of the tragic dimension invites, in what amounts to a classic dialectical reversal, a fresh consideration of the speculative dimension of the tradition. Adorno's work shows how dialectical thinking, ever torn between appeals to despair and redemption, can be said to animate and sustain the critical imagination in trying political times. "Since the possibility of changing the objective—namely societal and political—conditions is extremely limited today," Adorno says, attempts at political engagement are "necessarily restricted to the subjective dimension."[6] In other words, in this modern world, we find ourselves objectively condemned to the site of the ethical. And this is an unfortunate situation indeed, at once lamentable and dangerous, as "the lamenting subject threatens to become arrested in its condition and so to fulfill in its turn the law of the world's course." And yet, Adorno says in the very next breath, "fidelity to one's own state of consciousness and experience is forever in temptation of lapsing into infidelity, by denying the insight that transcends the individual and calls his substance by its name."[7] The latter part of this claim bears the unmistakable mark of the dialectical thinker, for no matter how real and true this lamentable situation may seem to us, no matter how real and true it may in fact be to us, it is never absolute. While dialectical thinking throws into the boldest possible relief the tragic nature of our extant reality, it does so in and through a simultaneous appeal to the transcendent, and in this way it provides a kind of built-in cognitive resistance to that resigned, withdrawn disposition often associated with the turn of ethics. Furthermore, as Adorno's remarks here would seem to underscore, we choose whether or not to apprehend and reflect upon our situation in a dialectical fashion. If in our time we find ourselves condemned to the subjective, condemned to the site of the ethical, then an embrace of dialectical thinking is at least part of a subjective response, indeed part of an individual ethical response, that, to say it again, might help cut into ethics as usual.

As this brief recap is meant to indicate, our focus throughout the book has been on how dialectical thinking might speak to a modern experience in which citizens have come to see themselves increasingly, and in the throes of neoliberal hegemony perhaps almost exclusively, as something less than capacious agents of robust democratic publics. Our question of *how we engage* today has led to a focus on certain aspects of dialectical thinking that might affect the psychic condition of the postpolitical subject. And while such thinking is meant to resist the political quietism of the ethical turn, certainly any emphasis on the subjective runs the risk of deteriorating into a mere therapeutics, an attempt simply to cope with a political situation thought to be beyond our control. In order ultimately to safeguard against a reflective spirit that procures an idealist and quietist way of living, we would need to attend also, through descriptive acknowledgment and normative aspiration, to a more collective aspect of a spirit of dialectical thinking, to the intersubjective experiences that nurture and sustain the possibility of collective reflection and real, shared human freedom. And certainly a restaging of the dialectical tradition reveals some potentially fruitful avenues here, for, as we have seen in a number of ways, and perhaps most pointedly in our discussion of James, an emphasis on the tragic nature of human action underscores our subjective vulnerability, our essential dependence upon one another. And simply to acknowledge this feature of our humanity—rather than to disavow it, as the prevailing liberal ideology, the notion of the "self-made man," so often tends to do—is to train focus on intersubjective experiences and on the need to reconstruct such experiences in order to renew and nurture viable sites of collective praxis.

But ultimately for our purposes a fuller and more affirmative vision of a renewed political would require a conversation with a different cadre of interlocutors, and it would require that we venture beyond the scope of this project, which is concerned more principally with how we engage with public life today, or at least with what has become of public life. Ours is a time in which, to borrow Sheldon Wolin's formulation, *politics* may be "continuous, ceaseless, and endless," but *the political*, understood as the moment when "collective power is used to promote or protect the wellbeing of the collectivity," is "episodic, rare," and increasingly so.[8] It is important to emphasize here in the conclusion that Sartre, Adorno, and James each implicitly counsel a sense of the "fugitive" nature of the political. They speak to a world in which the prospects for collective action are both grim and fleeting, a world in which ordinary women and men see themselves increasingly as private individuals just struggling to make ends meet. They speak, in other words, to a world without popular political form, a world without an established basis for any robust *ethos* of democratic engagement. And yet, they each draw upon a marginal intellectual tradition, upon what I have characterized throughout as a set of intellectual and rhetorical *resources*, that might provide some alternative ground on which to cultivate and sustain an active and politically incisive response. If ultimately the challenge of political theory is to describe, in vivid and honest terms, the nature of our human situation and then to determine what our political possibilities are and are not, then perhaps in our time the very possibility of a renewed political, the possibility of a more robust democratic public, depends, in the first instance, on our cultivation of a certain mode of reflective engagement, a distinctive spirit of critique. As I have argued in these pages, the modern dialectical tradition, and perhaps partly by virtue of its relative neglect in recent decades, provides today an inspiring and theoretically rich background upon which to wrestle with the challenges of an increasingly postpolitical moment.

NOTES

CHAPTER ONE. INTRODUCTION

1. See Karl Marx, "The Eighteenth Brumaire of Louis Bonaparte," in *The Marx-Engels Reader*, Second Edition, ed. R. Tucker (New York: Norton, 1977), 595.

2. "Innumerable introductions to the dialectic have been written," Jameson tells us, "although the tempo seems to be slowing down today" (Fredric Jameson, *Valences of the Dialectic* [New York: Verso, 2009], 3). I will mention here only a handful of recent studies that provide some intellectual and historical background and that are especially helpful for the story that I develop. In addition to Jameson's *Valences of the Dialectic*, 3–70, see: Jameson, "Persistencies of the Dialectic: Three Sites," *Science & Society* 62, 3 (Fall 1998), 358–372; Diana Coole, *Negativity and Politics: Dionysus and Dialectics from Kant to Poststructuralism* (New York: Routledge, 2000); Scott Warren, *The Emergence of Dialectical Theory: Philosophy and Political Inquiry* (Chicago: University of Chicago Press, 2008).

3. Jameson, *Valences of the Dialectic*, 4–5 (emphasis mine).

4. Indeed, as Jameson points out, the presence of the definite article focuses the reader's attention most squarely on the historical and intellectual legacy of Hegel and Marx. "To speak of the dialectic with the definite article cannot help but reinforce the more universalistic claims of this philosophy, as well as its unity. At the same time, this identification enhances its singularity, after the fashion of a proper name; and indeed, it is rare for the dialectic as such to be evoked in reference to any thinkers other than Hegel and Marx and people seeking to develop lines of thought affiliated with them" (Jameson, *Valences of the Dialectic*, 4).

5. Many of these images have come to fuel precisely these sorts of conjectures that we find ourselves obliged to confront, the often rather disingenuous caricatures of what dialectical thinking and the dialectical tradition are all about. Regarding the common presumption that dialectical thinking has to do with the logical movement from thesis to antithesis to synthesis, a presumption that is often attributed to Hegel but that is rather reflective of a shorthand popularized by a later interpreter, H. M. Chalybaeus, see G. E. Müller, "The Legend of 'Thesis-Antithesis-Synthesis,'" *Journal of the History of Ideas* 19, 3 (1958), 411–414. Regarding Engels's three "laws"—viz., the unity of opposites, the movement from quantity to quality, and the "negation of the negation"—see Friedrich Engels, *Dialectics of Nature* (New York: International Publishers, 1968). Regarding both the obstetric motif and the vision of rational reconciliation, perhaps it will suffice here simply to cite a prominent example, viz. Rosa Luxemburg's famous claim—derived, we should emphasize, from Marx's own

position in the 1859 preface to *A Contribution to the Critique of Political Economy*, which we will discuss in the next chapter—that "history . . . has the fine habit of always producing along with any real social need the means to its satisfaction, along with the task simultaneously the solution" (Rosa Luxemburg, *The Russian Revolution and Leninism or Marxism?* [Ann Arbor: University of Michigan Press, 1961], 70. The idea here is that history's problems always already prefigure their own resolution and that the task of dialectical inquiry is to play the role of midwife, to assist in the delivery of a movement beyond our control.

6. Jameson, "Persistencies of the Dialectic: Three Sites," 361.

7. Jameson, "Persistencies of the Dialectic: Three Sites," 366.

8. See G. W. F. Hegel, *Phenomenology of Spirit*, trans. A.V. Miller (New York: Oxford University Press, 1977), 49–50. I might add that Jameson seems likewise to raise some skepticism regarding the conventional reconciliatory staging of the dialectical narrative. Immediately after introducing the "diachronic" dimension of the dialectic, he acknowledges that "Marx has often, along with Hegel, been accused of having a 'philosophy of history' (which is evidently a bad thing; and also being somehow religious, replicating Christian historicism unconsciously, and projecting a salvational narrative of a movement of history towards some end of time—in short, of perpetuating the noxious doctrine of a telos); and in a lesser accusation, of being not only teleological but also a proponent of historical inevitability, whatever that may mean." But, he goes on to say referring specifically to Marx, "No reader of *The Eighteenth Brumaire of Louis Bonaparte* can believe any of these things," for there Marx "gives us to witness a narrative which is at every point a perpetual and dazzling, sometimes bewildering, cancellation of previously dominant narrative paradigms . . . [Marx's dialectic] constantly underscores the absolutely unforeseeable consequence, the bitterly ironic reversal, the inversion of human (individual) intention, and the progress inherent in the worst rather than the best, in failure rather than in success" (Jameson, "Persistencies of the Dialectic: Three Sites," 366). Again, we will return to these themes in chapter 2.

9. Jameson, "Persistencies of the Dialectic: Three Sites," 369. See also Jameson, *Valences of the Dialectic*, 43.

10. For a rich discussion of the concept of spirit in Hegel's philosophy, including an argument for its enduring critical theoretical import, particularly as a counterweight to the contemporary turn to ethics, see Raymond Geuss, *Outside Ethics* (Princeton, NJ: Princeton University Press, 2005), 40–66, 111–130. Geuss also raises some question as to whether or not Marx's "materialist" rejection of Hegelian idealism retains, in its (dialectical) orientation toward a historically unfolding socioeconomic "system," some trace of the Hegelian spirit. In the opening pages of chapter 2, I will suggest that Marx's "materialist" departure from Hegel's idealism is somewhat exaggerated, specifically as it relates to Marx's appropriation of Hegel's dialectical framework.

11. Heine draws a contrast between, on the one hand, the "servile" or conservative strain of Hegelian thinking and, on the other, its more "critical" and "progressive" dimensions. See John Edward Toews's discussion of "three brief characterizations of Hegel, drawn from the pen of the poet Heinrich Heine" in *Hegelianism: The Path Toward Dialectical Humanism, 1805–1841* (New York: Cambridge University Press, 1985), 95–97.

12. See Michel Foucault, *Politics and Truth*, ed. Sylvère Lotringer (New York: Semiotext(e), 2007), in particular the essay entitled "What Is Enlightenment?"; Foucault, "The Ethics of the Concern of the Self as a Practice of Freedom," in *The Essential Foucault: Selections from the 'Essential Works of Foucault 1954–1984,'* ed. P. Rabinow and N. Rose (New York: New Press, 2003) and Foucault, "Politics and Ethics: An Interview," in *The Foucault Reader*, ed. P. Rabinow (New York: Pantheon, 1984).

13. Foucault, *Politics and Truth*, 105. Foucault seems to embrace the language of ethos primarily because of its connection with embodied practice, which helps him to advance the idea that critique is informed not only by rational judgment but also by affective experience. This move is indicative of Foucault's departure from the more thoroughgoing rationalism of Habermas and the Frankfurt School. For more on this, see Amanda Anderson, *The Way We Argue Now: A Study in the Culture of Theory* (Princeton, NJ: Princeton University Press, 2006), esp. 9–12, 134–160, and Stephen K. White, "The Self-Understanding of Political Theory Today," *Political Theory* 34, 6 (2006), 785–790.

14. See Aristotle, *On Rhetoric*, ed. and trans. G. A. Kennedy (New York: Oxford University Press, 2007). The *OED* definition of ethos likewise underscores the importance of community: "the characteristic spirit, prevalent tone or sentiment, of a people or community." For a more thorough recent discussion of these issues and sources, see Stephen K. White, *The Ethos of a Late-Modern Citizen* (Cambridge, MA: Harvard University Press, 2009).

15. Jacques Rancière notes that "before signifying a norm or morality, the word *ethos* signifies two things: *ethos* is the dwelling and the way of being, the way of life corresponding to this dwelling" (Rancière, "The Ethical Turn of Aesthetics and Politics," *Critical Horizons* 7, 1 [2006], 2).

16. While this is not the place to engage thoroughly with Foucault's "philosophical ethos . . . of permanent critique," a few words may be worthy of note insofar as they speak to the political problem that animates our broader inquiry. Foucault's particular ethos has to do, he says, with the practice of "refusal," or with "the art of voluntary insubordination, that of reflected intractability," the "art of not being governed quite so much" (Foucault, *Politics and Truth*, 32, 29; see also Foucault, "Questions of Method: An Interview with Michel Foucault," in *After Philosophy: End or Transformation?*, ed. K. Baynes, J. Bohman, and T. McCarthy [Cambridge: MIT Press, 1987], 114). And in some ways, this ethos seems to reflect, albeit in ideological fashion, a rather well-established (neo)liberal order in which "society" appears as a mere aggregation of its parts, in which our individual capacities for "voluntary insubordination" appear far more substantial, far more promising, than they really are. Foucault does, after all, trace his ethos of critique back to Kant's famous essay on enlightenment, in which a sense of liberal optimism is attached to the "courage" of purportedly independent individuals. Furthermore, the very conception of critique at work here, this idea that critique has to do simply with an art of refusal, may speak rather directly, and affirmatively, to a postmodern moment in which the real attenuation of our capacities for political creativity and structural renewal are only exacerbated by a rather impolitic sense of how we ought to respond. For a more sympathetic account of this Foucauldian conception of critique as refusal, see David Hoy, *Critical Resistance: From Poststructuralism to Post-Critique* (Cambridge: MIT Press,

2004); for a richer theoretical defense of a Foucauldian "critical ethos," see James Tully, *Public Philosophy in a New Key: Volume I, Democracy and Civic Freedom* (New York: Cambridge University Press, 2008); and for an inspired critical discussion of how this notion of an ethos figures into recent theoretical work on democratic ethics and politics, see Antonio Y. Vázquez-Arroyo, "Democracy Today: Four Maxims," *Theory & Event* 13, 2 (2010).

17. See Theodor W. Adorno, *Minima Moralia: Reflections from Damaged Life*, trans. E. F. N. Jephcott (New York: Verso, 2006), 80–81, 151.

18. White, *The Ethos of a Late-Modern Citizen*, 3–4. For a more thorough discussion of "ontological figures" and an account of how these inform and sustain an ethical and political orientation or disposition, see Stephen K. White, *Sustaining Affirmation: The Strengths of Weak Ontology in Political Theory* (Princeton, NJ: Princeton University Press, 2000).

19. Of course we are dealing here with a set of problems related to the so-called turn to ethics in contemporary political theory. For some general background on this, see: Peter Baker, *Deconstruction and the Ethical Turn* (Gainesville: University Press of Florida, 1995); Todd Davis and Kenneth Womack (eds.), *Mapping the Ethical Turn: A Reader in Ethics, Culture, and Literary Theory* (Charlottesville: University of Virginia Press, 2001); Marjorie B. Garber, Beatrice Hanssen, and Rebecca L. Walkowitz (eds.), *The Turn to Ethics* (New York: Routledge, 2000); Chantal Mouffe, *On the Political* (New York: Routledge, 2005); and Rancière, "The Ethical Turn of Aesthetics and Politics." For a rich historical account of the French context, from which Foucault, Deleuze, Guattari, Derrida, and others have proven so influential in shaping the contemporary ethical turn, see Julian Bourg, *From Revolution to Ethics: May 1968 and Contemporary French Thought* (Montreal: McGill-Queens University Press, 2007).

20. Raymond Geuss, *Politics and the Imagination* (Princeton, NJ: Princeton University Press, 2010), 42. See also Geuss's critical commentaries on the ethical turn and its deleterious impact on our appreciation of "real politics" in *Outside Ethics* and *Philosophy and Real Politics* (Princeton, NJ: Princeton University Press, 2008).

21. Jean-Paul Sartre, cited in Simone de Beauvoir, *Force of Circumstance*, trans. R. Howard (New York: Harper and Row, 1977), 199.

22. Jean-Paul Sartre, *"What is Literature?" and Other Essays* (Cambridge, MA: Harvard University Press, 1988), 221–222. Commenting in the late 1950s on why Sartre abandoned his initial plan to write an ethics following publication of his wartime *Being and Nothingness*, Hazel Barnes notes that "Sartre evidently believes that so long as we live in a society based on falsehood and inequality, any individual ethics is at best a compromise" (Barnes, "Introduction" in Sartre, *Search for a Method*, trans. H. Barnes [New York: Vintage, 1968], xxv). These issues will surface again in our discussion of Sartre in chapter 3.

23. Max Horkheimer, "Traditional and Critical Theory," in *Critical Theory: Selected Essays*, trans. M. J. O'Connell (New York: Continuum, 1975), 207. Certainly Adorno and C. L. R. James, our other featured dialectical theorists, share this sentiment. More recently Jameson, one of the tradition's few contemporary legatees, has expressed similar concern, complaining that the "return to ethics as a philosophical sub-discipline and its subsequent colonization of political philosophy is one of the most regressive features and symptoms of the ideological climate of postmodernity" (Jameson, *Valences of the Dialectic*, 406).

24. Helpful discussions of the neoliberal condition include: Lisa Duggan, *The Twilight of Equality? Neoliberalism, Cultural Politics, and the Attack on Democracy* (Boston: Beacon Press, 2003); David Harvey, *A Brief History of Neoliberalism* (New York: Oxford University Press, 2005); Jodi Dean, *Democracy and Other Neoliberal Fantasies: Communicative Capitalism and Left Politics* (Durham, NC: Duke University Press, 2009); Wendy Brown, "Neoliberalism and the End of Liberal Democracy," in *Edgework: Critical Essays on Knowledge and Politics* (Princeton, NJ: Princeton University Press, 2005), 37–59; Wendy Brown, "Democracy and Bad Dreams," *Theory & Event* 10, 1 (2007); Wendy Brown, "We Are All Democrats Now," in Giorgio Agamben et al., *Democracy in What State?* (New York: Columbia University Press, 2011), 44–57; Sheldon S. Wolin, *Politics and Vision: Continuity and Innovation in Western Political Thought*, Second Edition (Princeton, NJ: Princeton University Press, 2004), 578–606.

25. Robert B. Pippin, *Hegel's Practical Philosophy: Rational Agency as Ethical Life* (New York: Cambridge University Press, 2008), 19.

26. Jameson, *Valences of the Dialectic*, 554.

27. Sartre, *The Emotions: Outline of a Theory*, trans. B. Frechtman (New York: Philosophical Library, 1948), 58; Sartre, *The Imaginary: A Phenomenological Psychology of the Imagination*, trans. J. Webber (New York: Routledge, 2004), 136.

28. "The whole" of dialectical rationality, Sartre says, is contained in Marx's famous claim, from the *Eighteenth Brumaire of Louis Bonaparte*, that "men make their own history . . . not under circumstances chosen by themselves, but under circumstances directly found, given and transmitted from the past" (Sartre, *Critique of Dialectical Reason, Vol. 1: Theory of Practical Ensembles*, trans. A. Sheridan-Smith (New York: Verso, 2004), 35; Marx, "The Eighteenth Brumaire of Louis Bonaparte," 595).

29. See Theodor W. Adorno, "Sociology and Empirical Research," in Adorno et al., *The Positivist Dispute in German Sociology*, trans. G. Adey and D. Frisby (London: Heinmann, 1976), 35, and Adorno, *Minima Moralia*, 86.

30. Adorno, *Minima Moralia*, 247; Robert Hullot-Kentor, *Things Beyond Resemblance: Collected Essays on Theodor W. Adorno* (New York: Columbia University Press, 2006), 199.

31. Cornelius Castoriadis, "C. L. R. James and the Fate of Marxism," in *C. L. R. James: His Intellectual Legacies*, ed. S. R. Cudjoe and W. E. Cain (Amherst: University of Massachusetts Press, 1995), 285.

32. See Walter Benjamin, "Left-Wing Melancholy," in *The Weimar Republic Sourcebook*, ed. A. Kaes, M. Jay, and E. Dimendberg (Berkeley: University of California Press, 1994), 304–306; Walter Benjamin, *The Origin of German Tragic Drama*, trans. John Osborne (London: Verso, 2009); and Wendy Brown, "Resisting Left Melancholy," in *Loss: The Politics of Mourning*, ed. D. L. Eng and D. Kazanjian (Berkeley: University of California Press, 2003), 458–466.

CHAPTER TWO. RESTAGING THE DIALECTIC

1. Karl Marx, *Economic and Philosophical Manuscripts of 1844*, trans. M. Milligan (Amherst, NY: Prometheus Books, 1988), 141–142.

2. Karl Marx, "Notebooks on Epicurean Philosophy," in Karl Marx and Friedrich Engels, *Collected Works*, Vol. 1 (New York: International Publishers, 1975–2005), 489. References to the *Collected Works* are hereafter cited as MECW.

3. Marx, *Economic and Philosophical Manuscripts*, 149.

4. Heinrich Marx, "Letter to Karl, 9 December 1837," in *MECW*, 1: 688.

5. Karl Marx, "The Critique of Hegel's *Philosophy of Right*," in MECW, 3: 91.

6. Marx, *Economic and Philosophical Manuscripts*, 149. Marx's 1843–1844 critique of Hegel indicates that his textual engagement with Hegel's dialectic was limited to a reading of the *Phenomenology of Spirit* and the so-called Lesser Logic, that is, the first volume of Hegel's *Encyclopedia of the Philosophical Sciences*. For additional historical background on Marx's encounter with Hegel and Hegelian philosophy, including Hegel's writings on dialectical logic, see Jarrold Seigel, *Marx's Fate: The Shape of a Life* (University Park: Pennsylvania State University Press, 1993); Warren Breckman, *Marx, The Young Hegelians, and the Origins of Radical Social Theory: Dethroning the Self* (New York: Cambridge University Press, 1999); and Allan Megill, *Karl Marx: The Burden of Reason (Why Marx Rejected Politics and the Market)* (Lanham, MD: Rowman and Littlefield, 2002).

7. Karl Marx, *Capital: A Critique of Political Economy: Vol. I*, trans. B. Fowkes (New York: Penguin, 1976), 103.

8. Marx, *Capital*, I: 103.

9. Karl Marx, "On Hegel," in *MECW*, 1: 577.

10. This sentiment is present throughout the 1843 *Contribution to the Critique of Hegel's Philosophy of Right* and the 1844 *Economic and Philosophical Manuscripts*, as we have seen. See also *The Holy Family* (1845), written primarily by Marx; while this text is generally quite hostile toward Hegel, it does suggest, at one point, that "Hegel very often gives a *real* presentation, embracing the *thing* itself, within the *speculative* presentation. This real development *within* the speculative development misleads the reader into considering the speculative development as real and the real as speculative" (Karl Marx and Friedrich Engels, *The Holy Family, or Critique of Critical Criticism: Against Bruno Bauer and Company*, in MECW, 4: 60–61).

11. Marx's widely publicized critique of Feuerbach (see Karl Marx, "Theses on Feuerbach," in *The Marx-Engels Reader*, Second Edition, ed. R. Tucker [New York: Norton, 1978], 143–145) tends to obscure the fact that the 1843–1844 critique of Hegel is strongly influenced by Feuerbach's insistence that ideas and concepts have their roots in material experience. At one point, Marx says that "*Sense-perception* (see Feuerbach) must be the basis of all science" (Marx, *Economic and Philosophical Manuscripts*, 111).

12. Karl Marx, *A Contribution to the Critique of Political Economy*, in *MECW*, 29: 263. For our purposes, the 1859 preface is significant in that it was written a year or so after Marx claims to have resurrected "by mere accident" his interest in Hegel's *Logic*, a year or so after he first expressed his interest in recovering "the *rational* aspect of the method which Hegel not only discovered but also mystified." As we noted earlier, this sentiment is rehashed in the 1873 afterword to *Capital*. See Karl Marx, "Letter to Engels, 16 January 1858," in *MECW*, 40: 249. Here is a lengthier sample of the relevant portion of the letter to Engels: "I am, by the way, discovering some nice arguments. E.g. I have completely demolished the theory of profit as hitherto propounded. What was of great use to me as regards *method* of treatment was Hegel's *Logic* at which I had taken another look *by mere accident*, Freiligrath having found and made me a present of several volumes of Hegel, originally the property of Bakunin.

If ever the time comes when such work is again possible, I should very much like to write 2 or 3 sheets making accessible to the common reader the *rational* aspect of the method which Hegel not only discovered but also mystified."

13. Two additional passages from the 1859 preface are helpful here. First, Marx says that "changes in the economic foundation lead sooner or later to the transformation of the whole immense superstructure. In studying such transformations it is always necessary to distinguish between the material transformation of the economic conditions of production, which can be determined with the precision of natural science, and the legal, political, religious, artistic or philosophic—in short, ideological forms in which men become conscious of this conflict and fight it out" (263). When Marx says that changes in the economic conditions "can be determined with the precision of natural science," I take it that he is *not* referring to dialectical or speculative science. In other words, developments in the modes of production unfold in a rather straightforward, mechanical way. Changes in consciousness, on the other hand, changes in "legal, political, religious, artistic or philosophic—in short ideological forms," unfold dialectically, which is why we run up against ideological tensions and contradictions, and which is why we must "fight it out." Second, Marx indicates that material reality essentially *prefigures* dialectical consciousness. Here is an extended excerpt: "No social order is ever destroyed before all the productive forces for which it is sufficient have been developed, and new superior relations of production never replace older ones before the material conditions for their existence have matured within the framework of the old society. Mankind thus inevitably sets itself only such tasks as it is able to solve, since closer examination will always show that the problem itself arises only when the material conditions for its solution are already present or at least in the course of formation. In broad outline, the Asiatic, ancient, feudal and modern bourgeois modes of production may be designated as epochs marking progress in the economic development of society. The bourgeois mode of production is the last antagonistic form of the social process of production—antagonistic not in the sense of individual antagonism but of an antagonism that emanates from the individuals' social conditions of existence—but the productive forces developing within bourgeois society create also the material conditions for a solution of this antagonism" (264). So our material reality, in our time the totality of bourgeois relations of production, conditions *both* the possibility of ideological contradictions *and* the possibility, indeed the inevitability, of their resolution—in our time, for Marx, a communistic resolution. This latter point, regarding the promise of resolution, will be important as we move into a discussion of Hegel.

14. Marx, *Capital*, I: 102.

15. Bertell Ollman sets out to make a point along these lines in his discussion of Marx's embrace of Hegel's "philosophy of internal relations" (Bertell Ollman, *Dance of the Dialectic: Steps in Marx's Method* [Chicago: University of Illinois Press, 2003], 36–50).

16. Marx, *Capital*, I: 102.

17. As Marx puts it in the final paragraph of the 1873 afterword, "The fact that the movement of capitalist society is full of contradictions impresses itself most strikingly on the practical bourgeoisie in the changes of the periodic cycle through which modern industry passes, the summit of which is the general crisis. That crisis

is once again approaching" (*Capital*, I: 103). Here we might also note a prominent passage from the *Economic and Philosophical Manuscripts*, in which "humanism," or what by 1859 will come to be known as the domain of the *superstructure*, and "naturalism," what will become the material *foundation*, are said to resolve themselves under conditions of communism: "the *genuine* resolution of the conflict between man and nature and between man and man—the true resolution between existence and essence, between objectification and self-confirmation, between freedom and necessity, between the individual and the species. Communism is the riddle of history solved, and it knows itself to be this solution" (Marx, *Economic and Philosophical Manuscripts*, 102–103).

18. For a more elaborate defense of this general claim, see Karl Ameriks, "The Legacy of Idealism in the Philosophy of Feuerbach, Marx, and Kierkegaard," in *The Cambridge Companion to German Idealism*, ed. K. Ameriks (New York: Cambridge University Press, 2000), 258–281.

19. On the question of how the division of labor is constitutive of class antagonisms, see also Karl Marx and Friedrich Engels, *The German Ideology* (Amherst, NY: Prometheus Books, 1998).

20. Again, the crucial passage cannot be overemphasized: "Mankind inevitably sets itself only such tasks as it is able to solve, since closer examination will always show that the problem itself arises only when the material conditions for its solution are already present or at least in the course of formation. . . . The bourgeois mode of production is the last antagonistic form of the social process of production—antagonistic not in the sense of individual antagonism but of an antagonism that emanates from the individuals' social conditions of existence—but the productive forces developing within bourgeois society create also the material conditions for a solution of this antagonism" (Marx, *Contribution to the Critique of Political Economy*, 264).

21. Marx, "Theses on Feuerbach," 145.

22. Hayden White, *Metahistory: The Historical Imagination in Nineteenth-Century Europe* (Baltimore: Johns Hopkins University Press, 1973), 94.

23. White, *Metahistory*, 94. See also Mark W. Roche, *Tragedy and Comedy: A Systematic Study and a Critique of Hegel* (Albany: State University of New York Press, 1997). Roche offers a helpful argument against the "common misconception that tragedy is for Hegel the highest form of drama." He shows that "for Hegel, comedy is philosophically (and historically) a later genre" (281). We will return to these issues later in the chapter.

24. G. W. F. Hegel, *The Philosophy of World History*, trans. J. Sibree (New York: Dover Publications, 1956), 10. Hegel's lectures on the philosophy of history provide the best fodder for an emphasis on teleology and thus on the comic staging of the dialectic. Hegel goes on to say, for example, that "[o]ur intellectual striving aims at realizing the conviction that what was *intended* by external wisdom, is actually *accomplished* in the domain of existent, active Spirit, as well as that of mere Nature. Our mode of treating the subject is, in this aspect, a Theodicæa—a justification of the ways of God" (15). Statements to this effect can be found elsewhere. At one point in the *Science of Logic*, for example, Hegel describes the "system of pure reason as the realm of pure thought. This realm is truth as it is without veil and in

its own absolute nature. It can therefore be said that this content is the exposition of God as He is in his eternal essence before the creation of nature and a finite Spirit" (G. W. F. Hegel, *Science of Logic*, trans. A.V. Miller [Atlantic Highlands, NJ: Humanities Press, 1969], 50).

25. In recent years, there has been a rather wide-ranging effort to background Hegel's commitment to a closed metaphysical system and to reveal a more "open" philosophy, and a consideration of the tragic dimensions of Hegel's thinking has been a significant component of this broader effort. Some of this work—for example that of Robert Pippin and Terry Pinkard, which I cite and consider in more detail later—focuses on Hegel's indebtedness to Kant. Other work—much of which emerges out of the twentieth-century French Hegelian tradition, in the wake of the influential readings of Alexandre Kojève and Jean Hyppolite—plays up the role of negativity in Hegel and sets out to explore the prospect of a dialectics without closure. See, for example, Judith Butler, *Subjects of Desire: Hegelian Reflections in Twentieth-Century France* (New York: Columbia University Press, 1987); Diana Coole, *Negativity and Politics: Dialectics and Dionysus from Kant to Poststructuralism* (New York: Routledge, 2000); Jean-Luc Nancy, *Hegel: The Restlessness of the Negative*, trans. J. Smith and S. Miller (Minneapolis: University of Minnesota Press, 2002); Catherine Malabou, *The Future of Hegel: Plasticity, Temporality, and Dialectic*, trans. L. During (New York: Routledge, 2005). See also Slavoj Žižek, *Tarrying with the Negative: Kant, Hegel, and the Critique of Ideology* (Durham, NC: Duke University Press, 1993); Fredric Jameson, *The Hegel Variations: On the Phenomenology of Spirit* (New York: Verso, 2010); and the essays collected in Slavoj Žižek, Clayton Crockett, and Creston Davis (eds.), *Hegel and the Infinite: Religion, Politics, and Dialectic* (New York: Columbia University Press, 2011). Karin de Boer's *On Hegel: The Sway of the Negative* (New York: Palgrave Macmillan, 2010) provides a well-researched and quite comprehensive look into the tragic dimensions of Hegel's thinking.

26. Robert B. Pippin, *Hegel's Practical Philosophy: Rational Agency as Ethical Life* (New York: Cambridge University Press, 2008), 19.

27. Scott Warren offers the best general survey of the modern dialectical tradition; for a helpful introduction to Kant, Hegel, Marx, and "the roots of contemporary dialectical theory," see Warren, *The Emergence of Dialectical Theory: Philosophy and Political Inquiry* (Chicago: University of Chicago Press, 2008), 28–61. Also helpful in terms of its survey of nineteenth-century dialectical thinking is Coole, *Negativity and Politics*, esp. 13–84.

28. The contributions of Robert Pippin and Terry Pinkard are among the most prominent here. In addition to Pippin's recent book on Hegel's practical philosophy (cited earlier), see Robert B. Pippin, *Hegel's Idealism: The Satisfactions of Self-Consciousness* (New York: Cambridge University Press, 1989); Terry Pinkard, *Hegel's Phenomenology: The Sociality of Reason* (New York: Cambridge University Press, 1994); Robert B. Pippin, *Idealism as Modernism: Hegelian Variations* (New York: Cambridge University Press, 1997); Robert B. Pippin, *Modernism as a Philosophical Problem: The Dissatisfactions of European High Culture*, Second Edition (Malden, MA: Blackwell, 1999); Terry Pinkard, *Hegel: A Biography* (New York: Cambridge University Press, 2000); Terry Pinkard, *German Philosophy, 1760–1860: The Legacy of Idealism* (New York: Cambridge University Press, 2002).

29. Immanuel Kant, *Critique of Pure Reason*, trans. P. Guyer and A. Wood (New York: Cambridge University Press, 1998), 100–101.

30. Immanuel Kant, "An Answer to the Question: What is Enlightenment?" in *Kant's Political Writings*, ed. H. S. Reiss (New York: Cambridge University Press, 1991), 54.

31. Immanuel Kant, *Groundwork of the Metaphysic of Morals*, trans. H. J. Paton (New York: Harper and Row, 1956), 116.

32. Kant, *Groundwork of the Metaphysic of Morals*, 107.

33. G. W. F. Hegel, *The Encyclopedia Logic: Part I of the Encyclopedia of the Philosophical Sciences with the Zusätze*, trans. T. F. Geraetz, W. A. Suchting, and H. S. Harris (Indianapolis: Hackett, 1991), 82.

34. Hegel, *Encyclopedia Logic*, 82.

35. Pippin, *Modernism as a Philosophical Problem*, 63.

36. Hegel, *Encyclopedia Logic*, 82 (emphasis mine).

37. This is certainly one way of interpreting the famous claim that "what is rational is actual and what is actual is rational" (G. W. F. Hegel, *Philosophy of Right*, trans. T. M. Knox [New York: Oxford University Press, 1967], 10). If we background the speculative dimension of this claim (a dimension that we will consider later in the chapter), we are left with the interpretation that Hegel wants simply to explain how, at any particular moment, we have come to accept a particular sense of what counts as rational or reasonable.

38. Hegel, *Encyclopedia Logic*, 82.

39. Pippin, *Modernism as a Philosophical Problem*, 68. See also Pippin, *Hegel's Practical Philosophy*, esp. chap. 4. Scott Warren offers a helpful summary of the general issue as well. Hegel, he says, "insists that any epistemological inquiry begin with the consideration of the genesis of knowledge itself. Although Hegel too wants to prove the objectivity of knowledge, he sees this as requiring a phenomenological reconstructive method of consciousness that can demonstrate the process of coming to knowledge presupposed by Kant's critique. What is dialectically radical about Hegel's project is his insistence on demonstrating the formative process of reflection leading up to the confrontation of consciousness with the object, while Kant takes this confrontation as his starting point" (Warren, *Emergence of Dialectical Theory*, 35).

40. G. W. F. Hegel, *Elements of the Philosophy of Right*, ed. A. Wood, trans. H. B. Nisbet (New York: Cambridge University Press, 1991), 43.

41. Consider, for example, a line from the *Phenomenology of Spirit*, in which Hegel says that "[w]hat observation knew as a *given* object in which the self had no part, is here a given custom, but a reality which is at the same time the deed and the work of the subject finding it. . . . It is in knowing that the law of his own heart is the law of all hearts, in knowing the consciousness of the self as the acknowledged universal order; it is a virtue, which enjoys the fruits of its sacrifice, which brings about what it sets out to do, viz. to bring forth its essence into the light of day, and its enjoyment in this universal life" (G. W. F. Hegel, *Phenomenology of Spirit*, trans. A.V. Miller [New York: Oxford University Press, 1977], 276–277).

42. G. W. F. Hegel, *Lectures on the Philosophy of World History: Introduction*, trans. H. B. Nisbet (New York: Cambridge University Press, 1975), 194. There are numerous passages to this effect throughout Hegel's corpus. In a late passage from

the *Encyclopedia*, for example, he says that "I am only truly free when the other is also free and is recognized by me as free" (G. W. F. Hegel, *Philosophy of Mind: Part Three of the Encyclopedia of the Philosophical Sciences, Together with the Zusätze*, trans. W. Wallace and A. V. Miller [New York: Oxford University Press, 1971], 171). In his *Science of Logic*, he characterizes this collective or universal freedom as the condition of peace, love, and blessedness: "The universal is therefore *free* power; it is itself and takes its other within its embrace, but without *doing violence* to it; on the contrary, the universal is, in its other, in peaceful communion with itself. We have called it free power, but it could also be called *free love* and *boundless blessedness*, for it bears itself towards its other as towards *its own self*; in it, it has returned to itself" (Hegel, *Science of Logic*, 603).

43. In, for example, *The Poverty of Philosophy*, Marx says that "[i]t is only in an order of things in which there are no more classes and class antagonisms that *social evolutions* will cease to be *political revolutions*. Till then, on the eve of every general reshuffling of society, the last word of social science will always be: 'Combat or Death: bloody struggle or extinction. It is thus that the question is inexorably put'" (Karl Marx, *The Poverty of Philosophy*, in *MECW*, 6: 212). In other words, *until* these class antagonisms are wiped away, *until* the partial and limited practical rationality is overcome by a collective consensus that is truly and self-sustainably universal, then human beings, understood in the moment as combative political subjects, will not rest satisfied with the material conditions of reality or with their conscious apprehension of it.

44. G. W. F. Hegel, *The Difference between Fichte's and Schelling's Systems of Philosophy*, trans. H. S. Harris and W. Cerf (Albany: State University of New York Press, 2007), 112.

45. Hegel, *Phenomenology of Spirit*, 10. See also the final paragraph of the book, where Hegel again speaks of "the *goal*" that teases the project along (493).

46. Hegel, *Phenomenology of Spirit*, 452–453.

47. G. W. F. Hegel, *Aesthetics: Lectures on Fine Art: Vol. II*, trans. T. M. Knox (New York: Oxford University Press, 1975), 1200.

48. Hegel, *Aesthetics*, II: 1199.

49. As Judith Butler puts it in a memorable passage: "For Hegel, tragic events are never decisive. . . . What seems like tragic blindness turns out to be more like the comic myopia of Mr. Magoo whose automobile careening through the neighbor's chicken coop always seems to land on all four wheels. Like such miraculously resilient characters of the Saturday morning cartoon, Hegel's protagonists always reassemble themselves, prepare a new scene, enter the stage armed with a new set of ontological insights—and fail again" (Judith Butler, *Subjects of Desire: Hegelian Reflections in Twentieth-Century France* [New York: Columbia University Press, 1999], 21).

50. For more on this see Roche, *Comedy and Tragedy*, cited previously, as well as Mark W. Roche, "Hegel's Theory of Comedy in the Context of Hegelian and Modern Reflections on Comedy," *Revue Internationale de Philosophie*, no. 221 (2003), 411–430. Roche notes that Hegel is attracted to the comic emphasis on subjectivity, specifically a subjectivity that is as yet unsubstantial and finite. In all types of comedy, according to Hegel, the subject tends to pursue private or particular interests that are out of step with the broader truths of ethical life. The subject thus sets him- or

herself up for failure, but this failure is always comical to an audience that looks on with "superior wisdom," as Hegel might put it, an audience that is able to recognize and laugh off this foolish behavior. William Desmond makes a similar point when he notes that, for Hegel, "the comic deals with the self-destruction of the false in its contrast and contradiction with the genuinely true" (William Desmond, *Beyond Hegel and Dialectic: Speculation, Cult, and Comedy* [Albany: State University of New York Press, 1992], 274).

51. White, *Metahistory*, 7. Building on the work of Northrop Frye, White identifies "at least four different modes of emplotment: Romance, Tragedy, Comedy, and Satire" (7). In our discussion of the dialectical tradition, we focus on the tragic and comic dimensions of a dialectical narrative, as White does in his discussions of both Hegel and Marx. For an extended account of various generic modes of explanation, see Northrop Frye, *Anatomy of Criticism: Four Essays* (Princeton, NJ: Princeton University Press, 2000).

52. White, *Metahistory*, 9.

53. White, *Metahistory*, 127. For the sake of presentation, we focus primarily on Hegel, but, as White shows, Marx's dialectical narrative is likewise shaped by a distinctively comic plot structure. In Marx, we come across an account that is oriented toward comic reconciliation, an account in which "the interaction between man and society progressively moves man toward a condition in which society itself will be dissolved and a genuine community, a communistic mode of existence, will be constituted as his true historic destiny" (287).

54. White, *Metahistory*, 281. Again, White draws a direct parallel between Hegel and Marx here: "Marx carries this comic conception even further; he envisioned nothing less than the dissolution of the 'society' in which the contradiction between consciousness and being had to be entertained as a fatality for all men in all times" (281–282).

55. White, *Metahistory*, 328.

56. Hegel, *Elements of the Philosophy of Right*, 197. A few pages earlier, Hegel makes a similar claim regarding the "accidental" nature of the individual: "Since the determinations of ethics constitute the concept of freedom, they are the substantiality or universal essence of individuals, who are related to them merely as accidents. Whether the individual exists or not is a matter of indifference to objective ethical life, which alone has permanence and is the power by which the lives of individuals are governed" (190).

57. Hegel, *Phenomenology of Spirit*, 490. We might note that in Marx, we find some ambiguity regarding this issue of how a grand dialectical narrative may be said to background the lives of individual subjects. On the one hand, Marx seems to attack Hegel on precisely this point. In the *Economic and Philosophical Manuscripts*, for example, he says that Hegel's dialectical "process must have a bearer, a subject. But the subject first emerges as a result. This result—the subject knowing itself as absolute self-consciousness—is therefore *God—absolute Spirit—the self-knowing and self-manifesting Idea*. Real man and real nature become mere predicates—symbols of this esoteric, unreal man and of this unreal nature" (Marx, *Economic and Philosophical Manuscripts*, 162). And yet, as is well known, Marx goes on to background individual agents in his own account of the broader trajectory of social and historical

development. As he says in *Capital*, "I do not by any means depict the capitalist and the landowner in rosy colors. But individuals are dealt with here only insofar as they are the personifications of economic categories, the bearers [*Träger*] of particular class-relations and interests. My standpoint, from which the development of the economic formation of society is viewed as a process of natural history, can less than any other make the individual responsible for relations whose creature he remains, specially speaking, however much he may subjectively raise himself above them" (Marx, *Capital*, I: 92).

58. Gillian Rose, *Dialectic of Nihilism: Poststructuralism and Law* (Oxford: Basil Blackwell, 1984), 3.

59. Desmond, *Beyond Hegel and Dialectic*, 304.

60. Desmond, *Beyond Hegel and Dialectic*, 252. Desmond goes on to say that "[t]he comic comes within the embrace of the dialectic: dialectic is the logical comedy of contradiction. The comedy has a happy ending in the sense that the dialectical debunking of the incongruity in the middle serves a more embracing reconstitution of unity" (306).

61. On this point, see Roche, *Tragedy and Comedy*, esp. chap 5. The rather straightforward observation here is that "[i]n the *Phenomenology* and the *Aesthetics*, comedy has an unambiguously later (and superior) position. Though Hegel may have had a stronger emotional attachment to tragedy, the systematic position of the two genres is beyond question" (399).

62. G. W. F. Hegel, *Natural Law: The Scientific Ways of Treating Natural Law, Its Place in Moral Philosophy, and Its Relation to the Positive Sciences of Law*, trans. T. M. Knox (Philadelphia: University of Pennsylvania Press, 1975), 105–108.

63. Hegel, *Natural Law*, 108.

64. Hegel, *Encyclopedia Logic*, 131.

65. Hegel, *Phenomenology of Spirit*, 123.

66. Hegel, *Science of Logic*, 28. Elsewhere Hegel says that "skepticism . . . is the dialectic of all that is determinate" (G. W. F. Hegel, *Lectures on the History of Philosophy, Vol. II*, trans. H. S. Haldane and F. H. Simon [Lincoln: University of Nebraska Press, 1995], 330).

67. Hegel, *Science of Logic*, 28.

68. Hegel, *Phenomenology of Spirit*, 51.

69. Hegel, *Phenomenology of Spirit*, 49–50. Hegel goes on to say that "[t]he skepticism that is directed against the whole range of phenomenal consciousness . . . renders Spirit for the first time competent to examine what truth is. For it brings about a state of despair about all the so-called natural ideas, thoughts, and opinions, regardless of whether they are called one's own or someone else's" (50). For a helpful discussion of the relationship between post-Kantian skepticism and the emergence of dialectical logic in Hegel, including a detailed analysis of this particular passage from the introduction to the *Phenomenology of Spirit*, see Allen Speight, "Skepticism, Modernity, and the Origins of Hegelian Dialectic," in *The Dimensions of Hegel's Dialectic*, ed. N. Limnatis (New York: Continuum, 2010), 140–156.

70. Hegel, *Encyclopedia Logic*, 131.

71. Hegel, *Phenomenology of Spirit*, 19. Hegel combines this expression with another metaphor; he says that we must not run from death but must have the

courage to welcome what is passing away. "Death, if that is what we want to call this non-actuality, is of all things the most dreadful, and to hold fast to what is dead requires the greatest strength. . . . the life of Spirit is not the life that shrinks from death and keeps itself untouched by devastation, but rather the life that endures it and maintains itself in it. It wins its truth only when, in utter dismemberment it finds itself."

72. In the natural law essay, Hegel ultimately privileges the "the tragedy which the Absolute eternally enacts with itself, by eternally giving birth to itself into objectivity, submitting in this objective form to suffering and death, and rising from its ashes into glory" (Hegel, *Natural Law*, 104). Regarding Hegel's use of the term *dialectic*, he does use this word at least once in the 1802–1803 natural law essay, albeit in passing and seemingly in an effort simply to draw attention to the importance of "relations" in any analysis of ethical life (88). It is not until 1807, in the *Phenomenology of Spirit*, that Hegel develops an explicitly dialectical logic and refers to it as such.

73. White, *Metahistory*, 9.

74. Warren, *Emergence of Dialectical Theory*, 40. See also Alexandre Kojève, *Introduction to the Reading of Hegel: Lectures on the Phenomenology of Spirit* (Ithaca, NY: Cornell University Press, 1980), esp. 169–171, and Karin de Boer, *On Hegel*, esp. fn. 3, 212. De Boer notes that, in the *Encyclopedia Logic*, Hegel uses the term *dialectic* to refer only to the second moment of negation, and he reserves the term *speculative* in reference to the positive synthesis, whereas in the *Science of Logic*, he abandons the distinction and uses the term *dialectic* to refer to all three aspects of speculative science. See Hegel, *Encyclopedia Logic*, 128–133 and Hegel, *Science of Logic*, 830–833.

75. Again, see Karin de Boer, *On Hegel*. In her efforts to tease out the tragic dimensions of Hegel's thinking, de Boer argues that Hegel's mature dialectical logic, his mature speculative science, puts strains on his ability to apprehend the genuinely tragic entanglements that befall ethical life. She points out that Hegel elevates the tragic in the early natural law essay, as we have seen, and this corresponds with the fact that, in the early Jena years, Hegel had not yet developed the contours of his mature dialectical logic. On this point, see also Michael Forster, "Hegel's Dialectical Method," in *The Cambridge Companion to Hegel*, ed. F. Beiser (New York: Cambridge University Press, 1993), 130–170.

76. Katrin Pahl, "The Way of Despair," in Žižek et al. (eds.), *Hegel and the Infinite*, 152.

77. White, *Metahistory*, 94. It may be helpful to elaborate just a bit more on White's rather complex argument. On White's account, Hegel shows how "those who pursue their own aims with a passion, a will and intelligence adequate to their immediate realizations—that is, the actual transformation of their societies in the light of their privately held conception of what a good life might be—will be tragic figures" (109–110); Hegel "implies that the life of every people or nation is, like the life of every heroic individual in history, a tragedy" (116); and yet Hegel's ultimate "purpose is to justify the transition from *the comprehension of the tragic nature of every specific civilization* to *the comic apprehension of the unfolding drama of the whole of history*" (117). In his discussion of Marx (281–330), White makes a similar argument

about how the tragic fate of any historical civilization is ultimately swept up in the comic nature of the broader dialectical trajectory of historical progress.

78. I thank my former teacher Frederick Dolan for this particular formulation.

79. Walter Kaufmann, *Nietzsche: Philosopher, Psychologist, Antichrist* (Princeton, NJ: Princeton University Press, 1974), 239.

80. Kaufmann, *Nietzsche: Philosopher, Psychologist, Antichrist*, 236.

81. Kaufmann, *Nietzsche: Philosopher, Psychologist, Antichrist*, 241. See also Nancy Love, *Marx, Nietzsche, and Modernity* (New York: Columbia University Press, 1986), esp. 102–111. Love develops an important defense of Kaufmann's reading of Nietzsche as a dialectical monist, and she uses this reading to develop a comparison between the dialectical histories of Marx and Nietzsche.

82. Presumably this is the point behind White's claim that "Nietzsche wanted to show that the dialectical process by which a human being moves from mere existence through alienation to reconciliation without the world is a function of comprehensible aesthetic impulses alone. . . . Tragic art is the dialectical art *par excellence*. It alone is capable, Nietzsche argued, of both impelling man to heroic collisions with reality and reclaiming man for life after those collisions" (White, *Metahistory*, 338–340).

83. Love, *Marx, Nietzsche, and Modernity*, 103.

84. Gilles Deleuze, *Nietzsche and Philosophy*, trans. H. Tomlinson (New York: Columbia University Press, 1983), 8.

85. Hegel, *Encyclopedia Logic*, 187.

86. Hegel, *Science of Logic*, 439.

87. Hegel, *Science of Logic*, 442.

88. Gilles Deleuze, *Difference and Repetition*, trans. P. Patton (New York: Columbia University Press, 1994), 49–50. It is worth citing the broader passage at some length here: "It is said that difference is negativity, that it extends or must extend to the point of contradiction once it is taken to the limit. This is true only to the extent that difference is already placed on a path or along a thread laid out by identity. It is true only to the extent that it is identity that pushes it to that point. Difference is the ground, but only the ground for the demonstration of the identical." Deleuze is perhaps the most outspoken post-Nietzschean critic of Hegelian dialectics, offering a sustained and influential analysis of the structural limitations of dialectical thinking. See also Deleuze, *Nietzsche and Philosophy*.

89. Friedrich Nietzsche, *On the Genealogy of Morals and Ecce Homo*, trans. W. Kaufmann and R. J. Hollingdale (New York: Vintage, 1989), 154. Nietzsche associates an "impoverishment of life" with "the affects grown cool, the tempo of life slowed down, dialectics in place of instinct, seriousness imprinted on faces and gestures."

90. Friedrich Nietzsche, *Human, All too Human: A Book for Free Spirits*, trans. R. J. Hollingdale (New York: Cambridge University Press, 1996), 12. See also Friedrich Nietzsche, *Beyond Good and Evil: Prelude to a Philosophy of the Future*, trans. W. Kaufmann (New York: Vintage, 1989), 10, where Nietzsche says that "one may doubt, first, whether there are any opposites at all, and secondly whether these popular valuations and opposite values on which the metaphysicians put their seal, are not perhaps merely foreground estimates, only provisional perspectives." See also Friedrich Nietzsche, *The Will to Power*, trans. W. Kaufmann and R. J. Hollingdale

(New York: Vintage, 1968), 297–298. There Nietzsche says that "duration, identity with itself, being are inherent neither in that which is called subject nor that which is called object: they are complexes of events apparently durable in comparison with other complexes—e.g., through the difference in tempo of the event (rest-motion, firm-loose: opposites that do not exist in themselves and that actually express only variations in degree that from a certain perspective appear to be opposites. There are no opposites: only from those of logic do we derive the concept of opposites—and falsely transfer it to things.)." Cf. Hegel, *Science of Logic*, 440, where Hegel simply disregards what will become the Nietzschean contention: "As regards the assertion that *there is* no contradiction, that it does not exist," Hegel says, "this statement need not cause us any concern."

91. See Friedrich Nietzsche, "'Reason' in Philosophy," in *Twilight of the Idols*, trans. D. Large (New York: Oxford University Press, 1998), 16–19.

92. Once again, it is Deleuze who, in his reading of Nietzsche, really drives home this point. "Dialectics," he says, "thrives on oppositions because it is unaware of far more subtle and subterranean differential mechanisms: topological displacements, typological variations" (Deleuze, *Nietzsche and Philosophy*, 157).

93. Nietzsche, *Will to Power*, 273.

94. Coole, *Negativity and Politics*, 87.

95. Michel Foucault, *Power/Knowledge: Selected Interviews and Other Writings, 1972–1977*, ed. C. Gordon; trans. C. Gordon, L. Marshall, J. Mepham, and K. Soper (New York: Pantheon Books, 1980), 144.

96. Coole, *Negativity and Politics*, 73.

97. Consider, for example, a passage from *Ecce Homo* in which Nietzsche says, "My formula for greatness in a human being is *amor fati*: that one wants nothing to be different, not forward, not backward, not in all eternity. Not merely to bear what is necessary, still less conceal it—all idealism is mendaciousness in the face of what is necessary—but to *love* it" (Nietzsche, *On the Genealogy of Morals and Ecce Homo*, 258).

98. Hegel, *Philosophy of Right*, 10.

99. Hegel, *Philosophy of Right*, 11.

100. Gillian Rose, *Hegel Contra Sociology* (New York: Verso, 2009), 56.

101. Rose, *Hegel Contra Sociology*, 56. It is worth citing Rose at some length here, as her formulation of the issue captures a sense of that tragic experience that we have been developing: "To read a proposition 'speculatively' means that the identity which is affirmed between subject and predicate is seen equally to affirm a lack of identity between subject and predicate. This reading implies an identity different from the merely formal one of the ordinary proposition. This different kind of identity cannot be prejudged, that is, it cannot be justified in a transcendental sense, and it cannot be stated in a proposition of the kind to be eschewed. This different kind of identity must be understood as a result to be achieved. From this perspective the 'subject' is not fixed, nor the predicates accidental: they acquire their meaning in a series of relations to each another. . . . This experience of lack of identity which natural consciousness undergoes is the basis for reading propositions as speculative identities. The subject of the proposition is no longer fixed and abstract with external, contingent accidents, but, initially, an empty name,

uncertain and problematic, gradually acquiring meaning as the result of a series of contradictory experiences. . . . Speculative experience of lack of identity informs propositions such as 'the real is the rational,' which have so often been misread as ordinary propositions" (52–53).

102. Once again, Gillian Rose offers an insightful formulation. She says that "[i]n the case of the proposition that the actual is rational, what has been overlooked is the explanatory coda that the truth of this proposition must be sought—'in dem *Schiene* des Zeitlichen,' in the illusion of the temporal, of history. . . . He [Hegel] is warning against an approach which would see illusion as rational, which makes illusion into the absolute principle of the whole. The proposition that the actual is rational is speculative. It refers to the experience of illusion, to the way bourgeois relations, or lack of identity are mistaken for rationality. This illusion must be acknowledged as real, but not made into the principle of rationality, nor can another principle of rationality be abstractly opposed to the prevailing illusion" (Rose, *Hegel Contra Sociology*, 87). See also Hegel's discussion of speculation in the *Encyclopedia Logic*. At one point, Hegel says that "the general character of the rational consists in being something unconditioned which therefore contains its determinacy within itself. In this sense, we know about the rational above all, because we know about God, and we know him as [the one] who is utterly self-determined. But also, the knowledge of a citizen about his country and its laws is a knowledge about what is rational, inasmuch as these things count for him as something unconditioned, and at the same time as a universal, to which he must subject his individual will" (Hegel, *Encyclopedia Logic*, 132). In other words, we experience the rationality of our country and its laws, the extant reality of the world around us, but, in a speculative move, we look beyond this world, toward an unconditioned or absolute rationality, and that beyond reveals our immediate present as false, negative, illusory.

103. Herbert Marcuse, *Reason and Revolution: Hegel and the Rise of Social Theory* (Amherst, NY: Humanity Books, 1999), 26–27.

104. Marcuse, *Reason and Revolution*, 312.

105. Simon Jarvis, *Adorno: A Critical Introduction* (New York: Routledge, 1998), 169. For more on the dialectical relationship between "is" and "ought," see Hegel, *Science of Logic*, 131–136 and Rose, *Hegel Contra Sociology*, esp. 201–217.

106. Hegel, *Science of Logic*, 389 (emphasis mine).

107. Simon Jarvis, "What Is Speculative Thinking?" *Revue internationale de philosophie* 227, 1 (2004), 69–83.

108. Hegel, *Encyclopedia Logic*, 47.

109. Nietzsche, *Will to Power*, 240.

110. See Friedrich Nietzsche, *Thus Spoke Zarathustra: A Book for All and None*, ed. A. Del Caro and R. Pippin; trans. A. Del Caro (New York: Cambridge University Press, 2006).

111. Hegel, *Encyclopedia Logic*, 60.

112. See G. W. F. Hegel, *Faith and Knowledge*, trans. W. Cerf and H. S. Harris (Albany: State University of New York Press, 1977), 190. For the remark about the "ladder" to absolute knowledge, see Hegel, *Phenomenology of Spirit*, 14.

113. Rose, *Hegel Contra Sociology*, 223.

114. Rose, *Hegel Contra Sociology*, 100.

115. Hegel, *Science of Logic*, 440–441.

116. It is important to emphasize again that the speculative dimensions of dialectical criticism are not the exclusive province of Hegelian idealism. This speculative interplay between the real and the rational survives whatever materialist reorientation we might ascribe to the tradition in the wake of Marx's influence. As Horkheimer indicates in an early essay on "Materialism and Morality," the "dialectical critique of the world is borne along" by "the battle-cries of the Enlightenment" or by certain ideals, such as freedom, equality, justice. And "the content of the ideas is not eternal, but is subject to historical change—not, as one might suppose, because 'Spirit' of itself capriciously infringed upon the principle of identity—but because the human impulses *which demand something better* take different forms according to the historical material with which they have to work" (Max Horkheimer, "Materialism and Morality," *Telos* 69 [1986], 108; emphasis mine). We see that for a materialist such as Horkheimer, dialectical critique is motivated by the human demand for a better world, and while the substance of any such demand is subject to change, such a demand, structurally speaking, helps to provoke and sustain a certain orientation toward an established reality that may well be a source of pain, suffering, and intense dependency, but that, as such, is not absolute. "The point," Horkheimer says, "is not to maintain concepts unchanged, *but to improve the lot of humanity*" (108; emphasis mine). For a helpful discussion of how Marx attends to these sorts of ethical impulses that emerge from changing material circumstances, see Cornel West, *The Ethical Dimensions of Marxist Thought* (New York: Monthly Review Press, 1991).

117. For an illuminating discussion of how Hayden White embraces the dialectical tradition in a "rhetorical" as opposed to a more rigidly "philosophical" or strongly foundationalist way, see Allan Megill, "The Rhetorical Dialectic of Hayden White," in *Refiguring Hayden White*, ed. F. Ankersmit, E. Domanska, and H. Kellner (Stanford, CA: Stanford University Press, 2009).

CHAPTER THREE. IN A MILIEU OF SCARCITY

1. Jean-Paul Sartre, "Interview with Michel Rybalka," in *The Philosophy of Jean-Paul Sartre*, ed. P. Schilpp (LaSalle, IL: Open Court, 1981), 30.

2. For a series of rich discussions on the omnipresence of the imagination in all forms of political thinking, see Raymond Geuss, *Politics and the Imagination* (Princeton, NJ: Princeton University Press, 2010) and *Philosophy and Real Politics* (Princeton, NJ: Princeton University Press, 2008). Without belittling the critical import of the imagination, Geuss nevertheless promotes what he calls a "realist" approach to political thinking, and the argument that I develop in this chapter may well contribute to such an approach. See also Bernard Williams, *In the Beginning Was the Deed: Realism and Moralism in Political Argument* (Princeton, NJ: Princeton University Press, 2005).

3. Michael Hardt and Antonio Negri, *Multitude: War and Democracy in the Age of Empire* (New York: Penguin, 2004), 310–311. See also Hardt and Negri, *Commonwealth* (Cambridge, MA: Harvard University Press, 2009).

4. See Sartre's interview with John Gerassi in Gerassi, *Jean-Paul Sartre: Hated Conscience of His Country, Vol. 1* (Chicago: University of Chicago Press, 1989), 179.

Helpful discussions of Sartre's intellectual development include: Thomas Flynn, *Sartre and Marxist Existentialism: The Test Case of Collective Responsibility* (Chicago: University of Chicago Press, 1986); Annie Cohen-Solal, *Sartre: A Life* (New York: The New Press, 2005 [1986]); and William McBride, *Sartre's Political Theory* (Bloomington: Indiana University Press, 1991). More recent commentaries include: Bernard-Henri Lévy, *Sartre: The Philosopher of the Twentieth Century*, trans. A. Brown (Malden, MA: Polity Press, 2003), which highlights, and largely condemns, the ways in which Sartre's evolving political allegiances inform his thinking; Sam Coombes, *The Early Sartre and Marxism* (New York: Peter Lang, 2008), which reads elements of Sartre's later Marxism into the earlier existentialist writings; and Joseph S. Catalano, *Reading Sartre* (New York: Cambridge University Press, 2010), which stresses philosophical continuity in Sartre's thought from *Being and Nothingness* through *Critique of Dialectical Reason* to *The Family Idiot*, Sartre's late and unfinished study of Flaubert. Curiously, neither Coombes nor Catalano mention colonialism (or racism), and so neither entertain the possibility that Sartre's evolving engagement with decolonization struggles may have affected the nature and development of his thinking. Helpful recent discussions of Sartre's evolving thinking about race and colonialism include Jonathan Judaken, "Sartre on Racism: From Existential Phenomenology to Globalization and 'the New Racism,'" in *Race after Sartre: Antiracism, Africana Existentialism, Postcolonialism*, ed. J. Judaken (Albany: State University of New York Press, 2008), 23–53, and Paige Arthur, *Unfinished Projects: Decolonization and the Philosophy of Jean-Paul Sartre* (New York: Verso, 2010).

5. Jean-Paul Sartre, *Search for a Method*, trans. H. Barnes (New York: Vintage, 1968), xxxiv. *Search for a Method*, first published in 1957, was included as a prologue to the original French publication of the *Critique of Dialectical Reason* in 1960. These two texts appear as separate volumes in English translation. I will refer to both texts under the rubric of "the *Critique*."

6. Sartre, *Critique of Dialectical Reason, Vol. 1: Theory of Practical Ensembles*, trans. A. Sheridan-Smith (New York: Verso, 2004), 15.

7. Sartre, *Search for a Method*, 90. As we will see, Sartre remains suspicious of any strongly deterministic Marxist materialism, but this new embrace of historical materialism does contrast with Sartre's position in the 1940s. On Sartre's earlier denunciation of historical materialism, see for example Sartre, "Materialism and Revolution," in *Literary and Philosophical Essays*, trans. A. Michelson (New York: Collier Books, 1967).

8. Yirmiyahu Yovel, "Dialectic without Mediation: On Sartre's Variety of Marxism and Dialectic," in *Varieties of Marxism*, ed. S. Avineri (The Hague: Martinus Nijhoff, 1977), 175–193.

9. Sartre, *Search for a Method*, xxxiv; Martin Jay, *Marxism and Totality: The Adventures of a Concept from Lukács to Habermas* (Berkeley: University of California Press, 1984).

10. See Mark Poster, *Sartre's Marxism* (New York: Cambridge University Press, 1982) and Joseph S. Catalano, *A Commentary on Jean-Paul Sartre's Critique of Dialectical Reason, Volume 1, Theory of Practical Ensembles* (Chicago: University of Chicago Press, 1968).

11. In his "Self-Portrait at Seventy," Sartre admits that an adequate account of dialectical reason would require a massive historical study; to complete the *Critique*,

he says, "I would have to go back to studying history" (Sartre, "Self-Portrait at Seventy," in *Life/Situations: Essays Written and Spoken*, trans. P. Auster and L. Davis [New York: Pantheon, 1977], 75). Ronald Aronson makes a convincing case that, by fall 1959, Sartre had come to recognize the naivety of his own political and theoretical optimism (Aronson, "Sartre's Turning Point: The Abandoned *Critique de la raison dialectique*, Volume Two," in P. Schilpp (ed.), *The Philosophy of Jean-Paul Sartre*).

12. On Sartre's rejection of pluralism and his concern about history losing its meaning, see Sartre, *Critique of Dialectical Reason*, I: 64; see also Hazel Barnes's "Introduction" to Sartre, *Search for a Method*, x. Even though ultimately Sartre abandons the *Critique*, he seems to maintain, throughout his life, this desire to articulate a singular, unified history. See, for example, Sartre and Benny Lévy, *Hope Now: The 1980 Interviews*, trans. A. von den Hoven (Chicago: University of Chicago Press, 1996), 66.

13. McBride has noted that "totalizations . . . are undertaken both by historical actors and, at a remove, by historians or by social theorists seeking to comprehend a segment of human history or society" (McBride, *Sartre's Political Theory*, 104). Another way to formulate my qualification: we can bracket the larger project of the grand social theorist, the attempt to "totalize" a multiplicity of human actions into a synthetic account of general historical trends, and still learn something from Sartre's discussion of historical actors who might be said to think and act dialectically.

14. Karl Marx and Friedrich Engels, *The Communist Manifesto*, trans. S. Moore (New York: Penguin, 2002), 223. Or consider Leon Trotsky's claim that "the important thing . . . is to see clearly. One can say of communism, above all, that it gives more clarity. We must liberate man from all that prevents his seeing" (Trotsky cited in Cedric Robinson, *Black Marxism: The Making of the Black Radical Tradition* [Chapel Hill: University of North Carolina Press, 2000], 208).

15. For a helpful discussion of *reflection* versus *contemplation*, see Jean-Paul Sartre, *Notebooks for an Ethics*, trans. D. Pellauer (Chicago: University of Chicago Press, 1992), 476–482, and Jean-Paul Sartre, *Anti-Semite and Jew*, trans. G. J. Becker (New York: Schocken, 1995), 90. Here Sartre suggests that this notion of critical reflection is connected to an ethic of authenticity, which consists "in having a true and lucid consciousness of [our] situation, in assuming the responsibilities and risks that it involves, in accepting it in pride or humiliation, sometimes in horror and hate."

16. Sartre, *Anti-Semite and Jew*, 59–60.

17. Consider, for example, a notable passage from *Being and Nothingness*, where Sartre describes the resistance of a rock that one is attempting to climb. "What my freedom cannot determine is whether the rock 'to be scaled' will or will not lend itself to scaling," he says. "This is part of the brute being of the rock. Nevertheless the rock can show its resistance to the scaling only if the rock is integrated by freedom in a 'situation' of which the general theme is scaling. For the simple traveler who passes over this road and whose free project is a pure aesthetic ordering of the landscape, the crag is not revealed as either scalable or as not-scalable; it is manifested only as beautiful or ugly" (Jean-Paul Sartre, *Being and Nothingness: A Phenomenological Essay on Ontology*, trans. H. Barnes [New York: Washington Square Press, 1984], 627). The point here is that the rock becomes difficult to scale only if we *project* onto that rock the idea that we want to climb it.

18. Sartre, *Being and Nothingness*, 265, 427–428, 765ff.

19. Sartre concludes *Being and Nothingness* with a famous (or perhaps infamous) promise some day to work out the ethical implications of his ontological analysis (798), and this parting promissory note has been seen as an implicit admission by Sartre that his monumental wartime contribution is critically and politically inadequate. Herbert Marcuse, for example, in his 1948 review, derides *Being and Nothingness* for its quietist and implicitly affirmative political orientation, describing it as a "decidedly undialectical" text (Marcuse, *Studies in Critical Philosophy*, trans. J. de Bres [London: New Left Books, 1972], 176). That said, clearly Sartre did not intend for *Being and Nothingness* to speak directly to the kinds of political concerns raised by critical theorists like Marcuse. We might also note here that Sartre's "ethics" has long been a topic of scholarly interest and debate. Of course Sartre drafted his fragmentary and posthumously published *Notebooks for an Ethics* in 1947–1948. In Rome in 1964, he gave an important lecture on ethics, and he planned to give another at Cornell University in 1965 (Sartre ultimately canceled the Cornell lecture in protest of the Vietnam War); almost seven hundred pages of notes for these lectures remain unpublished. For more on this, see Robert V. Stone in collaboration with Elizabeth A. Bowman, "Dialectical Ethics: A First Look at Sartre's Unpublished 1964 Rome Lecture Notes," *Social Text* 13/14 [Winter-Spring 1986], 195–215) and Thomas Anderson, *Sartre's Two Ethics: From Authenticity to Integral Humanity* (LaSalle, IL: Open Court, 1993). We will return to the 1964 Rome lecture in the concluding remarks to this chapter.

20. Simone de Beauvoir indicates that this shift had become quite significant by 1951: "In 1944, he [Sartre] thought that any situation could be transcended by a subjective movement . . . in 1951, he knew that circumstances sometimes steal our transcendence from us; in that case, no individual salvation is possible, only a collective struggle" (Simone de Beauvoir, *Force of Circumstance, Vol. I* [New York: Harper and Row, 1977], 242). While I will go on to emphasize the ways in which Sartre's evolving attentiveness to *racial* oppression affects his thinking about the constraining character of our social and material situation, we must also underscore Sartre's evolving attentiveness to *gendered* experiences and to the systemic oppression of women, an attentiveness that, we must admit, is never adequate or satisfactory but that is certainly inspired to a significant degree by Sartre's interactions with Beauvoir. For more on this, see Sonia Kruks, "Simone de Beauvoir: Teaching Sartre about Freedom," in *Sartre Alive*, ed. R. Aronson and A. van de Hoven (Detroit: Wayne State University Press, 1991).

21. Sartre, *Critique of Dialectical Reason*, I: 35; Karl Marx, "The Eighteenth Brumaire of Louis Bonaparte," in *The Marx-Engels Reader*, Second Edition, ed. R. Tucker (New York: Norton, 1978), 595.

22. Sartre, *Critique of Dialectical Reason*, I: 35.

23. Sartre, *Search for a Method*, 91, 93.

24. Sartre, *Critique of Dialectical Reason*, I: 79.

25. Poster, *Sartre's Marxism*, 50.

26. Sartre describes the "practico-inert" as "the *crystallized practice* of previous generations: individuals find an existence already sketched out for them at birth. . . . What is 'assigned' to them is a type of work, and a material condition

and a standard of living tied to this activity; it is a fundamental *attitude*, as well as a determinate provision of material and intellectual tools; it is a strictly limited field of possibilities" (Sartre, *Critique of Dialectical Reason*, I: 232).

27. Sartre, *Being and Nothingness*, 139.

28. Sartre, *Critique of Dialectical Reason*, I: 80. As Sartre remarks in the unfinished second volume, "The original force here is *need*. Need is the primary drive. It feeds ambition" (Sartre, *Critique of Dialectical Reason*, II: 423).

29. Sartre, *Critique of Dialectical Reason*, I: 87, 368.

30. Sartre, *Critique of Dialectical Reason*, II: 422; Sartre, *Critique of Dialectical Reason*, I: 735 (emphasis mine).

31. Sartre, *Critique of Dialectical Reason*, I: 128.

32. Sartre, *Critique of Dialectical Reason*, I: 220.

33. Sartre, *Critique of Dialectical Reason*, I: 127. See also 137: "We are united by the fact that we live in a world that is determined by scarcity." See also Sartre, *Critique of Dialectical Reason*, II: 28, where Sartre elaborates on this idea of scarcity as a *milieu*—"scarcity is never an abstract principle, or one external to the social ensemble. At every instant, it is a synthetic relation of all men to non-human materiality and of all men among themselves through this materiality, inasmuch as the ensemble of techniques, relations of production and historical circumstances gives this relation its determination and its unity."

34. Fredric Jameson, *Marxism and Form: Twentieth-Century Dialectical Theories of Literature* (Princeton, NJ: Princeton University Press, 1971), 233.

35. Sartre, *Critique of Dialectical Reason*, I: 128.

36. Sartre, *Critique of Dialectical Reason*, I: 128.

37. Sartre, *Critique of Dialectical Reason*, I: 131–132. Sartre goes on to offer one of the more memorable passages of the *Critique*: "Nothing—not even wild beasts or microbes—could be more terrifying for man than a species which is intelligent, carnivorous and cruel, and which can understand and outwit human intelligence, and whose aim is precisely the destruction of man. This, however, is obviously our own species *as perceived in others* [emphasis mine] by each of its members in the context of scarcity."

38. Sartre, *Critique of Dialectical Reason*, I: 54.

39. Sartre, *Critique of Dialectical Reason*, I: 147.

40. Sartre, *Critique of Dialectical Reason*, I: 148.

41. Sartre, *Search for a Method*, 132 (emphasis mine).

42. See, for example, the "Critique of the Gotha Program," where Marx points toward a future in which "all the springs of cooperative wealth flow more abundantly" (Marx, "Critique of the Gotha Program," in R. Tucker [ed.], *The Marx-Engels Reader*, 531).

43. Sartre, *Critique of Dialectical Reason*, I: 332.

44. These specific references to colonialism as an "infernal system" and a "hell" derive from the *Critique of Dialectical Reason*, I: 717–718. This language, and the language of "system" more broadly, can be traced back to a 1956 essay, originally a speech at an Algerian War protest rally in Paris, entitled "Colonialism Is a System," available in Sartre, *Colonialism and Neocolonialism*, trans. A. Haddour, S. Brewer, and T. McWilliams (New York: Routledge, 2006), 36–55.

45. Sartre, *Critique of Dialectical Reason*, I: 723.

46. Sartre, *Colonialism and Neocolonialism*, 58–59.

47. See Sartre's lengthy footnote on race in *Critique of Dialectical Reason*, I: 300, fn. 88.

48. Iris Marion Young, "Gender as Seriality: Thinking about Women as a Social Collective," in *Feminist Interpretations of Jean-Paul Sartre*, ed. J. Murphy (University Park: Pennsylvania State University Press, 1999), 213–216. Young focuses on the seriality of gender, but her analysis is immensely helpful for thinking about Sartre's concept of the serial collective as it applies to a range of collective identities. For another helpful account of seriality, see Sonia Kruks, "Identity Politics and Dialectical Reason: Beyond an Epistemology of Provenance," in J. Murphy (ed.), *Feminist Interpretations of Jean-Paul Sartre*, 229–252. For a helpful discussion of seriality as it pertains specifically to Sartre's thinking about race and colonialism, see Arthur, *Unfinished Projects*, esp. chap. 5.

49. Sartre, *Critique of Dialectical Reason*, I: 277. Joseph Catalano provides a helpful account of how "serial" collectives are experienced within the milieu of scarcity: "Seriality is our political impotence to remove scarcity; it arises from our false sense of privacy. Our privacy keeps our neighbor at a psychological distance from us, but, more importantly, it also keeps a part of our own self distant from another part of our self: We are kept too busy or too worried to reflect upon historical evils. Thus, whether it is the unspoken 'everyone for himself' or the more sympathetic 'every person is very much alone,' Sartre notes that we are wedded to our social isolation, which effectively keeps us politically impotent" (Catalano, *Reading Sartre*, 45).

50. Judaken, "Sartre on Racism," 30–37.

51. Sartre, *Critique of Dialectical Reason*, I: 300, fn. 88. Regarding Sartre's writings on race from the immediate postwar period see: Sartre, "Return from the United States: What I Learned about the Black Problem" [1945], trans. T. D. Sharpley-Whiting, in *Existence in Black: An Anthology of Black Existentialist Philosophy*, ed. L. Gordon (New York: Routledge, 1997), 81–90; Sartre, "The Respectful Prostitute" [1946], trans. L. Abel, in *No Exit and Three Other Plays* (New York: Vintage, 1989); Sartre, "The Oppression of Blacks in the United States" [1947–1948], in *Notebooks for an Ethics*, 561–574; Sartre, *Black Orpheus*, trans. S. Allen (Paris: Présence africaine, 1963 [1948]). For helpful secondary accounts of the development of Sartre's thinking about racism and colonialism, see Judaken, "Racism in Sartre," which outlines four distinct phases in Sartre's intellectual development, and Arthur, *Unfinished Projects*.

52. See Frantz Fanon, *Black Skin, White Masks*, trans. C. L. Markmann (New York: Grove, 1962), 138. For an illuminating account of Fanon's underappreciated influence on Sartre (underappreciated because scholarly focus tends to move in the other direction, to focus on Sartre's influence on Fanon), see George Ciccariello-Maher, "European Intellectuals and Colonial Difference: Césaire and Fanon beyond Sartre and Foucault," in J. Judaken (ed.), *Race after Sartre*, 129–154. Ciccariello-Maher points out that that, as a result of his evolving engagement with colonialism in the 1950s, Sartre comes to be "known as a preface writer. That is, through Sartre's simultaneous recognition of his own situation and need to totalize, he defers—in the role of preface writer—to decolonial thought. In a striking and largely unrecognized display of self-criticism," he, most notably in his preface to Fanon's 1962 *Wretched*

of the Earth, abandons "the idea that it was Europeans who 'removed the gag' for the anticolonial reality in which 'the mouths opened by themselves'" (138). The reference here is to Sartre's well-known rhetorical question, in his 1948 "Black Orpheus," which asks, "What would you [white Europeans] expect to find, when the muzzle that has silenced the voice of black men is removed? That they would thunder your praises?" (Sartre, *Black Orpheus*, 7). And the point here is that this rather paternalistic emphasis on the active role of European liberators is abandoned as Sartre comes to appreciate his own "situation" as a European intellectual, to appreciate his capacity, or incapacity, authentically to speak on behalf of the colonized and to respect the agency of the oppressed.

53. Sartre, *Colonialism and Neocolonialism*, 59–60.

54. Arthur, *Unfinished Projects*, 85–86.

55. See, for example, Raymond Aron, *Marxism and the Existentialists*, trans. R. Addis and J. Weightman (New York: Harper and Row, 1969), 169.

56. See Sartre, *Critique of Dialectical Reason*, I: 123ff; Poster, *Sartre's Marxism*, 55; Jay, *Marxism and Totality*, 356–357; and Ronald Aronson, *Sartre's Second Critique* (Chicago: University of Chicago Press, 1978), 48.

57. Sartre's orientation toward violence, ever a point of contention, has often been oversimplified and overemphasized as part of an attempt to caricature Sartre as an undisciplined radical with little to contribute to contemporary political theory. While this is not the place to explore Sartre's rather complex thinking on this subject, we might note that Sartre's postwar turn to dialectical thinking in many ways facilitates an appreciation of the scope and magnitude of the violence that is needed to maintain the system of colonial exploitation and racial oppression, and this appreciation is certainly part of an explanation for why Sartre finds himself hard-pressed to condemn the expression of violence in the struggle for decolonization. We might also note that his occasional defense of violence is perhaps best understood not as a categorical endorsement, not as an endorsement of violence as such, but rather as part of Sartre's own attempt to recognize and appreciate his own "situation" as a European intellectual, to recognize and appreciate the agency of the oppressed, to cede, perhaps to encourage, that agency, however it needs to manifest itself. For a more generous discussion of violence in Sartre, see Judith Butler, "Violence, Non-Violence: Sartre on Fanon," *Graduate Faculty Philosophy Journal* 27, 1 (2006), 3–24, and, for a more comprehensive discussion, Ronald Santoni, *Sartre on Violence: Curiously Ambivalent* (University Park: Pennsylvania State University Press, 2003).

58. Hardt and Negri, *Multitude*, 141; Hardt and Negri, *Commonwealth*, 131.

59. Hardt and Negri, *Multitude*, 310–311.

60. Hardt and Negri, *Multitude*, 311; Hardt and Negri, *Commonwealth*, 131–142.

61. Hardt and Negri, *Multitude*, 188. We might also note the work of J. K. Gibson-Graham who traces "the makings of a new political imaginary" around an attentiveness to an abundance or surplus of new ideas, new lines of communication, new modes of "economic being-in-common" (J. K. Gibson-Graham, *A Postcapitalist Politics* (Minneapolis: University of Minnesota Press, 2006).

62. Jürgen Habermas, "Jürgen Habermas on the Legacy of Jean-Paul Sartre," *Political Theory* 20, 3 (1992), 497. We might also note Merleau-Ponty's claim, in his commentary on Sartre's *Communists and Peace* [1968], that "[i]n Sartre there

is a plurality of subjects but no intersubjectivity" (Maurice Merleau-Ponty, *Adventures of the Dialectic*, trans. A. Bien [Evanston, IL: Northwestern University Press, 1973], 205).

63. Hardt and Negri, *Multitude*, 213–214.

64. In a discussion of Sartre's thinking about violence, William McBride makes a comment that might shed further light on the point that I want to make. "Such phenomena as love or friendship or social solidarity are real and really possible," McBride writes, "but . . . they can never be permanent and entirely without the potentiality of violent conflict. . . . 'Harmony theorists' tend to wish to deny the pervasive reality of violence by claiming that there can be such privileged, sheltered relationships of both a dyadic and perhaps even a communal sort, and moreover that it is on such ideal relationships that we ought to concentrate our attention. Sartre would maintain . . . that such an approach to social theory is at best self-deceptive, and is sometimes even a deliberate effort to encourage others not to reflect on the conflict-filled reality of the world around them, in the interest of preserving existing social hierarchies that have no rational basis" (McBride, *Sartre's Political Theory*, 20).

65. Sartre, "Interview with Michel Rybalka," 31.

66. To reinforce this point, I might call attention again to Sartre's thinking about the "exigent" character of racism in the modern world. In the mid-1940s, in *Anti-Semite and Jew*, Sartre alluded to Richard Wright's famous claim that racial division in the United States was not reflective of a "black problem" but was in fact a "white problem" (see Sartre, *Anti-Semite and Jew*, 152 and K. Kinneman and M. Fabre (eds.), *Conversations with Richard Wright* [Jackson: University Press of Mississippi, 1993], 88). And Wright's insinuation, of course, was that, in order to combat and ultimately overcome the problem, in order to eradicate the oppression and degradation of black Americans, white folks must be made to relinquish their privileged status. Sartre's postwar turn to dialectical thinking, which seems both to inform and be informed by his thinking about racism, only underscores the intense difficulty of this political project, this struggle for racial equality. The presumption, so common to this day, that the situation of black Americans can be improved without any real change to the living standards of white America simply obscures the fact that an American racial caste system endures largely because white Americans perceive—and perhaps subconsciously, as a result of what Sartre would call "internal, dialectical conditioning"—the needs of the racial "other," manifested in claims to racial equality, as a threat to their way of life.

67. Sartre, *Critique of Dialectical Reason*, I: 149.

68. Sartre, "1964 Rome Lecture," cited in Arthur, *Unfinished Projects*, 144.

69. Stone and Bowman, "Dialectical Ethics," 209. Paige Arthur, citing Thomas Anderson, points out that, for Sartre, "needs are not blind givens, but rather felt exigencies. They include freedom (of course) and bodily requirements to sustain life (nourishment, protein), but, as Anderson points out, Sartre ultimately went further, including 'our need for others, in particular for their love and valuation. He refers to our need for knowledge, for a meaningful life, and for culture, and insists that without the latter we would not become human'" (Arthur, *Unfinished Projects*, 144; see also Anderson, *Sartre's Two Ethics*).

70. Sartre, *Critique of Dialectical Reason*, I: 733.

71. See Stone and Bowman, "Dialectical Ethics," 209. Stone and Bowman go on to point out that "we will look in vain among Sartre's dialectical ethics for general rules or principles of right action. Clearly for Sartre, no such positive norm is required to justify revolutionary praxis. If 'need is its justification's own satisfaction,' then the moral burden of proof lies not on those who want reliably to satisfy their hunger and thirst, but instead on any who would allow systematic denial of these and other needs."

72. Sartre, "1964 Rome Lecture," cited in Stone and Bowman, "Dialectical Ethics," 207.

73. McBride, *Sartre's Political Theory*, 110. Certainly one could argue that Sartre is more ambiguous on this point. In his later interviews, for example, he seems to question sincerely this Hegelian notion that our subjective dependence upon others and the world is a necessarily negative phenomenon, something to be overcome. See Sartre and Lévy, *Hope Now: The 1980 Interviews*, 91.

74. Sartre, *Critique of Dialectical Reason*, II: 10.

CHAPTER FOUR. BETWEEN DESPAIR AND REDEMPTION

1. Walter Benjamin, "Theses on the Philosophy of History," in *Illuminations: Essays and Reflections*, trans. Harry Zohn; ed. Hannah Arendt (New York: Schocken, 1968), 253–264.

2. Benjamin, "Theses on the Philosophy of History," 253.

3. For a brief overview of the debate surrounding Benjamin's attempt to fuse theological motifs with Marxian materialism, see Susan Buck-Morss, *The Dialectics of Seeing: Walter Benjamin and the Arcades Project* (Cambridge: MIT Press, 1999), 245–249.

4. Jürgen Habermas, "Consciousness-Raising or Redemptive Criticism: The Contemporaneity of Walter Benjamin," *New German Critique* 17 (Spring, 1979), 51. Originally, "Bewusstmachende oder rettende Kritik: Die Aktualität Walter Benjamins," in *Zur Aktualität Walter Benjamins*, ed. Siegfried Unseld (Frankfurt am Main: Suhrkamp, 1972), 175–223.

5. Habermas, "Consciousness-Raising or Redemptive Criticism," 54.

6. As Habermas ultimately puts it, an "immanent relation to political praxis cannot be obtained at all from *redemptive* critique, as it can from a *consciousness-raising* one" ("Consciousness-Raising or Redemptive Criticism," 54).

7. David Kaufmann, "Adorno and the Name of God," *Flashpoint* 1, 1 (1996), 65. Much of Kaufmann's work is dedicated specifically to the question of why Adorno insists on using these religious tropes throughout his career. And Kaufmann does a fine job of countering, he might say *correcting*, much of the secularization of Adorno that, he argues, is prevalent in the Anglo-American scholarship. See Kaufmann, "Correlations, Constellations, and the Truth: Adorno's Ontology of Redemption," *Philosophy & Social Criticism* 26, 5 (2000), 62–80 and "Beyond Use, Within Reason: Adorno, Benjamin, and the Question of Theology," *New German Critique* 83, Special Issue on Walter Benjamin (Spring-Summer 2001), 151–173. See also Willem Von Reijen, "Redemption and Reconciliation in Benjamin and Adorno," in *The Possibility of the Impossible*, ed. N. Schafhausen, V. J. Müller, and M. Hirsch (New York: Lukas & Sternberg, 2003), 69–84; Eduardo Mendieta, "Religion as Critique: Theology as

Social Critique and Enlightened Reason," in *The Frankfurt School on Religion: Key Writings by the Major Thinkers*, ed. E. Mendieta (New York: Routledge, 2005), 1–17; and Raymond Geuss, "On the Usefulness and Uselessness of Religious Illusions" and "Adorno's Gaps," both in Geuss, *Outside Ethics* (Princeton, NJ: Princeton University Press, 2005), 111–130 and 234–247, respectively.

8. See Robert Hullot-Kentor, "Right Listening and a New Type of Human Being," in *Things Beyond Resemblance: Collected Essays on Theodor W. Adorno* (New York: Columbia University Press, 2006), 199. Elsewhere, in his translator's introduction to Adorno's early Kierkegaard book, Hullot-Kentor underscores the theological dimensions of Adorno's work: "theology is always moving right under the surface of all of Adorno's writings . . . theology penetrates every word" ("Critique of the Inorganic: Kierkegaard and the Construction of the Aesthetic" in *Things Beyond Resemblance*, 92; this essay was published originally in Adorno, *Kierkegaard: Construction of the Aesthetic*, trans R. Hullot-Kentor [Minneapolis: University of Minnesota Press, 1989]). We might note that Hullot-Kentor goes on to suggest that Adorno tones down or "sublimates" his theological references in his later works. I'll say more about this later.

9. Theodor W. Adorno, *Minima Moralia: Reflections from Damaged Life*, trans. E. F. N. Jephcott (New York: Verso, 2002), 247.

10. Here I am referring of course to Georg Lukács's polemical remarks in his 1962 preface to *The Theory of the Novel*, where he claims that "[a] considerable part of the leading German intelligentsia, including Adorno, have taken up permanent residence in the 'Grand Hotel Abyss' . . . a beautiful hotel, equipped with every comfort, on the edge of an abyss, of nothingness, of absurdity. And the daily contemplation of the abyss between excellent meals or artistic entertainments, can only heighten the enjoyment of the subtle comforts offered" (Lukács, *The Theory of the Novel*, trans. A. Bostock [Cambridge: MIT Press, 1971], 22). At issue here is Adorno's perceived elitism, his perceived flight from the real world of practical affairs, and the presumption that his musings on despair reflect merely a set of intellectual or philosophical interests. This caricature of Adorno was solidified by the famous, perhaps infamous, episode in the late 1960s when Adorno called on the police to break up student protests at the University of Frankfurt; in response, the SDS, the German Socialist Student Union, accused Adorno of political quietism and characterized him as a thinker of "sophisticated despair" (see Rolf Wiggershaus, *The Frankfurt School: Its History, Theories, and Political Significance*, trans. M. Robertson [Cambridge: MIT Press, 1994], 620). See also Lorenz Jäger, *Adorno: A Political Biography*, trans. S. Spencer (New Haven, CT: Yale University Press, 2004), 192–208 and, for a more sympathetic analysis of Adorno's response to the student protests of the late 1960s, Andrew Rubin, "The Adorno Files," in *Adorno: A Critical Reader*, ed. N. Gibson and A. Rubin (New York: Routledge, 2002). Certainly I will suggest that Adorno's musings on despair have significant ethical and political import.

11. This is Benjamin's phrase, which Adorno cites approvingly in "A Portrait of Walter Benjamin," in *Prisms*, trans. Samuel Weber and Shierry Weber (Cambridge: MIT Press, 1990), 240.

12. Simon Jarvis, "What is Speculative Thinking?," *Revue internationale de philosophie* 227, 1 (2004), 69–83.

13. Adorno, "Sociology and Empirical Research," in Adorno et al., *The Positivist Dispute in German Sociology*, trans. G. Adey and D. Frisby (London: Heinmann, 1976), 35; Adorno, *Minima Moralia*, 86.

14. See Jacques Derrida, *Specters of Marx: The State of the Debt, the Work of Mourning, and the New International*, trans. P. Kamuf (New York: Routledge, 1994); Derrida, "Marx & Sons," trans. G. M. Goshgarian, in *Ghostly Demarcations: A Symposium on Jacques Derrida's Specters of Marx* (New York: Verso, 1999); and Derrida, *Acts of Religion*, ed. G. Anidjar (New York: Routledge, 2002).

15. At one point in *Negative Dialectics*, Adorno describes physical suffering as the "unrest that makes knowledge move" and he calls pain and negativity "the moving forces of dialectical thinking." Adorno seems to suggest here that our thinking starts from the immediacy of bodily pain or physical suffering. But despair signals a far more mediated experience, and I will argue that the dialectical counterpoint of redemption is essential to any such experience. See Adorno, *Negative Dialectics*, trans. E. B. Ashton (New York: Continuum, 1973), 202–203. Ashton's is a controversial translation. See Dennis Redmond's alternative at http://www.efn.org/~dredmond/ndtrans.html. I generally follow Redmond's translation but maintain page references to the Ashton edition.

16. See Rubin, "The Adorno Files." For a discussion of the persistence of authoritarian tendencies, see, for example, Adorno's 1959 essay, "The Meaning of Working Through the Past," in *Critical Models: Interventions and Catchwords*, trans. H. Pickford (New York: Columbia University Press, 2005), 89–103. Recent helpful discussions of Adorno's exile and its impact on his critique of modernity include Gerhard Richter, "Nazism and Negative Dialectics: Adorno's Hitler in *Minima Moralia*," in *Thought-Images: Frankfurt School Writers' Reflection from Damaged Life* (Stanford: Stanford University Press, 2007), 147–190; and Antonio Y. Vázquez-Arroyo, "Minima Humana: Adorno, Exile, and the Dialectic," *Telos* 149 (Winter 2009), 105–125.

17. Numerous studies offer a more detailed survey of both Adorno's life and his wide-ranging critique of modernity, neither of which can be considered in great detail in the confines of the present chapter. In terms of biographies, see: Stefan Müller-Doohm, *Adorno: A Biography*, trans. R. Livingstone (Malden, MA: Polity Press, 2005) and Jäger, *Adorno: A Political Biography*. For helpful introductions to Adorno's overall work, see: Simon Jarvis, *Adorno: A Critical Introduction* (New York: Routledge, 1998); Gillian Rose, *The Melancholy Science: An Introduction to the Thought of Theodor W. Adorno* (New York: Columbia University Press, 1978); Martin Jay, *Adorno* (Cambridge, MA: Harvard University Press, 1984); and J. M. Bernstein, *Adorno: Disenchantment and Ethics* (New York: Cambridge University Press, 2001); as well as the essays collected in Jeffrey T. Nelson and Caren Irr (eds.), *Rethinking the Frankfurt School: Alternative Legacies in Critical Theory* (Albany: State University of New York Press, 2002) and Nigel Gibson and Andrew Rubin (eds.), *Adorno: A Critical Reader* (New York: Blackwell, 2002). For a recent attempt to glean a series of political theoretical teachings from Adorno's work, see Espen Hammer, *Adorno and the Political* (New York: Routledge, 2006).

18. See G. W. F. Hegel, *Phenomenology of Spirit*, trans. A. V. Miller (New York: Oxford University Press, 1977), 49.

19. Adorno, *Negative Dialectics*, 3.

20. This is of course a rather familiar move for intellectuals associated with the early Frankfurt School. See, for example, Marcuse's 1958 call for a return to theoretical reflection in face of Soviet-style Marxist practice: "If the proletariat no longer acts as the revolutionary class . . . it no longer furnishes the 'material weapons' for philosophy. The situation thus reverts: repelled by reality, Reason and Freedom become again the concern of philosophy. . . . [Theory] again not only anticipates political practice, runs ahead of it, but also upholds the objectives of liberation in the face of a failing practice. In this function, theory becomes again ideology—not as false consciousness, but as conscious distance and dissociation from, even opposition to, the repressive reality. And by the same token, it becomes a political factor of utmost significance" (Marcuse, *Soviet Marxism: A Critical Analysis* [New York: Columbia University Press, 1985], 126).

21. Fredric Jameson, *Late Marxism: Adorno, or, the Persistence of the Dialectic* (New York: Verso, 1990), 23.

22. Karl Marx, *Capital, Vol. 1*, trans. B. Fowkes (New York: Penguin, 1990), 135.

23. Adorno, "Subject and Object," in *Critical Models*, 248.

24. Jameson, *Late Marxism*, 24 (emphasis mine).

25. Adorno, "Sociology and Empirical Research," 80.

26. Adorno, *Negative Dialectics*, 154.

27. Adorno, *Negative Dialectics*, 149. For a more detailed account of Adorno's treatment of the concept and conceptuality, see Rose, *The Melancholy Science*, 43–46; Jameson, *Late Marxism*, 19–20; and Bernstein, *Adorno: Disenchantment and Ethics*, 263–329.

28. Adorno, *Negative Dialectics*, 146.

29. Martin Jay, *Marxism and Totality: The Adventures of a Concept from Lukács to Habermas* (Berkeley: University of California Press, 1984), 269.

30. Adorno, "Late Capitalism or Industrial Society?" Opening Address to the 16th German Sociological Congress (1968), trans. D. Redmond http://www.efn.org/~dredmond/AdornoSocAddr.html (2001), 7.

31. Adorno, "Late Capitalism or Industrial Society?," 7. See also Adorno, *Hegel: Three Studies*, trans. S. W. Nicholson (Cambridge: MIT Press, 1994), 27–28: "A world integrated through 'production,' through the exchange relationship, depends in all its moments on the social conditions of its production, and in that sense actually realizes the primacy of the whole over its parts; in this regard, the desperate impotence of every single individual now verifies Hegel's extravagant conception of the system. . . . The insatiable and destructive expansive principle of the exchange society, is reflected in Hegelian metaphysics. It describes the way the world actually is, not in historical perspective but in essence."

32. Jameson makes a similar point when he says that, on Adorno's account, the effects of exchange, or of material and mental reduction, "cannot simply be thought away by the thinking of a better thought, by new forms of philosophizing and more adequate (or even more Utopian) concepts. History already thinks the thinking subject and is inscribed in the forms through which it must necessarily think. 'Society precedes the subject'; thought's categories are collective and social; identity is not an option but a doom; reason and its categories are at one with the rise of civilization or capitalism, and can scarcely be transformed until the latter is transformed" (*Late Marxism*, 24).

33. Rose, *The Melancholy Science*, 18, 26, 79. For our purposes, Rose simply offers a slightly more focused articulation of a point that Adorno himself makes on a number of occasions, perhaps most notably in his defense of his well-known claim that, after Auschwitz, one cannot write poetry: "I once said that after Auschwitz one could no longer write poetry, and that gave rise to a discussion I did not anticipate when I wrote those words. I did not anticipate it because it is in the nature of philosophy—and everything I write is, unavoidably, philosophy, even if it is not concerned with so-called philosophical themes—that nothing is meant quite literally. Philosophy always relates to tendencies and does not consist of statements of fact. It is a misunderstanding of philosophy, resulting from its growing closeness to all-powerful scientific tendencies, to take such a statement at face value and say: 'He wrote that after Auschwitz one cannot write any more poems; so either one really cannot write them, and would be a rogue or a cold-hearted person if one did write them, or he is wrong, and has said something which should not be said.' Well, I would say that philosophical reflection really consists precisely in the gap, or, in Kantian terms, in the vibration, between these two otherwise so flatly opposed possibilities. I would readily concede that, just as I said that after Auschwitz one could not write poems—by which I meant to point to the hollowness of the resurrected culture of that time—it could equally well be said, on the other hand, that one must write poems, in keeping with Hegel's statement in his *Aesthetics* that as long as there is an awareness of suffering among human beings there must also be art as the objective form of that awareness" (Adorno, *Metaphysics: Concepts and Problems*, ed. R. Tiedemann; trans. E. F. N. Jephcott [Stanford, CA: Stanford University Press, 2000], 110–111).

34. I might note, incidentally, that herein lies a possible rejoinder to some of Habermas's concerns and confusions, which we noted at the outset, regarding the political import of a critique inspired by notions of redemption and the messianic. Adorno might suggest that such confusion is based at least in part on Habermas's overly literal reading of these references. I would wager that this sort of rejoinder, this accusation of an overly literal reading of Adorno's arguments, could be extended to Habermas's broader critique of Adorno in *The Philosophical Discourse of Modernity: Twelve Lectures*, trans. F. G. Lawrence (Cambridge: MIT Press, 1990).

35. These themes resound throughout *Minima Moralia*. See in particular the aphorisms entitled "Keeping One's Distance" and "Don't Exaggerate," both of which underscore the idea that, in order to generate and maintain a degree of critical distance, we sometimes need to invoke language that pushes our imaginations beyond the bounds of positive reality. See also some of Adorno's later essays from the 1950s, many of which deal with the "shocking" dimensions of surrealist literature, in Adorno, *Notes to Literature, Vol. I*, ed. R. Tiedemann; trans. S. W. Nicholson (New York: Columbia University Press, 1991).

36. See Adorno, *Philosophy of New Music*, trans. R. Hullot-Kentor (Minneapolis: University of Minnesota Press, 2006), 35. It is worth noting that *Philosophy of New Music* was drafted during the early 1940s and was meant as a kind of companion volume to *Minima Moralia*. See also Adorno's 1963 collection, *Quasi una Fantasia: Essays on Modern Music*, trans. R. Livingstone (New York: Verso, 1998), in which Adorno draws a distinction between "intentional language," which is essentially

positivistic in its concern to communicate unambiguous meaning, and music, which "points to true language" and which, in its ambiguity, is able to generate a degree of critical distance between our thinking, our listening, our conscious apprehension, on the one hand, and the ordinary routines of bourgeois modernity, on the other. While an adequate inquiry into Adorno's writings on music and aesthetic theory would require far more space than is available here, it is worth highlighting Adorno's remark that "the language of music . . . contains a theological dimension. What it has to say is simultaneously revealed and concealed. Its idea is the divine Name which has been given shape. It is demythologized prayer, rid of efficacious magic. It is the human attempt, doomed as ever, to name the Name, not to communicate meanings" (Adorno, "Language and Music: A Fragment" (1956), in *Quasi una Fantasia*, 2). The reference to the theological here is an attempt to underscore the distance between the immanent and the transcendent and to imagine the transcendent as a source of open-ended hope, the promise of alternative possibilities that we cannot know or articulate in any concrete way. We will return to this theme in the next section.

37. Adorno, "Discussion of Professor Adorno's Lecture 'The Meaning of Working Through the Past,'" in *Critical Models*, 305–306. For a very helpful discussion of the role of "exaggerations and other extremes" in Adorno's critical theory, see Lydia Goehr, "Reviewing Adorno: Public Opinion and Critique," in *Critical Models*, xxiii–xxvi.

38. Adorno, *Negative Dialectics*, 304.

39. Adorno, *Negative Dialectics*, 354.

40. Adorno, *Negative Dialectics*, 190.

41. Adorno, "Late Capitalism or Industrial Society?," 10. In yet another intriguing passage, Adorno writes, "The world's curse is not absolutely conclusive, nor is absolute despair; rather, despair is its conclusiveness. However void every trace of otherness in it, however much all happiness is marred by revocability: in the breaks that belie identity, entity is still pervaded by the ever broken pledges of that otherness. All happiness is but a fragment of the entire happiness men are denied, and are denied by themselves" (*Negative Dialectics*, 404).

42. Adorno, "Late Capitalism or Industrial Society?," 10.

43. Adorno, "Reason and Revelation," in *Critical Models*, 135; Benjamin, "Theses on the Philosophy of History," 253.

44. Adorno, *Negative Dialectics*, 144.

45. G. W. F. Hegel, *Hegel's Philosophy of Right*, trans. T. M. Knox (New York: Oxford University Press, 1967), 10.

46. See Hegel, *The Encyclopedia Logic: Part I of the Encyclopedia of Philosophical Sciences with the Zusätze*, trans. T. F. Geraets, W. A. Suchting, and H. S. Harris, (Indianapolis: Hackett, 2002), 47, where the point of dialectical logic is to help the thinker "cultivate one's spirit for higher things and to make efforts on behalf of that. We may hope that in our time a longing for something better has sprung up in the young."

47. Marcuse suggests something along these lines when he says that Hegel's dialectical approach is "originally motivated by the conviction that the given facts that appear to common sense as the positive index of truth are in reality the negation of truth, so that truth can only be established by their destruction," that "the

driving force of the dialectical method lies in this critical conviction," and ultimately that "Marx's dialectical criticism of reality was originally motivated by the same datum as Hegel's, namely, by the negative character of reality." See Marcuse, *Reason and Revolution: Hegel and the Rise of Social Theory* (Amherst, NY: Humanity Books, 1999), 26–27, 312.

48. Hent de Vries, *Minimal Theologies: Critique of Secular Reason in Adorno and Levinas*, trans. G. Hale (Baltimore: Johns Hopkins University Press, 2005), 279.

49. See de Vries, *Minimal Theologies*, 234–235, where he claims that "[o]ne must correct one important avenue in the reception of Adorno's work, which continues to portray him as, above all, a neo-Hegelian. . . . Adorno emphatically rejects every 'reconciliation' of contradictions, whether put forward as *real* or merely *realizable*."

50. De Vries, *Minimal Theologies*, 280.

51. Max Horkheimer, "Materialism and Morality," *Telos* 69 (1986), 108; Adorno, "Open Letter to Max Horkheimer" (1965), cited in de Vries, *Minimal Theologies*, 15.

52. Kaufmann, "Correlations, Constellations, and the Truth," 66.

53. Kaufmann, "Correlations, Constellations, and the Truth," 71.

54. Max Horkheimer and Theodor W. Adorno, *Dialectic of Enlightenment: Philosophical Fragments*, trans. E. F. N. Jephcott (Stanford, CA: Stanford University Press, 2002), 17.

55. Adorno, "Resignation," in *Critical Models*, 292.

56. Adorno, "Resignation," 292–293.

57. By now I hope that I have implicitly dispelled any possible concern that I overemphasize the sentiment expressed in our guiding passage, but it may be worthwhile at least to note an explicit comment about this. The potential concern here would be that, by focusing on Adorno's references to redemption and the messianic in a single aphorism from *Minima Moralia*, I threaten to take the passage out of context, to extend Adorno's theological references beyond their province, perhaps even to confuse Adorno's earlier thinking with his more mature works of the 1960s. Some scholars have suggested that Adorno's earlier writings exhibit more theological inflection than do the later ones and that the early theology may be part of a response to the helplessness and despair that Adorno (and Horkheimer) witnessed at the hands of the Hitler regime in the 1930s and 1940s. Robert Hullot-Kentor, for example, notes how Adorno's early book on Kierkegaard—which "appeared in bookstores on February 27, 1933, the day that Hitler declared a national emergency and suspended the freedom of the press, marking the transition from chancellor to dictator"—is concerned fundamentally with the idea of hope and is written in a "context of theological interests." But Hullot-Kentor goes on to point out that, in Adorno's later works, including a revised version of the Kierkegaard book, we see a "sublimation of the theological," and ultimately, "in *Aesthetic Theory* (1969), his last work, the idea of hope no longer sails in on a silken pillow" (Hullot-Kentor, "Critique of the Organic: Kierkegaard and the Construction of the Aesthetic," in *Things Beyond Resemblance*, 92; see also Hullot-Kentor's introduction to his translation of Adorno, *Kierkegaard: Construction of the Aesthetic*, trans. R. Hullot-Kentor (Minneapolis: University of Minnesota Press, 1989), x–xxiii. Plainly Adorno continues to speak of God, of redemption, of hope, certainly of despair, in, for example, *Negative Dialectics* (1966), especially in the final section on "meditations on metaphysics." I

will suggest, at the very least, that, whether or not Adorno sublimates the theological in his later writings, the meaning and significance of his remarks in the "Finale" remain central to his thinking about critique and dialectical reflection, as we see in his essay on "Resignation," which was written in 1969, and in his account of the relationship between the immanent and the transcendent in his *Aesthetic Theory*, which Adorno was in the process of completing at the time of his death. Regarding this question about just how central theological motifs are to Adorno late in his life, we might note that, in an interview with *Der Spiegel* on the eve of Adorno's funeral, Horkheimer saw fit to underscore, in Stefan Müller-Doohm's words, "theological motifs, he [Horkheimer] emphasized that Adorno's 'negativism implied the affirmation of something "other,"' which, however, is not susceptible to definition. This was not a negative theology 'in the sense that there is no God, but in the sense that God cannot be represented.' Horkheimer was evidently attempting to identify the legacy of Jewish thought in Adorno. The notion of truth as temporal knowledge that is always gradually unfolding could be combined with the prohibition on graven images, as could the concept of being mindful of the messianic aspect of redemption or reconciliation: hope for the sake of those who are without hope" (Müller-Doohm, *Adorno: A Biography*, 485).

58. Adorno, *Against Epistemology: A Metacritique: Studies in Husserl and the Phenomenological Antinomies*, trans. W. Domingo (Cambridge: MIT Press, 1984), 11.

59. Adorno, "Goldmann and Adorno: To Describe, Understand, and Explain," in Lucien Goldmann, *Cultural Creation in Modern Society*, trans. B. Grahl (St. Louis, MO: Telos Press, 1976), 131.

60. Rolf Tiedemann, "Editor's Foreword," in Adorno, *Lectures on Negative Dialectics: Fragments of a Lecture Course 1965/1966*, ed. R. Tiedemann; trans. R. Livingstone (Malden, MA: Polity Press, 2010), xii. See also Adorno, *Hegel: Three Studies*, 53.

61. Tiedemann, "Editor's Foreword," xiv.

62. See Tiedemann, "Editor's Foreword," xiv; see also Adorno, *Lectures on Negative Dialectics*, 82.

63. Adorno, *Negative Dialectics*, 11.

64. Adorno, *Negative Dialectics*, 5.

65. Adorno, *Negative Dialectics*, 141.

66. Adorno, *Negative Dialectics*, 149. We might note that in a later piece, in his 1968 address to the German Sociological Association, Adorno says that "[t]he *telos* of the dialectical view of society runs contrary to the global view," by which Adorno means that a dialectical approach aims to counter "totality" by pursuing a kind of "micrology" or, again, those excessive remainders that necessarily haunt that "totality" (Adorno, "Sociology and Empirical Research," 38–39).

67. Adorno, *Negative Dialectics*, 10.

68. See Bernstein, *Adorno: Disenchantment and Ethics*, 348–349. My discussion here owes much to Bernstein's analysis.

69. Adorno, "Something's Missing: A Discussion between Theodor W. Adorno and Ernst Bloch on the Contradictions of Utopian Longing" (1964), in Ernst Bloch, *The Utopian Function of Art and Literature: Selected Essays*, trans. J. Zipes and F. Mecklenburg (Cambridge: MIT Press, 1996), 3–4; emphasis mine.

70. See Adorno's discussion of a postdialectical "changed philosophy," which would—or *could*, as Adorno tends to resist substantive speculation—be adequate to a world free of system and contradiction. "The changed philosophy itself would be infinite in the sense of scorning solidification in a body of innumerable theorems. Its substance would lie in the diversity of objects that impinge upon it and of the objects it seeks, a diversity not wrought by any schema; to those objects, philosophy would truly give itself, mistaking its own image for concretion" (*Negative Dialectics*, 13).

71. Jameson, *Late Marxism*, 27–28.

72. In a way, my questions build on a line of inquiry developed by Romand Coles. Coles worries that Derrida "sometimes overestimates the ateleological," and that, in light of such an overestimation, we must be careful to never let the "call to anticipate the unanticipatable . . . become a comfortable deconstructionist mantra lulling us to abandon the work of determinate democratic theory and practice in favor of messianic gestures toward 'the new' and 'possibility.'" See Coles, *Beyond Gated Politics: Reflections for the Possibility of Democracy* (Minneapolis: University of Minnesota Press, 2005), 178, 156–157.

73. Derrida, *Specters of Marx*, 59.

74. See Derrida, "Marx & Sons," 248, and *Specters of Marx*, 168.

75. Derrida, "Force of Law," in *Acts of Religion*, 281.

76. See Karl Marx, "Contribution to the Critique of Hegel's *Philosophy of Right*," in *The Marx-Engels Reader*, Second Edition, ed. R. Tucker (New York: Norton, 1978), 20–21, and Marx, "The German Ideology," in *The Marx-Engels Reader*, 162. See also Derrida, "Marx & Sons," 248. Derrida does think of this messianic force as a "*real* movement" or, as he puts it, "the coming of an eminently real, concrete event . . . the most irreducible heterogeneous otherness."

77. Marx, "Contribution to the Critique of Hegel's *Philosophy of Right*," 21.

78. Derrida, *Margins of Philosophy*, trans. A. Bass (Chicago: University of Chicago Press, 1984), 67. See also, Derrida, "Marx & Sons," 249, where messianicity signals a "way of thinking the event 'before' or independently of all ontology."

79. Derrida, *Margins of Philosophy*, 27 (my emphasis).

80. On the concept of *Gelassenheit*, see Martin Heidegger, *Discourse on Thinking*, trans. J. Anderson and H. Freund (New York: Harper and Row, 1966).

81. Derrida, *Specters of Marx*, 168.

82. Derrida, "For a Justice to Come: An Interview with Jacques Derrida," in *The Derrida-Habermas Reader*, ed. L. Thomassen (Chicago: University of Chicago Press, 2006), 268.

83. Jacob Taubes, *The Political Theology of Paul*, trans. D. Hollander (Stanford, CA: Stanford University Press, 2004), 74.

84. Adorno, *Minima Moralia*, 86.

85. Adorno, "Sacred Fragment: Schoenberg's Moses und Aron," in *Quasi Una Fantasia*, 226.

86. Adorno, *Negative Dialectics*, 403.

87. Adorno, *Negative Dialectics*, 377–378. We might note that Adorno returns to this chromatic metaphor in a very effective way in his *Aesthetic Theory*. "To survive reality at its most extreme and grim," he says, "artworks that do not want to sell themselves as consolation must equate themselves with that reality. Radical

art today is synonymous with dark art; its primary color is black. . . . Still, black art bears features that would, if they were definitive, set their seal on historical despair; to the extent that change is always still possible they too may be ephemeral" (Adorno, *Aesthetic Theory*, trans. R. Hullot-Kentor [Minneapolis: University of Minnesota Press, 1997], 39–40). He goes on to say that "[t]he tenebrous has become the plenipotentiary of . . . utopia," and because "utopia—the yet-to-exist—is draped in black . . . it is the imaginary reparation of the catastrophe of world history; it is freedom, which under the spell of necessity did not—and may not ever—come to pass" (135). While an adequate engagement with the *Aesthetic Theory* is beyond the scope of this chapter, these passages reinforce precisely the argument that I make regarding the dialectical interconnection between the immanent and the transcendent. They also reinforce our emphasis on Adorno's language, his rhetoric, his "extreme" formulations of dark, tenebrous despair, on the one hand, and possibility, utopia, reparation, on the other.

88. Adorno, *Lectures on Negative Dialectics*, 95.

89. Adorno, "Discussion to Lecture: 'The Meaning of Working Through the Past,'" 298.

90. See Theodor W. Adorno and Herbert Marcuse, "Correspondence on the German Student Movement," *New Left Review* 233 (January-February 1999), 123–126; Esther Leslie, "Introduction to Adorno/Marcuse Correspondence on the German Student Movement," *New Left Review* 233 (January-February 1999); and Wiggershaus, *The Frankfurt School: Its History, Theories, and Political Significance*, esp. 609–636.

91. Adorno, "The Meaning of Working Through the Past," 93. Later, in front of students in 1967, he expressed his "fear that the democratic spirit which is only just developing in Germany might be stifled by authoritarian practices" (Adorno, cited in Müller-Doohm, *Adorno: A Biography*, 452).

92. Adorno, *Minima Moralia*, 39.

93. Adorno, "Critique," in *Critical Models*, 285.

94. Adorno and Hellmut Becker, "Education for Maturity and Responsibility," *History of the Human Sciences* 12, 3 (1999), 21. See also Adorno, "Democratic Leadership and Mass Manipulation," in *Studies in Leadership: Leadership and Democratic Action*, ed. A. W. Gouldner (New York: Harper and Brothers, 1950), 418–435; Adorno, "The Meaning of Working Through the Past"; and Adorno, "Discussion to Lecture: 'The Meaning of Working Through the Past.'" I thank Shannon Mariotti for alerting me to the first two essays listed here, on education and leadership.

95. Adorno, "Discussion to Lecture: 'The Meaning of Working Through the Past,'" 300.

96. Adorno, "Critique," in *Critical Models*, 281.

97. Adorno, *Negative Dialectics*, 389.

CHAPTER FIVE. THE INSTINCTIVE DIALECTIC

1. Karl Marx, *Economic and Philosophical Manuscripts of 1844*, trans. M. Milligan (Amherst, NY: Prometheus Books, 1988), 102.

2. Marx, *Economic and Philosophical Manuscripts*, 105.

3. Marx, *Economic and Philosophical Manuscripts*, 108.

4. Erich Fromm, *Marx's Concept of Man* (New York: Continuum, 2004), v.

5. Marx, *Economic and Philosophical Manuscripts*, 148–149. The passage continues: "The *real*, active orientation of man to himself as a species being, or his manifestation as a real species being (i.e., as a human being), is only possible by his really bringing out of himself all the *powers* that are his as the *species* man—something which in turn is only possible through the cooperative action of all mankind, as the result of history."

6. Fromm, *Marx's Concept of Man*, 53.

7. Judith Butler, "Restaging the Universal," in J. Butler et al., *Contingency, Hegemony, Universality: Contemporary Dialogues on the Left* (New York: Verso, 2000), 38. Or consider the words of James's West Indian contemporary Aimé Césaire: "And that is the great thing I hold against pseudo-humanism: that for too long it has diminished the rights of man, that its concept of those rights has been—and still is—narrow and fragmentary, incomplete and biased and all things considered, sordidly racist" (Aimé Césaire, *Discourse on Colonialism*, trans. Joan Pinkham [New York: Monthly Review, 2000], 37). These kinds of concerns have been leveled for many years and from many angles. For a general overview of post- or antihumanist concerns, see Kate Soper, *Humanism and Anti-Humanism* (La Salle, IL: Open Court, 1986) and, more recently, Tony Davies, *Humanism*, Second Edition (New York: Routledge, 2008).

8. James, *The Black Jacobins: Toussaint L'Ouverture and the San Domingo Revolution*, Revised Edition (New York: Vintage, 1989). A select bibliography of James's works includes his critical study of Melville, *Mariners, Renegades, and Castaways: The Story of Herman Melville and the World We Live In* (Hanover, NH: University Press of New England, 2001); his semi-autobiographical work on the sport of cricket, *Beyond a Boundary* (London: Stanley Paul, 1990); his writings on Marxist organization, some of which are collected in Martin Glaberman (ed.), *Marxism for Our Times: C. L. R. James on Revolutionary Organization* (Jackson: University Press of Mississippi, 1999); and his writings on black America, some of which are collected in Scott McLemee (ed.), *C. L. R. James and the 'Negro Question'* (Jackson: University Press of Mississippi, 1996). For a range of writings on politics, history, literature, and culture, and for a more extensive bibliography, see Anna Grimshaw (ed.), *The C. L. R. James Reader* (Cambridge, MA: Blackwell, 1992). A number of James's shorter essays and excerpts from some of his longer pieces are available online from the C.L.R. James Institute (http://www.clrjamesinstitute.org) and from the Marxist Internet Archive (http://www.marxists.org). For a detailed biography of James, see Kent Worcester, *C. L. R. James: A Political Biography* (Albany: State University of New York Press, 1996); Paul Buhle, *C. L. R. James: The Artist as Revolutionary* (New York: Verso, 1988); and Frank Rosengarten, *Urbane Revolutionary: C. L. R. James and the Struggle for a New Society* (Jackson: University Press of Mississippi, 2008). For a helpful introduction to James's political theory, see Anthony Bogues, *Caliban's Freedom: The Early Political Thought of C. L. R. James* (Chicago: Pluto Press, 1997).

9. James, "Letters to Literary Critics," in A. Grimshaw (ed.), *The C. L. R. James Reader*, 230.

10. Cornelius Castoriadis, "C. L. R. James and the Fate of Marxism" [originally a lecture at Harvard University, April 4, 1992], in *C. L. R. James: His Intellectual*

Legacies, ed. S. R. Cudjoe and W. E. Cain (Amherst: University of Massachusetts Press, 1995), 285.

11. On this point, it is worth quoting White at some length: "Hegel's Comic conception of history was based ultimately in his belief in the right of life over death; 'life' guaranteed to Hegel the possibility of an ever more adequate form of social life throughout the historical future. Marx carries this Comic conception even further; he envisioned nothing less than the dissolution of that 'society' in which the contradiction between consciousness and being had to be entertained as a fatality for all men in all times. It would not, then, be unjust to characterize the final vision of history which inspired Marx in his historical and social theorizing as a Romantic one. But his conception did not envisage humanity's redemption as a deliverance from time itself. Rather, his redemption took the form of a reconciliation of man with a nature denuded of its fantastic and terrifying powers, submitted to the rule of technics, and turned to the creation of a genuine community, to the end of creating individuals who are free because they no longer have to struggle with one another for their own selfhood, but only with themselves" (Hayden White, *Metahistory: The Historical Imagination in Nineteenth-Century Europe* [Baltimore: Johns Hopkins University Press, 1973], 281–282). Romance, White says earlier on, is "symbolized by the hero's transcendence." It is "a drama of the triumph of good over evil, of virtue over vice, or light over darkness, and of the ultimate transcendence of man over the world" (8–9). While ultimately it may be misguided to characterize Marx as a "romantic," many scholars have pointed out that elements of romantic thinking are implicit in the work of both Marx and Engels, especially in the writings of the mid-1840s. For more on this, see Michael Löwy and Robert Sayre, *Romanticism Against the Tide of Modernity*, trans. C. Porter (Durham, NC: Duke University Press, 2001), esp. 89–99. See also Jürgen Habermas's discussion of Marx's "Romantic socialism" in "What Does Socialism Mean Today? The Rectifying Revolution and the Need for New Thinking on the Left," trans. B. Morgan, *New Left Review* 183 (1990), esp.15.

12. Bottomore's translation of the *Economic and Philosophical Manuscripts* appeared originally in the 1961 publication of Fromm's *Marx's Concept of Man*.

13. For James's introduction to the original mimeograph, see James, "On Marx's Essays from the Economic-Philosophical Manuscripts" [1947], in *At the Rendezvous of Victory: Selected Writings* (London: Allison and Busby, 1984), 65–72. For some historical background on these translations and on James's early engagement with the *Economic and Philosophical Manuscripts*, see Robert A. Hill, "Literary Executor's Afterword," in James, *American Civilization*, ed. A. Grimshaw and K. Hart (New York: Blackwell, 1993), 313–314. See also Bill Schwartz, "C. L. R. James's *American Civilization*," in *Beyond Boundaries: C. L. R. James and Postnational Studies*, ed. C. Gair (Ann Arbor, MI: Pluto Press, 2002), 150–151.

14. Here we might note a retrospective remark by Grace Lee (Boggs), which captures the humanist aspirations of James, Dunayevskaya, and Lee in the mid-1940s: "We read and reread practically everything that Marx ever wrote, looking for support for our position that the concern of every revolutionist worthy of the name must be *not* property relationships or just higher wages or more efficient plans but the liberation of the natural and acquired powers of human beings—or, as Hegel put it, not Substance but Subject. You can imagine our joy, therefore, when we discovered

Marx's 1844 Economic-Philosophical essays which, I am proud to say, we were the first to publish in English translation" (Grace Lee Boggs, "C. L. R. James: Organizing in the U.S.A., 1938–1953," in *C. L. R. James: His Intellectual Legacies*, ed. S. R. Cudjoe and W. E. Cain [Amherst: University of Massachusetts Press, 1995], 170).

15. James, *American Civilization*, 248. For further discussion of James's critique of Cartesian dualism and the impact of this critique on James's humanist commitments, see Brett St. Louis, *Rethinking Race, Politics, and Poetics: C. L. R. James and the Critique of Modernity* (New York: Routledge, 2007), 160–161.

16. See Anna Grimshaw and Keith Hart, "American Civilization: An Introduction," in C. L. R. James, *American Civilization* (New York: Blackwell, 1993), 20; and Anna Grimshaw and Keith Hart, "James, de Tocqueville, and Baudrillard" (The C.L.R. James Institute, 2001), (http://www.clrjamesinstitute.org/baudrill.html).

17. James, *American Civilization*, 184.

18. James, *American Civilization*, 65. To be sure, James maintains a self-conscious ambivalence toward Whitman, whom he admires as a "genuine democrat," driven by a "conviction of the worth of the individual as an individual in work and play and all aspects of life," and aware, perhaps all too aware, that "this individual could only find his fullest expression with other individuals equal to himself."

19. James, *American Civilization*, 159.

20. Löwy and Sayre, *Romanticism Against the Tide of Modernity*, 25. Löwy and Sayre develop the somewhat provocative claim that "Romanticism is essentially a reaction against the way of life in capitalist societies," that romantic thinking "represents a critique of modernity, that is of modern capitalist civilization, in the name of values drawn from the past (the precapitalist, premodern past)" (17). Frank Rosengarten has suggested that "James did not go quite so far as Löwy and Sayre in their conception of Romanticism as an anticapitalist movement, but he came close to it." I am not exactly sure *how* James stopped short of Löwy and Sayre's conception; he certainly came very close to it. See Rosengarten, *Urbane Revolutionary*, 184.

21. James, *American Civilization*, 119.

22. James, *American Civilization*, 169. For another notable example of this sentiment, see James, "Every Cook Can Govern" [1956], in *The Future in the Present: Selected Writings* (London: Allison and Busby, 1977), 167. In what is one of many nostalgic references to what James regards as the fully integrated character of ancient Greek democracy, he speaks of a "perfect balance, instinctive and unconscious, between individual and the city-state which gave him [the Greek citizen] the enormous force and the enormous freedom of his personality."

23. This notion of the "integrated personality" is perhaps simply James's shorthand for the familiar "humanist" idea that we cannot carve out our own individual freedom in isolation, that our individual freedom is dependent upon the freedom of others, indeed upon the freedom of all. Here we might draw a parallel between James and Sartre, who, as I noted in chapter 3, initiates his shift toward humanism, his shift away from the existential individualism of *Being and Nothingness*, by announcing in 1946, in "Existentialism Is a Humanism," that "if existence really does precede essence, man is responsible for what he is . . . and when we say that man is responsible for himself, we do not mean that he is responsible for his own individuality, but that he is responsible for all men" (Jean-Paul Sartre,

Existentialism and Human Emotions, trans. B. Frechtman (New York: Philosophical Library, 1957), 16.

24. Martin Halliwell and Andy Mousley, *Critical Humanism: Humanist/Anti-Humanist Dialogues* (Edinburgh: Edinburgh University Press, 2003), 33.

25. James, *Mariners, Renegades, and Castaways*, 89. See also James, "On Marx's Essays from the Economic-Philosophical Manuscripts," esp. 69, and *Notes on Dialectics: Hegel, Marx, Lenin* (Westport, CT: Lawrence Hill, 1980), 175, where James says that "man, by becoming revolutionary, continuously active and creative, would become truly human."

26. James, *American Civilization*, 171.

27. Löwy and Sayre, *Romanticism Against the Tide of Modernity*, 22.

28. James, *Modern Politics: A Series of Lectures on the Subject Given at the Trinidad Public Library* (Detroit: Bewick Editions, 1973), 3–5. See also James, *American Civilization*, 162: "Integration was the source of the miraculous outpouring of creative genius which distinguished the Greeks."

29. James, "Letter of March 20, 1957," in A. Grimshaw (ed.), *The C. L. R. James Reader*, 270.

30. Robin D. G. Kelley, "The World the Diaspora Made: C. L. R. James and the Politics of History," in *Rethinking C. L. R. James*, ed. G. Farred (Cambridge, MA: Blackwell, 1996), 119. See also Kelley's "Introduction" in James, *A History of Pan-African Revolt* (Chicago: Charles H. Kerr, 1995), 1–33.

31. See, for example, Aimé Césaire, "Poetry and Knowledge," in *Refusal of the Shadow: Surrealism and the Caribbean*, trans. M. Richardson and K. Fijalkowski (New York: Verso, 1996). For further discussion of the "primitivism" implicit to Césaire's humanism, see Mara de Gennaro, "Fighting Humanism on Its Own Terms," *differences* 14, 1 (Spring 2003).

32. Césaire, *Discourse on Colonialism*, 44.

33. For further discussion of the romantic dimensions of Césaire's humanism, see Jane Hiddleston, "Aimé Césaire and Postcolonial Humanism," *Modern Language Review* 105 (2010). Hiddleston argues that "the putative 'return' to African roots [in Césaire's work] turns out to have been a gesture of recreation rather than a movement back to an origin" (92). In addition to Césaire, I might highlight the Romantic humanist dimensions of the Antiguan writer and activist Tim Hector, one of James's most stimulating intellectual disciples. In his own defense of the creative self-activities of ordinary people, in an effort to inspire grassroots political activities throughout the postcolonial Caribbean, Hector, following James, draws upon an idealized image of both classical Greek democracy and premodern African communities. For more on this, see Matthew Quest, "Legislating the Caribbean General Will: The Later Political Thought of Tim Hector, 1979–2002," *The C.L.R. James Journal* 13, 1 (2007). For a more wide-ranging introduction to the life and ideas of Tim Hector, see Paul Buhle, *Tim Hector: A Caribbean Radical's Story* (Jackson: University Press of Mississippi, 2006).

34. Fanon suggests that any nostalgic gesture toward an idealized past bespeaks an implicit commitment to, or perhaps an accommodation of, some sort of reified and necessarily worn-out conception of "man." As he puts it, "I do not want to make myself the man of any past. I do not want to exalt the past at the expense of my

present and of my future" (Fanon, *Black Skin, White Masks*, trans. C. L. Markmann (New York: Grove Press, 1967), 226). See also Fanon's critique of a romanticized "national culture" in *The Wretched of the Earth*, trans. C. Farrington (New York: Grove Press, 1963), 237–238. I intend to show how James enriches and tempers his own romanticism in ways that may appease some of Fanon's concerns.

35. For an elaboration on this sentiment, and for more on the black radical tradition more generally, see Cedric Robinson, *Black Marxism: The Making of the Black Radical Tradition* (Chapel Hill: University of North Carolina Press, 2000).

36. Halliwell and Mousley, *Critical Humanism*, 19.

37. See the "Introduction" to James's *Notes on Dialectics*.

38. James, *Beyond a Boundary* (London: Stanley Paul, 1990), 149. See also 29.

39. James, *Beyond a Boundary*, 149–150.

40. See James, *Notes on Dialectics*, 7. Where "Lenin had come to the conclusion that you could not understand *Capital* without an understanding of the Hegelian *Logic*," James "came to the conclusion that a fundamental investigation still remained to be done, on Hegel's *Science of Logic* (with that had to be associated the smaller *Logic*, a section of Hegel's *Encyclopedia*)." We might also note here that, throughout his life, James insisted on his affiliation with the legacy of Lenin. When asked in an interview in 1980 to reflect in his "greatest contributions," James says plainly, "My contributions have been, number one, to clarify and extend the heritage of Marx and Lenin." See James, "Interview with James Early, Ethelbert Miller, Paul Buhle, and Noel Ignatin," in *C. L. R. James: His Life and Work*, ed. P. Buhle (New York: Allison and Busby, 1986), 164. In the words of Kent Worcester, "even in the 1960s and 1970s James had nothing but the highest regard for Lenin as a revolutionary leader, whom he thought of as a democrat and an ally of both the working class and the peasantry" (Worcester, "C. L. R. James and the American Century," in *C. L. R. James: His Intellectual Legacies*, 182).

41. For more on this, see Andrew J. Douglas, "Democratizing Dialectics with C. L. R. James," *The Review of Politics* 70, 3 (2008), 420–441.

42. See James, *Notes on Dialectics*, 33.

43. James makes these "transfers" repeatedly throughout the text—for example, "Let us *transfer* this to the labour movement. These transfers are rough but Hegel intended them to be made" (James, *Notes on Dialectics*, 17).

44. John McClendon recently published the first book-length study of James's *Notes on Dialectics*, which may be worthy of passing mention here if only in order to show how a conventional reading of James and the dialectical tradition can usurp James's remarkably creative treatment of Hegel. McClendon's book is an attempt to find an appropriate label for James. Through an "internal critique" of *Notes*, McClendon seeks a "comprehensive apprehension of [James's] locus as a Marxist-Leninist philosopher" (John H. McClendon III, *C. L. R. James's Notes on Dialectics: Left-Hegelianism or Marxism-Leninism?* [Lanham, MD: Lexington Books, 2005], xv). He argues that James fatally departs from his own expressed commitment to dialectical materialism and "becomes ensnared in dogmatism" by virtue of his tacit adherence to a politically bankrupt brand of Hegelian idealism (for an introduction to this complex claim, a claim that McClendon will develop in detail throughout his book, see xxii). According to McClendon, "James overlooks how Marx

and Lenin approach Hegel's dialectic and therefore he cannot replicate Marx and Lenin's mode of apprehending Hegel's *Logic*, that is, penultimately James does not reclaim their materialist reading and ultimately the materialist inversion of Hegel's idealist dialectics" (119). As may be apparent already, I am generally sympathetic to the claim that James departs from a strong dialectical materialism and, at least at times, seems to develop a more left-Hegelian or perhaps Hegelian-Marxian theoretical orientation. But because McClendon approaches James from the perspective of Marxist-Leninist doctrine and frames his reading in terms of Marxism-Leninism, McClendon determines in advance the character of James's Hegel. In other words, McClendon reads *Notes on Dialectics* only in terms of what we might call the major narrative and does not allow the minor narrative to come forth in any way. We should note also that McClendon does not appear to pick up on James's "transfers" from Hegel and instinctive dialectic to the theoretical dialectic of Marx and Lenin.

45. James, *Notes on Dialectics*, 56, 26, 31. We might note here that James has been criticized for essentially butchering Hegel and Kant, for, as McClendon puts it, neglecting the "locus of German idealism," and for misunderstanding Marx and Lenin and their materialist inversion of Hegelian dialectics. But we must keep in mind that James is not interested in getting Hegel right. "I shall interpret freely," he says (*Notes on Dialectics*, 95). "I do not *guarantee* these interpretations. The point is once they are down we begin to get somewhere. I am not afraid of mistakes" (79). James plays rather freely with Hegel, just as he plays rather freely with Kant ("I am doing injustice to Kant, I am sure, and committing crimes against philosophical terminology" [19]) and just as he plays rather freely with the very language of dialectics. My interpretation is based on an admittedly generous reading of James and of the more nuanced figuration of dialectical reflection that emerges in what I have referred to as James's "minor narrative." In many ways, and as I noted at the outset of this chapter, I threaten to move beyond James. But my reading is, I think, more in tune with James's rather remarkable intellectual and political creativity. I might note also that McClendon would almost certainly describe mine as an "anachronistic" reading. McClendon wants to distance his own approach from any reading that is, as he puts it, "arrogantly presentist in orientation." He warns against any temptation to link James to "contemporary political and ideological fads and trends" and to "interpret James in the mode of an external retrospective" that would thereby "distort the integrity of James's corpus" (McClendon, *C. L. R. James's Notes on Dialectics*, 18). In reading James, I just get the sense that he would want us to interpret him in the way that he interprets Hegel, not as a figure to be understood rightly or wrongly but as a source of creative inspiration for emerging generations of readers with their own ethical and political problems.

46. James, *Notes on Dialectics*, 25. For the reference in Hegel, see *Science of Logic*, trans. A. V. Miller (Atlantic Highlands, NJ: Humanities Press International, 1969), 24. See also Hegel, *Phenomenology of Spirit*, trans. A. V. Miller (New York: Oxford University Press, 1977), 51.

47. On James's assessment of Hegel's materialism, see "Dialectical Materialism and the Fate of Humanity," esp. 166. "Hegel," James says, "led his *Logic* into an impossible and fantastic idealism about world-spirit, etc. But the basis of his work was solidly materialistic."

48. James, *Notes on Dialectics*, 29. There are potentially some interesting affinities between James's emphasis on desire in Hegel and some of the contributions of the twentieth-century French Hegelians Jean Hyppolite and Alexandre Kojève. Both Hyppolite and Kojève published their major works on Hegel in 1947, the same year James began drafting *Notes on Dialectics*. James read and spoke French, but as far as I know, he never commented on or even acknowledged his French contemporaries.

49. We might note that James develops an approach to Hegel that looks a bit like the approach that Adorno pursues almost twenty years later. In his 1966 *Negative Dialectics*, for example, Adorno says that the "bodily moment informs knowledge that suffering should not be, that it should be otherwise. . . . Hence the specifically material converges with the critical, with socially transformative praxis" (Theodor W. Adorno, *Negative Dialectics*, trans. E. B. Ashton [New York: Continuum, 1973], 203). And certainly these remarks ought to be read in tandem with Adorno's lectures on Hegel from the same period, where he emphasizes the "experiential" character of Hegel's thought, or the idea that Hegel "brought infinitely more concreteness into his philosophical ideas . . . and not because his speculative imagination was balanced by a sense of reality but by virtue of the approach his philosophy takes—by virtue, one might say, of the experiential character of his speculation itself" (Adorno, *Hegel: Three Studies* [Cambridge: MIT Press, 1993], 67). Whatever affinities we may be able to draw in hindsight between James's and Adorno's readings of Hegel, we ought to keep in mind that James's personal engagement with Adorno, and with the Frankfurt School in general, was always a bit curious. In *Notes on Dialectics*, James acknowledged his debt to Marcuse's *Reason and Revolution*, and he met Adorno and Horkheimer in New York in the 1940s. But James's popular democratic enthusiasm, perhaps his generally more hopeful tenor, seems to have prevented any productive interaction with his more somber, more politically disillusioned German counterparts. For a brief discussion of James's encounter with the early Frankfurt School theorists, see Buhle, *C. L. R. James: The Artist as Revolutionary*, 106.

50. James, *American Civilization*, 184.

51. James, *American Civilization*, 138. This passage derives from James's discussion of certain sadistic trends in post-Depression popular arts. Kent Worcester provides a nice delineation of James's concern here: "The Depression ushered in an era of unparalleled savagery in the popular arts. For the first time, the 'funnies' (comic strips) depicted acts of depravity and murder. Mass anxieties mounted in the 1930s, and then pushed even deeper into the collective unconscious after 1945 . . . all connoting the crisis of American civilization, the gap between the desire for meaningful individualism versus the drudgery and manipulation of everyday life." See Worcester, *C. L. R. James: A Political Biography*, 109.

52. For a helpful discussion of how James, as well as Grace Lee and Raya Dunayevskaya—the other major intellectuals associated with the Johnson-Forest Tendency in the 1940s—move beyond any simple notion of proletarian class struggle, see Harry Cleaver, *Reading Capital Politically* (San Francisco: AK and Anti/Theses, 2000). See also Brian W. Alleyne, "C. L. R. James: Critical Humanist," in C. Gair (ed.), *Beyond Boundaries: C. L. R. James and Postnational Studies*, 189. Alleyne notes that "James's vision of what modernity might become was inspired by transcendent

emancipatory political projects like the French and Haitian Revolutions, yet he was demonstrably aware that such ideas and projects were ideals whose realization had constantly to be struggled for—they were always unfinished. This openness, rare in a Marxist who began his career in the 1930s, is manifested in James's early attempts to incorporate non-class aspects of social differentiation more seriously into his revolutionary praxis." We might also note that James's more broadly inclusive language may signal an effort to redeem his public image before a wider American audience. By 1950, he was under suspicion of "un-American activities," his visa had expired, and he found himself subject to increasing scrutiny by immigration officials. Both *American Civilization* and his 1953 study of Herman Melville, much of which was written while he was imprisoned during deportation proceedings, were part of an effort to distance himself from Communism and to exhibit at least a qualified celebration of American democratic values and traditions.

53. For a rich account of James's intellectual development in the 1930s and 1940s, including a special focus on James's evolving appreciation for the autonomous political struggles of women and men of African descent, see Robinson, *Black Marxism*, 251–286.

54. In other writings from this period, James is more explicit in his identification of the distinctive democratic promise of black Americans or his faith in grassroots political activity born of the intense frustrations that black Americans knew only too well. In a 1948 address to the SWP, an address given to an overwhelmingly orthodox Marxist audience, James concluded by saying: "Let us not forget that in the Negro people, there sleep and are now awakening passions of a violence exceeding, perhaps, as far as these things can be compared, anything among the tremendous forces that capitalism has created. Anyone who knows them, who knows their history, is able to talk to them intimately, watches them at their own theatres, watches them at their dances, watches them in their churches, reads their press with a discerning eye, must recognize that although their social force may not be able to compare with the social force of a corresponding number of organized workers, the hatred of bourgeois society and the readiness to destroy it when the opportunity should present itself, rests among them to a degree greater than in any other section of the population in the United States" (James, "The Revolutionary Answer to the Negro Problem in the USA," in A. Grimshaw [ed.], *The C. L. R. James Reader*, 188–189).

55. Hegel, *The Encyclopedia Logic: Part I of the Encyclopedia of Philosophical Sciences with the Zusätze*, trans. T. F. Geraets, W. A. Suchting, and H. S. Harris (Indianapolis, IN: Hackett Publishing, 2002), 187. Hegel, *Science of Logic*, 439; James, *Notes on Dialectics*, 92. See Hegel, *Science of Logic*, 442, where Hegel claims that "every determination, every concrete thing, every Notion . . . [must] pass over into contradictory moments."

56. James, *Notes on Dialectics*, 92.

57. Hegel, *Science of Logic*, 42.

58. James, *Notes on Dialectics*, 91–92.

59. Jean-Paul Sartre, *Black Orpheus*, trans. S. Allen (Paris: Présence africaine, 1963), 55.

60. See Robinson, *Black Marxism*, 285–286.

61. Louis Althusser, *For Marx*, trans. Ben Brewster (New York: Verso, 2005), 229. Althusser is a rich and complex thinker, and this is not the place to embark on a detailed discussion of the humanism/antihumanism debates spawned by his work. For a more detailed comparative analysis of James and Althusser, see McClendon, *C. L. R. James's Notes on Dialectics*, 181–238, and Alrick Cambridge, "C. L. R. James: Freedom through History and Dialectics," in *Intellectuals in the Twentieth-Century Caribbean*, ed. Alistair Hennessey (London: McMillan Caribbean, 1992), 163–178.

62. In many ways, James would seem to fall in line with E. P. Thompson's critique of Althusser's antihumanism (see E. P. Thompson, *The Poverty of Theory* [New York: Monthly Review, 1978]). For more on Althusser, Thompson, and the debates about the human as subject and object of knowledge, see John Sanbonmatsu, *The Postmodern Prince: Critical Theory, Left Strategy, and the Making of a New Political Subject* (New York: Monthly Review, 2004), esp. 103–114.

63. David Scott, *Conscripts of Modernity: The Tragedy of Colonial Enlightenment* (Durham, NC: Duke University Press, 2004). See also Scott, "Tragedy's Time: Postemancipation Futures Past and Present," in *Rethinking Tragedy*, ed. R. Felski (Baltimore: Johns Hopkins University Press, 2008).

64. See A. Grimshaw (ed.), *The C. L. R. James Reader*, 425 n. 14. Grimshaw indicates that James lectured on Shakespeare's *Hamlet* as part of a 1953 Columbia series on "Human Personality in Great Tragedy." Elsewhere, James indicates that he lectured on tragic motifs in "Aeschylus (*Orestia* and *Prometheus Bound*), then on Shakespeare, Milton, Rousseau and the characters of Dostoyevsky's *Karamazov* and *The Possessed*" (James, "Letters to Literary Critics," 231). See also, Scott, *Conscripts of Modernity*, 256 n. 16, where Scott indicates that James lectured on tragedy between 1949 and 1952. For a discussion of debates about tragedy between James and some of his Johnson-Forest Tendency comrades—notably Grace Lee Boggs and William Gorman, both of whom were trained philosophers—see Rosengarten, *Urbane Revolutionary*, 190–191.

65. James, "Letters to Literary Critics," 220. James emphasizes his debt to Aristotle and Hegel in numerous places. See *Mariners, Renegades, and Castaways*, 70—"Except for Aristotle, nearly 2500 years ago, and Hegel who wrote a generation before Melville, no critic of literature has written so profoundly of the art of great writing."

66. James, "Letters to Literary Critics," 231.

67. James, *Mariners, Renegades, and Castaways*, 70.

68. See Aristotle, *The Basic Works of Aristotle*, ed. and trans. Richard McKeon (New York: Random House, 1941), 1461. On the essential agreement between Aristotle and Hegel on the priority of action in tragic drama, see Allen Speight, *Hegel, Literature, and the Problem of Agency* (New York: Cambridge University Press, 2001), esp. 47. Speight writes, "[I]t is well known that for Aristotle tragedy turned on the notion of *hamartia*, a mistake such as Oedipus', rather than on the sort of larger, presumably unavoidable social conflict that we associate with Hegel's reading of *Antigone*. While this view of a difference between a tragedy of *hamartia* and a tragedy of conflict in the ethical realm is essentially right, it misses an important and underlying point of agreement between Aristotle and Hegel: the notion that tragedy, at root, is *about action*."

69. James, "Notes on Hamlet," in A. Grimshaw (ed.), *The C. L. R. James Reader*, 245.

70. Here we might note a possible comparison between James's account of Toussaint and Sartre's depiction of Patrice Lumumba as a "Black Robespierre" (Jean-Paul Sartre, "The Political Thought of Patrice Lumumba," in *Colonialism and Neocolonialism* [New York: Routledge, 2006], 175). Sartre published a eulogic essay on Lumumba in 1963, the same year that James reissued *The Black Jacobins*. And as James effectively doubles down on his characterization of Toussaint as a tragic figure, an embodiment of the contradictions of the "New World" at the turn of the nineteenth century, Sartre likewise reads Lumumba's tragic failures as a reflection of, an embodiment of, an increasingly total, and increasingly tragic, neocolonial situation.

71. In his *Preface to Criticism*, written in or around 1955, James discusses the importance of how action is received by the popular audience in both Greek and Shakespearean tragic drama. The meaning, the significance, the success or failure of the actors, as characters, depends upon how their dramatic action is judged by the spectators. And here I might underscore James's emphasis on the *popular* audience, as opposed to the intentions of the actors or the producers, or the judgments of elite intellectuals or trained critics. For example, in a discussion of the 1953 filmic production of *Julius Caesar*, starring Marlon Brando, James claims that "the modern popular audience turned away from the last act . . . and in doing so, it was right and the producers, following the critics, were wrong." See James, "Preface to Criticism," in A. Grimshaw (ed.), *The C. L. R. James Reader*, 255–260. For an additional discussion of action in tragic drama, see Stuart Hall, "A Conversation with C. L. R. James," in G. Farred (ed.), *Rethinking C. L. R. James*, 19–20.

72. Scott, *Conscripts of Modernity*, 164–165.

73. James, *American Civilization*, 36–37.

74. James, *Mariners, Renegades, and Castaways*, 3.

75. Aristotle, *The Basic Works of Aristotle*, 1461.

76. Wilson Harris, "A Unique Marxist Thinker," in P. Buhle (ed.), *C. L. R. James: His Life and Work*, 230. Cf. Jameson, who likewise underscores the experience of "shock" or "breathlessness" induced by dialectical thinking, "something of the sickening shudder we feel in an elevator's fall or in the sudden dip of an airliner" (Fredric Jameson, *Marxism and Form: Twentieth-Century Dialectical Theories of Literature* [Princeton, NJ: Princeton University Press, 1971], 308).

CHAPTER SIX. CONCLUSION

1. Fredric Jameson, "Interview," in *Lukács after Communism: Interviews with Contemporary Intellectuals*, ed. Eva L. Corredor (Durham, NC: Duke University Press, 1997), 93. Jameson, for his part, goes on to say, "this is not any particularly new idea with me. Lenin had already said that no one could understand *Das Kapital* who had not already worked his way through Hegel's logic. . . . I think the coming years will show an unconscious need for the dialectic which some of us on the left ought to have the mission to satisfy."

2. As may be expected from a critic shaped by his engagements with Sartre and Adorno, as well as other legatees of the dialectical tradition, Jameson has long

been suspicious of the turn to ethics. "Ethical thought," he said years ago, "projects as permanent features of human 'experience,' and thus as a kind of 'wisdom' about personal life and interpersonal relations, what are in reality the historical and institutional specifics of a determinate type of group solidarity of class cohesion" (Fredric Jameson, *The Political Unconscious: Narrative as a Socially Symbolic Act* [Ithaca, NY: Cornell University Press, 1982], 59; for a more recent articulation of this sentiment, see Fredric Jameson, *Valences of the Dialectic* [New York: Verso, 2009], 406). And Jameson has long sought to retain from the dialectical tradition a critical apparatus that is unabashedly systematic in orientation, one that can apprehend global capital in its totalizing character, one that can inform a systematic and total—that is, *revolutionary*—political response. It is a claim that resounds throughout his work: "it is capitalism which totalizes, which constitutes a total system, not its critics," and for this reason alone, Jameson suggests, we might give the dialectical tradition another look (see Fredric Jameson, "Persistencies of the Dialectic: Three Sites," *Science & Society* 62, 3 [Fall 1998], 367). For an accessible discussion of some of these issues, see Ian Buchanan, *Fredric Jameson: Live Theory* (New York: Continuum, 2006), as well as the essays collected in Caren Irr and Ian Buchanan (eds.), *On Jameson: From Postmodernism to Globalization* (Albany: State University of New York Press, 2005).

3. See Stephen K. White, *Sustaining Affirmation: The Strengths of Weak Ontology in Political Theory* (Princeton, NJ: Princeton University Press, 2000). "Weak ontologies," White says, "respond to two pressing concerns. First, there is the acceptance of the idea that all fundamental conceptualizations of self, other, and world are contestable. Second, there is the sense that such conceptualizations are nevertheless necessary or unavoidable for an adequately reflective ethical and political life. The latter insight demands from us the affirmative gesture of constructing foundations, the former prevents us from carrying out this task in a traditional fashion" (8).

4. Raymond Geuss, *Philosophy and Real Politics* (Princeton, NJ: Princeton University Press, 2008), 25.

5. Raymond Geuss, *Politics and the Imagination* (Princeton, NJ: Princeton University Press, 2010), 42.

6. Theodor W. Adorno, "Education After Auschwitz," in *Critical Models: Interventions and Catchwords*, trans. H. W. Pickford (New York: Columbia University Press, 2005), 192.

7. Theodor W. Adorno, *Minima Moralia: Reflections from Damaged Life*, trans. E. F. N. Jephcott (New York: Verso, 2002), 16.

8. Sheldon S. Wolin, "Fugitive Democracy," in *Democracy and Difference: Contesting the Boundaries of the Political*, ed. Seyla Benhabib (Princeton, NJ: Princeton University Press, 1996), 31. For a more recent discussion of the "fugitive" character of the political, see Sheldon S. Wolin, *Politics and Vision: Continuity and Innovation in Western Political Thought*, Expanded Edition (Princeton, NJ: Princeton University Press, 2004), 601–606; Sheldon S. Wolin, *Democracy Incorporated: Managed Democracy and the Specter of Inverted Totalitarianism* (Princeton, NJ: Princeton University Press, 2008), 259–292.

INDEX